HAS THE CHURCH REPLACED ISRAEL?

A THEOLOGICAL EVALUATION

MICHAEL J. VLACH

B&H
ACADEMIC
NASHVILLE, TENNESSEE

ISBN: 978-0-8054-4972-3

Published by B&H Publishing Group
Nashville, Tennessee

Dewey Decimal Classification: 230

Subject Heading: ISRAEL \ DOCTRINAL THEOLOGY \ CHURCH

Printed in the United States of America

10 11 12 13 14   •   20 19 18 17 16

To my wife, Holly, who also longs for His appearing and the restoration of all things—including Israel.

Contents

Contents

Abbreviations

AB	Anchor Bible
ABRL	Anchor Bible Reference Library
ANTC	Abingdon New Testament Commentaries
ACCS	Ancient Christian Commentary on Scripture
ACW	*Ancient Christian Writers* Series. 1946–
ANF	*Ante-Nicene Fathers*
BSac	*Bibliotheca sacra*
BECNT	Baker Exegetical Commentary on the New Testament
CBQ	*Catholic Biblical Quarterly*
CD	*Church Dogmatics*
DB	*Dictionaire de la Bible.* Edited by F. Vigouroux. 5 vols. 1895–1912.
DJG	*Dictionary of Jesus and the Gospels*
EBC	*Expositor's Bible Commentary*
GTJ	*Grace Theological Journal*
HTR	*Harvard Theological Review*
IB	*Interpreter's Bible*
IBC	Interpretation: A Bible Commentary for Teaching and Preaching
ICC	International Critical Commentary
IVPNTCS	IVP New Testament Commentary Series
JETS	*Journal of the Evangelical Theological Society*
KJV	King James Version
LCC	Library of Christian Classics
LW	*Luther's Works*
NAC	New American Commentary
NACSBT	New American Commentary Studies in Bible and Theology
NASB	New American Standard Bible
NCBC	New Century Bible Commentary
NEB	New English Bible
NIB	*New Interpreter's Bible*

NIBCNT	New International Biblical Commentary on the New Testament
NICNT	New International Commentary on the New Testament
NIDNTT	*New International Dictionary of New Testament Theology*, ed. Colin Brown
NIV	New International Version
NIVAC	New International Version Application Commentary
NPNF¹	*Nicene and Post-Nicene Fathers, Series 1*
NPNF²	*Nicene and Post-Nicene Fathers, Series 2*
NT	New Testament
NTC	New Testament Commentary
PG	Patrologia graeca
PL	Patrologia latina
PSB	*The Princeton Seminary Bulletin*
RevExp	*Review and Expositor*
RSV	Revised Standard Version
TDNT	*Theological Dictionary of the New Testament*
TNTC	Tyndale New Testament Commentaries
WA	*Weimarer Ausgabe* (*D. Martin Luthers Werke: Kritische Gesammtausgabe*)
WBC	Word Biblical Commentary
WPC	Westminster Pelican Commentaries
WTJ	*Westminster Theological Journal*

Introduction

The relationship between Israel and the church continues to be a controversial topic. Anyone who has an interest in the doctrines of Israel, the church, and the end times is probably aware of this fact. At the heart of the controversy is the question, Does the church replace, supersede, or fulfill the nation Israel in God's plan, or will Israel be saved and restored with a unique identity and role? The position that the church is the "new" or "true" Israel that replaces or fulfills national Israel's place in the plan of God has often been called "replacement theology" or "supersessionism." More recently, some have argued for the title "fulfillment theology."

Ever since my days as a seminary student in the early 1990s, I have been intrigued by the Israel-church issue. Not only has this topic interested me, but I have been fascinated by the disagreement in the Christian community on this issue. There simply is no consensus on the relationship between Israel and the church. That is, in part, the reason I decided to make the Israel-church relationship my main area of study in my doctoral program. I was frustrated with how the Israel-church topic was often addressed. In short, I found that supersessionists often had their passages and arguments that they believed supported supersessionism, yet they did not adequately grapple with the passages and arguments put forth by those who were nonsupersessionists. And likewise, I found that those who promoted a nonsupersessionist view in which national Israel would be saved and restored often did not engage the arguments put forth by supersessionists. This frustration caused me to interact seriously with the main points both sides were making in order to determine which position was closer to the truth.

My goal with this book is similar. I will evaluate the doctrine of replacement theology and address whether the Bible teaches that the church is the complete replacement or fulfillment of national Israel. As will become evident, the relationship between Israel and the church is complex. Not only are there many passages to take into consideration, but there are significant hermeneutical issues to grapple with as well. One hermeneutical topic looms especially large—how the NT applies OT passages that speak of Israel's future. As will be shown, one's hermeneutical assumptions will largely determine where one lands on the relationship between Israel and the church.

Whenever we address a complex theological issue, the subject of methodology is important. For example, where do we start? What passages do we emphasize? What hermeneutic should we use? What are the implications of our conclusions on other doctrines? What threshold must be crossed to have confidence that one view is correct and another is wrong? All these questions are relevant for understanding the Israel and church issue.

Thus, we need to ask, "What does supersessionism need to prove to be considered a biblical doctrine?" I would like to offer what I think is reasonable criteria that can guide us in the process of evaluating supersessionism. In order for supersessionism to be correct, three things must be proved. First, supersessionists need to explain how God can make multiple eternal and unconditional promises and covenants to the nation Israel and then not fulfill these promises with this specific group. If God is true and does not lie, how can He promise the nation Israel certain things and then not complete the fulfillment with the group to whom the promises were made? It will not be enough to claim that the church is the new or true Israel. What also must be addressed is how God can promise certain blessings to a certain people without the fulfillment of these promises involving these same people.

Second, in order for supersessionism to be accepted as true, it must be shown that the church is now considered the new or true Israel. It needs to be proven that Gentile Christians are now part of Israel and that they rightly can be identified as Jews. There must be proof that the titles of "Israel" and "Jew" have now been transcended or broadened to include believing Gentiles.

Third, supersessionists need to show that the church inherits national Israel's covenants and promises in such a way that we should not expect a future fulfillment of these with national Israel. Now one may ask, "If one proves the second point above, does this not automatically prove the third?" Our answer to that is not necessarily. I am not convinced that if it can be shown that the church is called "Israel" or that Gentile Christians are now "Jews" in some sense, this necessarily rules out a fulfillment of covenant promises to national Israel. Perhaps God is expanding the concept of "Israel" and "Jews" to include Gentiles but is not doing so at the expense of believing ethnic Jews. C. E. B. Cranfield claimed that Rom 2:28–29 identifies believing Gentiles as true Jews, yet he also believed that Rom 9–11 explicitly rejects a replacement theology in which the church is viewed as replacing Israel in the plan of God.[1] Likewise, I am not convinced that if a passage like Gal 6:16 indicates believing Gentiles are part of the "Israel of God" (which I do not believe) this means the nation

---

[1] C. E. B. Cranfield, *A Critical and Exegetical Commentary on the Epistle to the Romans*, ICC (Edinburgh: T&T Clark, 1975), 1:176.

Israel has no future role or purpose in the plan of God. In sum, supersessionists need to show positively that the church is the complete fulfillment of Israel and show negatively that the nation Israel never again will have a unique identity or role in God's plan.

For reasons that will be made known, supersessionism does not satisfy any of these requirements and, therefore, is not a biblical doctrine. There are compelling scriptural reasons in both Testaments to believe in a future salvation and restoration of the nation Israel. Plus, nowhere do I see a passage or collection of passages that revokes this expectation.

In researching this subject, I have found that most of the arguments supersessionists offer for holding that the church is the complete replacement or fulfillment of Israel are based on implications they believe are true but in reality are not biblically accurate or logically consistent. For example, supersessionists claim that the unity between Jews and Gentiles expressed in Eph 2:11–22 means there can be no functional role for national Israel in the future, but this simply is not the case since spiritual unity does not necessarily cancel ethnic and functional distinctions between groups. Or supersessionists argue that the application of "Israel" language to the church in passages like 1 Pet 2:9–10 and Rom 9:24–26 means that the church is now the new Israel. But the OT predicted the day would come when Gentiles would assume the language used to describe Israel but not in the sense of assuming Israel's identity (see Isa 19:24–25). Or supersessionists claim that since Jesus is the fulfillment of the seed of Abraham (see Gal 3:16), then the promises to the believing ethnic seed of Abraham through Jacob are no longer in effect. But the concept of "seed of Abraham" is not an either-or concept. There are multiple senses of "seed of Abraham" in Scripture with no one sense cancelling out the meaning of the others. Also, supersessionists, in rightly claiming that Jesus is the fulfillment of the OT, mistakenly assume that the details of OT prophecies are absorbed into Christ in some Hindu or Platonic-like way that makes the specifics of these prophecies no longer relevant. In actuality, though, the NT often affirms OT expectations concerning Israel as a nation, the temple, the coming of a personal Antichrist, and the Day of the Lord. In contrast, the nonsupersessionist position is built on many explicit biblical passages that predict a coming salvation and restoration of the nation Israel.

Supersessionists, therefore, find themselves in the difficult situation of having to prove that explicit predictions of Israel's restoration do not mean what they meant when these predictions were first written. The task of the nonsupersessionist, though, is simpler and less risky. His main task is to show that no passage or passages clearly overturn what God has explicitly declared regarding Israel's future. Our view is that the NT harmonizes with the

OT but does not change its meaning. I fear that the supersessionist position is tampering with the strongest biblical evidence possible—multiple explicit declarations in both Testaments that the nation Israel will be saved and restored.

I will also argue that supersessionists have made a foundational error concerning God's intended purpose for Israel. Contrary to the supersessionist position, it is not God's intention for everyone who believes to become part of "Israel." Through Abraham, the nation Israel was created as a vehicle to bring blessings to "all the families of the earth" (Gen 12:2–3), but it has never been God's intent to make everyone who believes "Israel." Israel, through the ultimate Israelite, Jesus Christ, is the means for world-wide blessing, but Israel is not an end in itself. Thus, the error of supersessionism goes beyond just a misunderstanding of certain passages about Israel and the church; this view misses the purpose of Israel itself, which is to glorify God by bringing blessings to all people groups.

As for how this book will operate, I will offer a historical, hermeneutical, and theological analysis of supersessionism. The historical chapters will document how supersessionism came to be accepted by the Christian church. I will also show that while the early church often went beyond the NT in viewing the church as Israel, there was a strong consensus that national Israel would be saved, and some even held to what could be considered a restoration of Israel. I will also survey the doctrine of supersessionism in history until the present. Supersessionism has a long history dating back to the second century, but this view has also received a stiff challenge from the nonsupersessionist position since the time of the Reformation. I also will document how the supersessionist position has lost its grip on many Christians and denominations in the last 100 years.

This book will then shift to hermeneutical and theological issues related to the Israel-church relationship. Most of the discussion in these sections will focus on NT passages. There is a reason for this. Scholars on both sides of the supersessionism issue admit that the OT authors predicted a restoration of the nation Israel to her land with a role to play among the nations that included leadership and service.[2] Thus, the fact that Israel is promised a restoration in the OT is not disputed by most scholars. What is disputed, though, is how the NT understands the OT promises to Israel. Supersessionists claim that the NT transfers, interprets, or reinterprets OT promises to Israel and applies them to the church in a way that rules out a

---

[2]For instance, Riddlebarger, who takes a supersessionist view, states, "Another eschatological theme in the Old Testament is the promise that the nation of Israel will be gloriously restored in the distant future." K. Riddlebarger, *A Case for Amillennialism: Understanding the End Times* (Grand Rapids: Baker, 2003), 54.

future fulfillment with national Israel. In other words, supersessionists claim that the OT authors themselves believed in a future restoration of the nation Israel when they penned their prophecies, but these prophecies are being fulfilled or redirected in a way unforeseen by the OT writers to the exclusion of the original intent.

My approach of focusing mostly on NT passages should not be thought of as a capitulation to supersessionists and their insistence on NT priority over the OT. Far from it. I will argue that the integrity of OT passages must be maintained and emphasized. The eschatological message of the OT regarding Israel is not transcended and made into something other than what was originally intended. By focusing on NT passages, I intend to show that the NT's message concerning Israel is largely continuous with what the OT predicted. Thus, the NT, when properly understood, does not support supersessionism. In reality, it advocates the salvation and restoration of Israel.

The reader should also be aware that this book is primarily about the doctrine of supersessionism and whether the nation Israel will experience a national salvation and restoration. It is not a book about which view of the millennium is correct, nor is it a comprehensive discussion of ecclesiology or eschatology. For instance, my discussion of the church is limited mostly to how the church has been understood in regard to Israel. Also, this work is not a defense or refutation of any particular eschatological system such as covenant theology or dispensationalism. Certainly, the millennium and other eschatological issues are organically related to the Israel-church issue, and I am not denying the importance of those issues, but these topics are not the focus here. Likewise, our goal here is not to evaluate the systems of covenant theology and dispensationalism. *The main issue of this book is whether the Bible indicates that the NT church is the replacement or fulfillment of Israel and whether national Israel has any future role in God's plan.* Thus, I will deal directly with the passages and arguments most related to this issue.

One final note is needed. Many works that have addressed the issue of supersessionism have done so from the perspective of emphasizing the often ugly anti-Semitism of the Christian church throughout history. I appreciate those works and find them helpful and necessary.[3] For this book, though, I have purposely avoided much discussion of anti-Semitism. It is undeniable that anti-Jewish bias has often gone hand in hand with the supersessionist view, and it has influenced in a negative way how many

---

[3]For a helpful treatment of this topic, see B. E. Horner, *Future Israel: Why Christian Anti-Judaism Must Be Challenged*, NACSBT (Nashville: B&H, 2007).

view the OT and Israel. This point is relevant and cannot be ignored. Yet while there is a strong historical connection between anti-Semitism and the doctrine of supersessionism, I cannot rightly say that all supersessionists are inherently anti-Jewish. Some accept supersessionism because they believe it is biblical. So this book will focus mostly on the hermeneutical and theological beliefs associated with supersessionism, yet in doing so I acknowledge that anti-Jewish sentiments have often greased the pole on the slide toward replacement theology.

While there are many issues to consider when it comes to the Israel-church issue, I believe the Bible teaches that the nation Israel has a future. God will save and restore Israel for His glory and His electing purposes (Rom 11:28–29, 33–36). Thus, supersessionism is not a biblical doctrine. The great spiritual blessings poured out on believing Jews and Gentiles in the church today are consistent with, and not contrary to, God's future purposes to bring glory to Himself by saving and restoring the nation Israel. As Paul declared concerning Israel, "I ask, then, has God rejected His people? Absolutely not! . . . God has not rejected His people whom He foreknew" (Rom 11:1–2).

Part 1

Introduction to Supersessionism

Chapter 1

What Is Supersessionism?

As with any theological topic, defining terms is important for being accurate and avoiding misunderstandings. So what is the doctrine of replacement theology or supersessionism? Giving a title to the view that the church replaces, supersedes, or fulfills Israel as the people of God has not been without controversy or debate. As Woudstra observes, "The question whether it is more proper to speak of a replacement of the Jews by the Christian church or of an extension (continuation) of the OT people of God into that of the NT church is variously answered."[1]

A common designation used in scholarly literature to identify this position is *supersessionism*. The term *supersessionism* comes from two Latin words: *super* (on or upon) and *sedere* (to sit). It carries the idea of one person sitting on another's chair, displacing the latter.[2] The title "replacement theology" is often viewed as a synonym for *supersessionism*.[3] This title appears to be the most common designation in popular literature, at least for now.

The title *replacement theology* is not well received by some. Several have noted that they would rather be known as "fulfillment theologians" or some other title that is more positive. Lehrer, for example, shies away from the term *replacement theology* since he does not see the church replacing the nation Israel. He says, "Instead I would rather use the term 'fulfillment theology.' Israel was simply a picture of the true people of God, which the

---

[1] M. H. Woudstra, "Israel and the Church: A Case for Continuity," in *Continuity and Discontinuity: Perspectives on the Relationship Between the Old and New Testaments*, ed. J. S. Feinberg (Wheaton, IL: Crossway, 1988), 237. Woudstra believes that the terms, *replacement* and *continuation* are both acceptable and consistent with biblical teaching. See also G. B. Caird, *New Testament Theology* (Oxford: Clarendon, 1994), 55.

[2] C. M. Williamson, *A Guest in the House of Israel: Post-Holocaust Church Theology* (Louisville, KY: Westminster/John Knox, 1993), 268, n. 9.

[3] Diprose views the titles *replacement theology* and *supersessionism* as synonymous. He also notes that the title *replacement theology* is a "relatively new term in Christian theology." R. E. Diprose, *Israel in the Development of Christian Thought* (Rome: Istituto Biblico Evangelico Italiano, 2000), 31, n. 2.

church fulfills."[4] Unfortunately, for those who desire a different label, the titles *replacement theology* and *supersessionism* are better established and do not appear to be going away any time soon. Plus, many theologians who espouse a supersessionist view have used the terms *replace* and *replacement* in regard to Israel and the church. It is not the case that non-supersessionists[5] have imposed the title *replacement theology* against the will of supersessionists unfairly. Those who espouse the supersessionist view are partly responsible for this title since they often have used *replacement* or similar terminology themselves.

I have no trouble with the designation *replacement theology* because with the supersessionist view there is a taking away or transferring of what national Israel was promised to another group. One can use *fulfillment* terminology as some prefer, but in the end the result is the same—promises and covenants that were made with the nation Israel are no longer the possession of national Israel. Israel's promises and covenants now allegedly belong to another group that is not national Israel. This other group may be called the "new" or "true" Israel, but this does not change the fact that what was promised to one people group—national Israel—is now the possession of another group to the exclusion of national Israel.[6] Thus, the title *replacement theology* appears appropriate. Those who say, "I'm not a replacement theologian; I'm a fulfillment theologian" are not making the criticisms of replacement theology moot. Nor does it make the whole discussion of replacement theology irrelevant. Those who approach this issue should not be sidetracked by claims that "replacement theology" does not exist, only "fulfillment theology." In my study, I have found that those who teach that the church is the complete replacement or fulfillment of Israel use the same basic arguments. It is not as though replacement theology comes with its own set of arguments while fulfillment theology has a different compilation of arguments. The position is the same while some call it one thing and others call it another. If all of a sudden the title *fulfillment*

---

[4]S. Lehrer, *New Covenant Theology: Questions Answered* (n.p.: Steve Lehrer, 2006), 203. Lehrer is a leading representative of New Covenant Theology. Some view the church more as the *continuation* or *fulfillment* of national Israel. See H. Ridderbos, *Paul: An Outline of His Theology*, trans. J. R. De Witt (Grand Rapids: Eerdmans, 1975), 333–34; M. J. Erickson, *Christian Theology*, 2nd ed. (Grand Rapids: Baker, 1999), 1058–59.

[5]In this book I will use the terms *nonsupersessionism* and *nonsupersessionists* in contrast to supersessionism. For our purposes, a nonsupersessionist is one who does not believe that the church is the complete replacement or fulfillment of national Israel. A nonsupersessionist, as I define it, also holds to a future salvation and restoration of the nation Israel.

[6]As will be made clear later, the nation that will see the promises fulfilled will be the *believing* nation of Israel.

theology became accepted by all, it would not change any of the arguments or points presented in this book.

So how should we handle this issue of terminology? First, we should focus more on the concept than the title. While I often use the titles *supersessionism* and *replacement theology*, I am addressing an idea more than trying to further the acceptance of a title. Second, we should respect those who prefer "fulfillment" terminology over "replacement." If I am talking to a person who feels this way, I do not say, "You are not a fulfillment theologian; you are a replacement theologian! Too bad!" That approach is not helpful. Yet the titles *replacement theology* and *supersessionism* are well established. I will use mostly these two designations in this work. I prefer the term *supersessionism* because it can encompass the concepts of "replace" and "fulfill."

DEFINING SUPERSESSIONISM

Several theologians have offered definitions of *supersessionism* or *replacement theology*. According to Walter C. Kaiser Jr., "Replacement theology . . . declared that the Church, Abraham's spiritual seed, had replaced national Israel in that it had transcended and fulfilled the terms of the covenant given to Israel, which covenant Israel had lost because of disobedience."[7] Diprose defines *replacement theology* as the view that "the Church completely and permanently replaced ethnic Israel in the working out of God's plan and as recipient of OT promises to Israel."[8]

Soulen argues that supersessionism is linked with how some view the coming of Jesus Christ: "According to this teaching [supersessionism], God chose the Jewish people after the fall of Adam in order to prepare the world for the coming of Jesus Christ, the Savior. After Christ came, however, the special role of the Jewish people came to an end and its place was taken by the church, the new Israel."[9] Ridderbos asserts that there is a positive and negative element to the supersessionist view: "On the one hand, in a positive sense it presupposes that the church springs from, is born out of Israel; on the other hand, the church takes the place of Israel as the historical people of God."[10]

These definitions from Kaiser, Diprose, Soulen, and Ridderbos appear consistent with statements of those who have explicitly declared that the

---

[7]W. C. Kaiser Jr., "An Assessment of 'Replacement Theology': The Relationship Between the Israel of the Abrahamic–Davidic Covenant and the Christian Church," *Mishkan* 21 (1994): 9.

[8]Diprose, *Israel in the Development of Christian Thought*, 2.

[9]K. Soulen, *The God of Israel and Christian Theology* (Minneapolis: Fortress, 1996), 1–2.

[10]Ridderbos, *Paul*, 333–34.

church is the replacement of Israel. Bruce K. Waltke, for instance, declares that the NT teaches the "hard fact that national Israel and its law have been permanently replaced by the church and the New Covenant."[11] According to LaRondelle, the NT affirms that "Israel would no longer be the people of God and would be *replaced* by a people that would accept the Messiah and His message of the kingdom of God."[12] LaRondelle believes this "people" is the church who replaces "the Christ-rejecting nation."[13] Boettner, too, writes, "It may seem harsh to say that 'God is done with the Jews.' But the fact of the matter is that He is through with them as a unified national group having anything more to do with the evangelization of the world. That mission has been taken from them and given to the Christian Church (Matt. 21:43)."[14]

Supersessionism, therefore, appears to be based on two core beliefs: (1) the nation Israel has somehow completed or forfeited its status as the people of God and will never again possess a unique role or function apart from the church, and (2) the church is now the true Israel that has permanently replaced or superseded national Israel as the people of God. In the context of Israel and the church, supersessionism is the view that *the NT Church is the new and/or true Israel that has forever superseded the nation Israel as the people of God*. The result is that the church has become the sole inheritor of God's covenant blessings originally promised to national Israel in the OT. This rules out a future restoration of the nation Israel with a unique identity, role, and purpose.[15]

VARIATIONS WITHIN SUPERSESSIONISM

While all supersessionists affirm that the church has superseded national Israel as the people of God, there are variations within supersessionism. Thus, this is not a one-size-fits-all perspective. Three major forms of supersessionism have been recognized: punitive supersessionism, economic supersessionism, and structural supersessionism.

---

[11]B. K. Waltke, "Kingdom Promises as Spiritual," in *Continuity and Discontinuity*, 274. He also states, "The Jewish *nation* no longer has a place as the special people of God; that place has been taken by the Christian community which fulfills God's purpose for Israel" (275). Emphasis in original.

[12]H. K. LaRondelle, *The Israel of God in Prophecy: Principles of Prophetic Interpretation* (Berrien Springs, MI: Andrews University Press, 1983), 101. Emphasis in original.

[13]Ibid.

[14]L. Boettner, *The Millennium* (Philadelphia: P&R, 1957), 89–90. According to Bright, "The New Testament triumphantly hails the Church as Israel . . . the true heir of Israel's hope." J. Bright, *The Kingdom of God: The Biblical Concept and Its Meaning for the Church* (Nashville: Abingdon, 1953), 226.

[15]I use this term *restoration* strategically, and by it I mean more than just a salvation of Israel. By *restoration* I mean a return of Israel to her land and a role to the nations in an earthly millennium.

Punitive Supersessionism

"Punitive" or "retributive" supersessionism emphasizes Israel's *disobedience* and *punishment* by God as the reason for its displacement as the people of God. Or in other words, Israel is replaced by the church because the nation acted wickedly and has forfeited the right to be the people of God.

As Fackre explains, this form of supersessionism "holds that the rejection of Christ both eliminates Israel from God's covenant love and provokes divine retribution."[16] With punitive supersessionism, according to Soulen, "God abrogates God's covenant with Israel . . . on account of Israel's rejection of Christ and the gospel."[17] Because the Jews reject Christ, "God in turn angrily rejects and punishes the Jews."[18] In sum, with punitive supersessionism, God has rejected the Jews because of their disobedience and their rejection of Christ.

Belief in punitive supersessionism was common in the patristic era. Hippolytus (c. 205), for example, promoted punitive supersessionism when he declared, "And surely you [the Jews] have been darkened in the eyes of your soul with a darkness utter and everlasting. . . . Furthermore, hear this yet more serious word: 'And their back do you bend always.' This means, in order that they may be slaves to the nations, not four hundred and thirty years as in Egypt, nor seventy as in Babylon, but bend them to servitude, he says, 'always.'"[19]

Origen (c. 185–254), too, espoused a form of punitive supersessionism: "And we say with confidence that they [the Jews] will never be restored to their former condition. For they committed a crime of the most unhallowed kind."[20] Lactantius (c. 304–313) also asserted that the Jews were abandoned by God because of their disobedience: "For unless they [the Jews] did this [repent], and laying aside their vanities, return to their God, it would come to pass that He would change His covenant, that is, bestow the inheritance of eternal life upon foreign nations, and collect to Himself a more faithful people out of those who were aliens by birth. . . . On account of these impieties of theirs He cast them off forever."[21]

Punitive supersessionism was also held by Martin Luther. For him, the destruction of Jerusalem was proof of God's permanent rejection of Israel: "'Listen, Jew, are you aware that Jerusalem and your sovereignty, together

---

[16]G. J. Fackre, *Ecumenical Faith in Evangelical Perspective* (Grand Rapids: Eerdmans, 1993), 148.

[17]Soulen, *The God of Israel and Christian Theology*, 30.

[18]Ibid.

[19]Hippolytus, *Treatise Against the Jews* 6, *ANF* 5:220.

[20]Origen, *Against Celsus* 4.22, *ANF* 4:506.

[21]Lactantius, *The Divine Institutes* 4.11, *ANF* 7:109.

with your temple and priesthood, have been destroyed for over 1,460 years?' . . . For such ruthless wrath of God is sufficient evidence that they assuredly have erred and gone astray. . . . Therefore this work of wrath is proof that the Jews, surely rejected by God, are no longer his people, and neither is he any longer their God."[22]

Economic Supersessionism

A second form of supersessionism is "economic" supersessionism. This view is not as harsh as punitive supersessionism since it does not emphasize Israel's disobedience and punishment as the primary reason for its permanent displacement as the people of God. Instead, it focuses on God's plan in history for the people of God to transfer from an ethnic group (Israel) to a universal group not based on ethnicity (church). In other words, economic supersessionism asserts that God planned from the beginning for Israel's role as the people of God to expire with the coming of Christ and the establishment of the church.

According to Soulen, economic supersessionism is the view that "carnal Israel's history is providentially ordered from the outset to be taken up into the spiritual church."[23] With this form of supersessionism, national Israel corresponds to Christ's church in a merely prefigurative and carnal way. Thus, Christ, with His advent, "brings about the obsolescence of carnal Israel and inaugurates the age of the spiritual church."[24]

With economic supersessionism, Israel is not replaced primarily because of its disobedience but rather because its role in the history of redemption expired with the coming of Jesus. It is now superseded by the arrival of a new spiritual Israel, the Christian church. For those who adopt an economic supersessionist view, the key figure in bringing about this expiration of national Israel's role in redemptive history is Jesus Christ. According to Bultmann, "The new *aeon* has dawned in the Christ-event."[25] As a result, "the people of God, the true Israel, is present in the Christian community."[26]

Economic supersessionism, according to Soulen, "logically entails the ontological, historical, and moral obsolescence of Israel's existence after Christ."[27] With His coming, Jesus, the ultimate Israelite, fulfills all God's

---

[22]Martin Luther, "On the Jews and Their Lies," in *LW* 47:138–39. See also *WA* 53:418.

[23]Soulen, *The God of Israel and Christian Theology*, 181, n. 6.

[24]Ibid., 29.

[25]R. Bultmann, "Prophecy and Fulfillment," in *Essays on Old Testament Hermeneutics*, ed. C. Westermann, trans. J. C. G. Greig (Richmond, VA: John Knox, 1969), 71.

[26]Ibid.

[27]Soulen, *The God of Israel and Christian Theology*, 30. Dubois writes, "Now that the messiah has come, the church—*versus Israel*—has taken the place of the 'old' Israel and the Jewish people no longer has any reason to occupy the historic land of Israel." M. J. Dubois, "Israel and Christian Self-Understanding," in *Voices from Jerusalem: Jews and Christians Reflect on the Holy Land*, ed. D. Burrell and Y. Landau (New York: Paulist, 1992), 65. Emphasis in original.

plans and promises regarding Israel. All those who are in Jesus, then, are the true Israel. This appears to be the approach of V. S. Poythress:

> Because Christ is an Israelite and Christians are in union with Christ, Christians partake of the benefits promised to Israel and Judah in Jeremiah. With whom is the new covenant made? It is made with Israel and Judah. Hence it is made with Christians by virtue of Christ the Israelite. Thus one might say that Israel and Judah themselves undergo a transformation at the first coming of Christ, because Christ is the final, supremely faithful Israelite. Around him all true Israel gathers.[28]

While punitive supersessionism was popular in the early church, several early church fathers also espoused economic supersessionism.[29] Melito of Sardis, for example, declared, "The people [Israel] was precious before the church arose, and the law was marvelous before the gospel was elucidated. But when the church arose and the gospel took precedence the model was made void, conceding its power to the reality. . . . The people was made void when the church arose."[30]

A more recent advocate of economic supersessionism is Karl Barth.[31] He stated,

> The first Israel, constituted on the basis of physical descent from Abraham, has fulfilled its mission now that the Saviour of the world has sprung from it and its Messiah has appeared. Its members can only accept this fact with gratitude, and in confirmation of their own deepest election and calling attach themselves to the people of this Saviour, their own King, whose members the Gentiles are now called to be as well. Its mission as a natural community has now run its course and cannot be continued or repeated.[32]

---

[28]V. S. Poythress, *Understanding Dispensationalists*, 2nd. ed. (Phillipsburg, NJ: P&R, 1994), 106. See also J. W. Wenham, *Christ and the Bible* (Downers Grove, IL: InterVarsity, 1972), 106–7.

[29]Pelikan points out that Gen 49:10 was sometimes used by the early fathers as evidence that the "historic mission of Israel" came to an "end with the coming of Jesus." J. Pelikan, *The Emergence of the Catholic Tradition (100–600)*, vol. 1 of *The Christian Tradition: A History of the Development of Doctrine* (Chicago: University of Chicago Press, 1971), 56; cf. Justin, *First Apology* 32, ANF 1:173.

[30]Melito of Sardis, *On Pascha*, trans. S. G. Hall (Oxford: Clarendon, 1979), 21.

[31]According to Soulen, "Barth's theology of consummation embodies the logic of economic supersessionism as clearly as any in the history of the church. The incarnation brings Israel's history to a conclusion in principle, after which Israel's sole legitimate destiny is to be absorbed into the spiritual church." Soulen, *The God of Israel and Christian Theology*, 92–93.

[32]K. Barth, *CD* III/2, 584.

In line with an economic supersessionist viewpoint, N. T. Wright asserts that "Israel's purpose had come to its head in Jesus' work."[33] As a result, "those who now belonged to Jesus' people . . . claimed to be the *continuation of Israel in a new situation*."[34] Wright also argues that "Jesus intended those who responded to him to see themselves as the true, restored Israel."[35]

Structural Supersessionism

According to Soulen, there is a third form of supersessionism—*structural supersessionism*. Unlike the first two forms of supersessionism we have looked at, which are primarily theological positions concerning Israel, structural supersessionism is more of a hermeneutic or perspective concerning the Jewish Scriptures.

In explaining the concept of structural supersessionism, Soulen asserts that there has been a deeply engrained bias against the Jewish Scriptures of the OT on the part of Christians. Soulen links this form of supersessionism with how Christians have traditionally understood the biblical canon: "The problem of supersessionism in Christian theology goes beyond the explicit teaching that the church has displaced Israel as God's people in the economy of salvation. At a deeper level, the problem of supersessionism coincides with the way in which Christians have traditionally understood the theological and narrative unity of the Christian canon as a whole."[36]

According to Soulen, whereas punitive and economic supersessionism are "explicit doctrinal perspectives," structural supersessionism concerns how the standard canonical narrative as a whole has been perceived.[37] Thus, "structural supersessionism refers to the narrative logic of the standard model whereby it renders the Hebrew Scriptures largely indecisive for shaping Christian convictions about how God's works as Consummator and as Redeemer engage humankind in universal and enduring ways."[38]

Soulen argues that the standard canonical narrative model, which the church has accepted since Justin Martyr and Irenaeus, turns on four key episodes: (1) God's intention to create the first parents, (2) the fall, (3) Christ's incarnation and the inauguration of the church, and (4) the

---

[33]N. T. Wright, *The New Testament and the People of God* (Minneapolis: Fortress, 1992), 457.

[34]Ibid. Emphasis in original. According to Wright, these who make up the redefined Israel were able to draw upon Israel's images, read Israel's Scriptures, and "fulfill Israel's vocation on behalf of the world" (457–58).

[35]N. T. Wright, *Jesus and the Victory of God* (Minneapolis: Fortress, 1996), 316. Emphasis in original.

[36]Soulen, *The God of Israel and Christian Theology*, 33.

[37]Ibid., 181, n. 6.

[38]Ibid.

final consummation.[39] He says two facts stand out from the narrative content of this standard model.

First, the foreground of this standard model emphasizes God's engagement with human creation in "cosmic and universal terms."[40] Second, the foreground of this model "completely neglects the Hebrew Scriptures with the exception of Genesis 1–3!"[41] The standard model tells how God engaged Adam and Eve as Consummator and how God's consummating plan for them was disrupted at the fall. The story, however, then "leaps to the Apostolic Witness" and the "deliverance of humankind from the fall through Jesus Christ."[42]

Thus, according to Soulen, God's purposes as Consummator and Redeemer "engage human creation in a manner that simply outflanks the greater part of the Hebrew Scriptures and, above all, their witness to God's history with the people of Israel."[43] What is the result of this leap over the Hebrew Scriptures? God's identity as the God of Israel and His history with the Jewish people "become largely indecisive for the Christian conception of God."[44]

Putting it together, Soulen is claiming that most supersessionists have adopted a hermeneutical approach that ignores or removes the Hebrew Scriptures of the OT from having a voice. Clearly, those who hold a supersessionist view will deny the claim of Soulen or call it something different from "structural supersessionism." But in my view, what Soulen is discussing is accurate and is similar to the supersessionist concept of "New Testament priority" in which the NT is viewed as superseding the original meanings of OT passages. I will have more to say on this later in this book. For now, though, I agree with Soulen's assessment. I also concur with Craig Soulen when he states that the "structural nature of supersessionism" has established "the deep set tradition of excluding ethnic, national Israel from the theological reading of Scripture."[45]

---

[39]Ibid., 31.
[40]Ibid.
[41]Ibid.
[42]Ibid., 32.
[43]Ibid.
[44]Ibid., 33.
[45]C. A. Blaising, "The Future of Israel as a Theological Question," *JETS* 44 (2001): 442.

Chapter 2

Supersessionism and the Future of Israel

In light of our discussion so far, it might seem natural to assume that the doctrine of supersessionism always leads to the view that Israel has absolutely no future whatsoever in God's plan. God is done with Israel and that's that. While this certainly is the case for many supersessionists, others believe in or are open to some future significance for Israel as a nation or the Jews as a group. Thus, this chapter will highlight some important distinctions and beliefs within the doctrine of supersessionism in regard to Israel.

SALVATION AND RESTORATION

Two terms are important for understanding what some supersessionists believe about Israel. These terms are *salvation* and *restoration*. In short, some supersessionists believe there will be a future *salvation* of Israel, but no supersessionists hold that there will be a *restoration* of the nation Israel.

So what is the difference between Israel's salvation and their restoration? Belief in the salvation of the nation Israel means that in the last days the Jews as a group will believe in Christ and be saved. In short, *salvation* means simply that many Jews will believe in Christ and be saved. The concept of *restoration*, on the other hand, includes the ideas of Israel being saved and replanted in their land and given a unique role and mission to the nations. The restoration of Israel means that Israel will have a role and a place that is uniquely theirs.

Those who are nonsupersessionists believe in both concepts. They believe Israel as a nation will be *saved*, and they also believe Israel will be *restored* as a national entity. In fact, belief in a restoration of Israel is the main factor that distinguishes all supersessionists from all nonsupersessionists. Put simply, no supersessionists believe in Israel's restoration, but all nonsupersessionists believe in Israel's restoration.

In regard to Israel's future, there are two major variations on the future of Israel among supersessionism. "Strong supersessionism" asserts that Israel will not experience salvation as a nation. "Moderate supersessionism," though, holds that the nation Israel will experience salvation. Thus, the major distinguishing factor between supersessionists is whether they believe in a future salvation of Israel.

MODERATE SUPERSESSIONISM

Below are statements from various moderate supersessionists who hold that the church is the new Israel but still hold to a future for national Israel. Ridderbos, for instance, believes there is "tension-filled unity" concerning Israel's rejection and its election.[1] He asserts that "the church takes the place of Israel as the historical people of God."[2] For him, "this means a new definition of the people of God, and likewise a new concept of Israel."[3] This belief, though, does not lead him to conclude that the historical people of Israel have permanently lost their role in the history of redemption.[4] For Ridderbos, the historical bond between God and Israel continues to be maintained with real significance: "Thus, on one hand Paul is able to see the church of the gentiles as endowed with all the privileges and blessings of Israel, and to see it occupy the place of unbelieving Israel, and yet on the other hand to uphold to the full the continuation of God's original redemptive intentions with Israel as the historical people of God."[5]

According to Ridderbos, this tension regarding Israel's rejection and election is consistent: "There is therefore no contradiction between the definition of the essence of the New Testament church as the people of God and holding to Israel as the object of God's irrevocable gift of grace and calling."[6]

This dialectical approach concerning Israel's acceptance and rejection is found often in church history. Tertullian, for example, declared that the church had overcome Israel as the people of God and that Israel had been

---

[1]H. Ridderbos, *Paul: An Outline of His Theology*, trans. J. R. De Witt (Grand Rapids: Eerdmans, 1975), 356.

[2]Ibid., 333–34.

[3]Ibid., 334.

[4]Ibid., 355.

[5]Ibid., 360–61.

[6]Ibid., 360.

"divorced" by God.[7] Yet he also encouraged Christians to "rejoice" at the coming "restoration of Israel."[8]

Hood asserts that there was a "dualistic view" concerning the fate of the Jews among theologians of the Middle Ages.[9] According to Hood, "medieval Christians believed Jews would eventually accept Christ and be saved, but they also saw them as dangerous infidels who had been rejected and punished by God."[10] Hood notes that Thomas Aquinas, like other medieval theologians of his day, accepted the supersessionism theory as a "given," yet Aquinas also held to a future salvation of the Jews.[11] Aquinas attempted to deal with the "dualities" of this view. As Aquinas states, "He [Aquinas] made an effort to explain how it was possible for Jews to be at the same time chosen *and* rejected, ignorant *and* malicious Christ-killers, damned *and* destined for salvation."[12]

Calvin's views on Israel also appear to evidence a rejection-acceptance tension. According to VanGemeren, "some have seen the utter rejection of Israel in Calvin's writing, whereas others have also viewed the hope for national Israel."[13] Williamson, for example, believes there is a tension in Calvin's writings on this issue when he states, "On the one hand, Calvin strongly insisted that God's promise to and covenant with the people Israel was unconditional, unbreakable, and gracious. . . . On the other hand, Calvin often makes statements exactly opposing the above."[14]

At times, Calvin made statements consistent with supersessionism. For him, the "all Israel" who will be saved in Rom 11:26 is a reference to the church composed of Jews and Gentiles.[15] He also took the interpretation that the "Israel of God" in Gal 6:16 refers to "all believers, whether Jews

---

[7]Tertullian, PL 2:598.

[8]Ibid., 2:996.

[9]J. Y. B. Hood, *Aquinas and the Jews* (Philadelphia: University of Pennsylvania Press, 1995), xii.

[10]Ibid.

[11]Aquinas believed in a future conversion of the Jews based on his view of Romans 11. See T. Aquinas, *Sancti Thomae de Aquino Super Epistolam B. Pauli ad Romanos lectura*, 11.4, http://www.unav.es/filosofia/alarcon/cro05.html, accessed January 26, 2004. Especially significant is the statement in which Aquinas asserted that Paul believed all Jews will be saved in a general sense.

[12]Hood, *Aquinas and the Jews*, xii. Emphases in original.

[13]W. VanGemeren, "Israel as the Hermeneutical Crux in the Interpretation of Prophecy," *WTJ* 45 (1983): 142.

[14]C. M. Williamson, *A Guest in the House of Israel: Post-Holocaust Church Theology* (Louisville, KY: Westminster/John Knox, 1993), 131.

[15]J. Calvin, *The Epistles of Paul the Apostle to the Romans and to the Thessalonians*, ed. D. W. Torrance and T. F. Torrance, trans. R. Mackenzie (Grand Rapids: Eerdmans, 1961), 255.

or Gentiles, who were united into one church."[16] At other times, though, Calvin made statements that seem to indicate he believed in some form of a future for the Jewish people. For example, in his commentary on Isa 59:20, he stated,

> Paul quotes this passage, (Rom. xi. 26,) in order to shew that there is still some remaining hope among the Jews; although from their unconquerable obstinacy it might be inferred that they were altogether cast off and doomed to eternal death. But because God is continually mindful of his covenant, and "his gifts and calling are without repentance," (Rom. xi. 29) Paul justly concludes that it is impossible that there shall not at length be some remnant that come to Christ, and obtain that salvation which he has procured. Thus the Jews must at length be collected along with the Gentiles that out of both "there may be one fold" under Christ. (John x. 16). . . . Hence we have said that Paul infers that he [Christ] could not be the redeemer of the world, without belonging to some Jews, whose fathers he had chosen, and to whom this promise was directly addressed.[17]

More recently, a dualistic view of Israel can be found in the writings of Ladd. Ladd asserted that the church is now the new "spiritual Israel."[18] Yet he also believed "the New Testament clearly affirms the salvation of literal Israel."[19] He based this conclusion on his study of Romans 11. Commenting on Rom 11:26 and its statement that "all Israel will be saved," Ladd declared, "It is difficult to escape the conclusion that this means literal Israel."[20]

Erickson, too, holds that the church is the new Israel, yet he also believes in a salvation of national Israel: "To sum up then: the church is the new Israel. It occupies the place in the new covenant that Israel occupied in the old. . . . There is a special future coming for national Israel, however, through large-scale conversion to Christ and entry into the church."[21] He also says, "There is, however, a future for national Israel. They are still the special people of God."[22]

---

[16]J. Calvin, "Commentaries on the Epistles of Paul to the Galatians and Ephesians," in *Calvin's Commentaries*, trans. W. Pringle (Edinburgh: Calvin Translation Society, 1844–56; repr., Grand Rapids: Baker, 1999), 21:186.

[17]J. Calvin, "Commentary on the Book of the Prophet Isaiah," in *Calvin's Commentaries*, 8:269.

[18]G. E. Ladd, "Historic Premillennialism," in *The Meaning of the Millennium: Four Views*, ed. R. G. Clouse (Downers Grove, IL: InterVarsity, 1977), 25.

[19]Ibid., 28.

[20]Ibid., 27.

[21]M. J. Erickson, *Christian Theology*, 2nd ed. (Grand Rapids: Baker, 1999), 1053.

[22]Ibid.

Grudem, in his discussion of Israel and the church, espouses a supersessionist view when he states that "many New Testament verses . . . understand the church as the 'new Israel' or new 'people of God.'"[23] Yet he also declares that the Jews have a future in the plan of God: "I affirm the conviction that Rom. 9–11 teaches a future large-scale conversion of the Jewish people."[24] The Catholic theologian Rahner said Israel still possesses some role in salvation history: "The church is made up of Jews and pagans. . . . But the unfinished role of Israel in salvation history is also recognized (cf. Rom. 9–11)."[25]

As these quotations show, it is possible to believe the church is the new Israel while still holding to a large-scale conversion of the Jews. This salvation, though, is usually viewed as an incorporation into the Christian church. While affirming a future salvation of the Jews, supersessionists do not see this salvation as inferring any special role for Israel apart from the church. As Erickson explains,

> In Romans 9 and Galatians 3, for example, it is difficult to escape the conclusion that Paul regarded the church, Jew and Gentile alike, as the true heir to the promises originally made to national Israel. It does appear that there will be a period of special favor toward the Jews and that they will in large numbers turn to God. It seems likely, however, that this will be brought about through their being converted and integrated into the church rather than through God resuming the relationship He had with them, as the chosen or covenant nation, in the Old Testament.[26]

So in addition to affirming the existence of three variations of supersessionism—punitive, economic, and structural—it is also valid to affirm that there are variations within supersessionism on the future of Israel. A stronger form of supersessionism holds that there is no special future whatsoever for national Israel or ethnic Jews as a group. A milder or more moderate form of supersessionism holds that the church supersedes national Israel as the people of God, but it also asserts that there will be a future *en masse* salvation of Jews into the Christian church.

---

[23]W. Grudem, *Systematic Theology: An Introduction to Biblical Doctrine* (Grand Rapids: Zondervan, 1994), 861.

[24]Ibid., n. 17.

[25]K. Rahner, *Foundations of Christian Faith: An Introduction to the Idea of Christianity*, trans. W. V. Dych (New York: Seabury, 1978), 338.

[26]M. J. Erickson, *A Basic Guide to Eschatology* (Grand Rapids: Baker, 1998), 123–24.

Part 2

Supersessionism in Church History

Chapter 3

Factors Leading to Supersessionism

Supersessionism has been a popular view for many Christians throughout church history. But just how did many come to accept supersessionism? In later chapters, I will survey the history of supersessionism in the patristic, medieval, Reformation, and modern eras, but in this chapter, I will discuss the historical, political, theological, and hermeneutical factors that contributed to the rise and acceptance of the supersessionist view. Thus, in this chapter I will focus on why supersessionism developed as an accepted doctrine. Later I will discuss what significant theologians of church history had to say about the Israel-church issue.

VIEWS ON THE ORIGIN OF SUPERSESSIONISM

Church historians generally agree that supersessionism originated and developed early in the church's history.[1] The precise time supersessionism began, though, is more difficult to ascertain. Some, for example, hold that it began with the teachings of the NT writers.[2] Others point to Justin (c. 100–165) as the key figure in the origin and development of supersessionism.[3] Justin is important because he was the first church father explicitly to identify the church as "the true spiritual Israel."[4] Blaising, on the other hand, asserts that supersessionism first arose after the suppression of the Bar Kokhba revolt against Rome in AD 135.[5] Others have argued for a later date for the replacement view. Kaiser, for instance,

---

[1]See A. E. McGrath, *Christian Theology: An Introduction*, 2nd. ed. (Malden, MA: Blackwell, 1998), 461–62.

[2]B. K. Waltke, for instance, asserts that the New Testament teaches the "hard fact that national Israel and its law have been permanently replaced by the church and the New Covenant." B. K. Waltke, "Kingdom Promises as Spiritual," in *Continuity and Discontinuity: Perspectives on the Relationship Between the Old and New Testaments*, ed. J. S. Feinberg (Wheaton, IL: Crossway, 1988), 274.

[3]For information on how Justin is perceived, see J. S. Siker, *Disinheriting the Jews: Abraham in Early Christian Controversy* (Louisville, KY: Westminster John Knox, 1991), 15. According to Siker, A. von Harnack viewed Justin as inaugurating a new era in how Christians perceived themselves in relation to Israel (15–16).

[4]Justin, *Dialogue with Trypho* 11, *ANF* 1:200.

[5]C. A. Blaising, "The Future of Israel as a Theological Question," *JETS* 44 (2001): 435.

believes that supersessionism has its origins in the "political-ecclesiastical alliance forged between Eusebius Pamphilius and the Emperor Constantine."[6] For Kaiser, a theology of replacement arose in the fourth century when "the church began to adopt an anti-Jewish stance that had an enormous effect on its theological constructions."[7]

Historically, though, the rise and acceptance of supersessionism preceded Justin. Justin is important in regard to supersessionism, but he was not the originator of this view. Instead, he reflected what many in the church had already come to accept concerning Israel and the church. As R. L. Saucy has observed, Justin's statement "was only the capstone of a developing tendency in the church to appropriate to itself the attributes and prerogatives that formerly belonged to historical Israel."[8] Siker, too, rightly states that "Justin marks the end of an era, the culmination of a process in formative Christianity that had begun much earlier."[9] Likewise, the political-ecclesiastical alliance between Eusebius and Constantine solidified the replacement position as the official view of the church, yet the seeds of supersessionism predate this alliance by two centuries.

The rise of supersessionism can be traced to events in the first two centuries of the church. During this period, several political, historical, and cultural developments converged that led some to believe that the church had superseded Israel as the people of God.[10] Before looking specifically at these factors, though, a word of caution is necessary. The origin of supersessionism is a complex topic. Thus, simplistic notions that any one person or event was the sole beginning point of this position must be avoided. In addition, it is difficult to locate a precise date when supersessionism formally became accepted.

Three factors contributed to the acceptance of supersessionism in the early church: (1) the increasing Gentile composition of the early church,

---

[6]W. C. Kaiser Jr., "An Assessment of 'Replacement Theology': The Relationship Between the Israel of the Abrahamic–Davidic Covenant and the Christian Church," *Mishkan* 21 (1994): 9.

[7]W. C. Kaiser Jr., "An Epangelical Response," in *Dispensationalism, Israel and the Church: The Search for Definition*, ed. C. A. Blaising and D. L. Bock (Grand Rapids: Zondervan, 1992), 361.

[8]R. L. Saucy, *The Case for Progressive Dispensationalism: The Interface Between Dispensational and Nondispensational Theology* (Grand Rapids: Zondervan, 1993), 212. Saucy also notes, "With Justin's statement, the developing tendency of replacement was complete. There was no longer any place for historical Israel in salvation history. The prophecies addressed to this people henceforth belonged to the church" (212). Richardson, too, observes that Justin's statement was "not itself the great divide" but "the sign of something more profound," the long-standing tendency for Christianity to view itself "as the heir of all which Israel once possessed." P. Richardson, *Israel in the Apostolic Church* (Cambridge: Cambridge University Press, 1969), 1.

[9]Siker, *Disinheriting the Jews*, 16.

[10]According to Wylen, "There was no sudden rift between Christians and Jews, but rather an ever-widening chasm that grew over the years. Some of the causes were doctrinal. Others were social and historical." S. M. Wylen, *The Jews in the Time of Jesus* (Mahwah, NJ: Paulist, 1996), 190.

(2) the church's perception of the destructions of Jerusalem in AD 70 and 135, and (3) a hermeneutical approach that allowed the church to appropriate Israel's promises to itself. Together these factors contributed to the belief that the church had permanently replaced Israel as God's people.

INCREASING GENTILE COMPOSITION OF THE EARLY CHURCH

In its earliest years, the church consisted almost exclusively of Jewish Christians who were under the direction of Jewish apostles. Koester points out that "one could with justification designate the whole first generation of Christians as 'Jewish Christian.'"[11] As time progressed, however, the church's population became increasingly Gentile, and the influence of the Jewish community decreased significantly.[12] Wilson notes this shift from a Jewish to a Gentile church: "After the apostles died, the next generation of leaders was mostly gentile, especially in the great centers of Christian growth, which included Antioch and Rome. The church had begun within Judaism as an all-Jewish sect, but by the early part of the second century its adherents—especially in the Diaspora—were predominately non-Jews."[13]

The failed second Jewish revolt against the Romans under Bar Kokhba in AD 132–35 contributed to the declining Jewish influence in the church. Part of this was due to the decree of the Roman leader Hadrian who forbade Jews from entering Jerusalem after the rebellion. This event affected the leadership of the Jerusalem church. According to Eusebius, 15 Jews had occupied the position of bishop in Jerusalem,[14] but after Hadrian's decree, Jerusalem had its first Gentile bishop—Marcus.[15]

---

[11]H. Koester, *History and Literature of Early Christianity*, trans. H. Koester (New York: Walter de Gruyter, 1982), 198. "For approximately ten years after the ascension of Christ, early Christians consisted entirely of Jewish converts." H. W. House, "The Church's Appropriation of Israel's Blessings," in *Israel, the Land and the People: An Evangelical Affirmation of God's Promises*, ed. H. W. House (Grand Rapids: Kregel, 1998), 83. See also M. R. Wilson, *Our Father Abraham: Jewish Roots of the Christian Faith* (Grand Rapids: Eerdmans, 1989), 41.

[12]See Eusebius, *Church History* 4.6.4, *NPNF*[2] 1:177–78.

[13]Wilson, *Our Father* Abraham:, 79.

[14]Eusebius, *Church History* 4.5.1–3, *NPNF*[2] 1:176. "The chronology of the bishops of Jerusalem I have nowhere found preserved in writing; for tradition says that they were all short lived. But I have learned this much from writings, that until the siege of the Jews, which took place under Adrian, there were fifteen bishops in succession there all of whom are said to have been of Hebrew descent, and to have received the knowledge of Christ in purity, so that they were approved by those who were able to judge of such matters, and were deemed worthy of the episcopate. For their whole church consisted then of believing Hebrews who continued from the days of the apostles until the siege which took place at this time; in which siege the Jews, having again rebelled against the Romans, were conquered after severe battles. But since the bishops of the circumcision ceased at this time, it is proper to give here a list of their names from the beginning."

[15]Eusebius, *Church History* 4.6.4, *NPNF*[2]1:178.

The Jewish Christians who eventually returned to Jerusalem after the failed revolt continued to have an influence in the church, but their influence was "in other places" as House states, "Christianity had become for all intents and purposes a Gentile religion."[16] Eusebius took note of this shift from a Jewish to a Gentile church that happened as a result of the failed revolt:

> And thus, when the city had been emptied of the Jewish nation and had suffered the total destruction of its ancient inhabitants, it was colonized by a different race, and the Roman city which subsequently arose changed its name and was called Aelia, in honor of the emperor Aelius Adrian. And as the church there was now composed of Gentiles, the first one to assume the government of it after the bishops of the circumcision was Marcus.[17]

The impact of this development was a marginalizing of Jewish influence on the church. As House points out, "With the end of the Second Jewish War against Rome, Jewish influence and importance became marginalized. It had become so irrelevant to the majority of the church that by the fourth century, at the council of Nicea, eighteen members had come from Palestine. Every one was Gentile and not a single Jewish bishop attended."[18]

According to Siker, Jewish Christians "were eventually absorbed into an overwhelmingly Gentile Christianity."[19] As a result, the church increasingly became the *ecclesia ex gentibus* (church of the Gentiles). This growing Gentile presence in the church led to "theological questions regarding the status of the Jews before God."[20]

THE CHURCH'S PERSPECTIVE ON THE TWO DESTRUCTIONS OF JERUSALEM

The destruction of Jerusalem by the Romans in AD 70[21] and 135[22] had significant implications for how non-Christian Jews and Christians viewed each other. In the eyes of many Jews, Jewish Christians were traitors for

---

[16]House, "The Church's Appropriation of Israel's Blessings," 93. See also J. L. Gonzalez, *The Story of Christianity* (San Francisco: HarperSanFrancisco, 1984), 1:22.

[17]Eusebius, *Church History* 4.6.4, *NPNF*[2] 1:177–78.

[18]House, "The Church's Appropriation of Israel's Blessings," 93.

[19]Siker, *Disinheriting the Jews*, 195.

[20]Ibid.

[21]In 63 BC, Pompey conquered Jerusalem and brought the city under Roman control. In AD 66, Jewish zealots, who chafed under the authority of Rome, took military action to remove the yoke of Rome from Israel. In AD 70, however, the Romans destroyed the city of Jerusalem and its temple.

[22]This second uprising against Rome was led by Bar Kokhba, whom many Jews believed to be the Messiah. Under his leadership hundreds of Jewish villages fought for freedom from the Romans. The revolt, however, was a disaster as more than half a million Jews died.

not helping their countrymen in these battles against the Romans. As a result, Jewish opposition to Christianity increased. As House observes, "After A.D. 70, and especially after A.D. 135, the Jewish religion increasingly became the enemy of the gospel of Christ and the followers of Christ."[23]

The Christian church, however, had a different perspective on the two failed Jewish revolts. The destruction of Jerusalem by the Romans in AD 70 and 135 was viewed by many in the church as God's judgment against Israel. Justin, for example, in his *Dialogue with Trypho*, argued that these destructions of Jerusalem were God's judgment on the Christ-rejecting Jews. He stated that the Jews "justly suffer" and that the Jewish cities were rightly "burned with fire."[24] He also described the Jews as "desolate" and forbidden to go to Jerusalem.[25] In speaking to the Jews about the destructions of Jerusalem, he said, "Accordingly, these things have happened to you in fairness and justice, for you have slain the Just One . . . and now you reject those who hope in Him."[26]

This belief that the two failed revolts were evidence of God's rejection of Israel was evident also in the writings of Origen (c. 185–254): "For what nation is an exile from their own metropolis, and from the place sacred to the worship of their fathers, save the Jews alone? And these calamities they have suffered, because they were a most wicked nation, which, although guilty of many other sins, yet has been punished so severely for none, as for those that were committed against our Jesus."[27]

Origen also said, "And a sign that she [Israel] has received the bill of divorce is this, that Jerusalem was destroyed along with what they called the sanctuary of the things in it which were believed to be holy."[28]

According to Alexander, the AD 70 destruction of Jerusalem handed Christians "a propaganda coup" in that it gave them the opportunity to argue that the catastrophe was "a divine judgment on Israel for the rejection of Jesus."[29] The same was also true concerning the failed second Jewish revolt in AD 135. Simon asserts that the destruction of Jerusalem in AD 135 "appeared to Christians as the confirmation of the divine

---

[23]House, "The Church's Appropriation of Israel's Blessings," 96.

[24]Justin, *Dialogue with Trypho* 16, *ANF* 1:202.

[25]Ibid.

[26]Ibid.

[27]Origen, *Against Celsus* 2.8, *ANF* 4:433.

[28]Origen, *Commentary on the Gospel of Matthew* 19, *ANF* 9:507.

[29]P. S. Alexander, "'The Parting of the Ways,'" in *Jews and Christians: The Parting of the Ways A.D. 70 to 135*, ed. J. D. G. Dunn (Grand Rapids: Eerdmans, 1999), 20.

verdict on Israel."[30] Richardson states, "The war of A.D. 132–5 did what the Synagogue Ban did not: to all intents and purposes it severed the two groups, freeing later Christians from the need to assert close contact with Judaism and providing for them evidence of the full 'judgment' of God upon Israel."[31] Thus, these two destructions, especially the one in AD 135, caused many in the church to believe that God had permanently rejected Israel and that the church was the new Israel. As McDonald notes, "The church fathers concluded from God's evident rejection of the Jews, demonstrated by the destruction of their Temple, and their displacement from Jerusalem, that the Christians themselves constituted the 'new Israel.'"[32]

HERMENEUTICAL ISSUES

Hermeneutical issues were also important in the development and acceptance of supersessionism. House points to three significant factors. The first involved the church's use of the Jewish Scriptures. He says, "The church not only appropriated the special status of the Jewish people, it took over their Bible, the Septuagint (LXX)."[33] For example, in addressing Trypho about truths concerning Jesus, Justin declared, "Are you acquainted with them, Trypho? They are contained in your Scriptures, or rather not yours, but ours."[34] The second significant hermeneutical factor was the rise of Greek philosophical interpretation and, in particular, the adoption of the allegorical method of interpretation by many in the church. As House writes,

> By the end of the first century the allegorical method had gained considerable sway in the church. The more literal interpretation of the New Testament authors and post-apostolic fathers gave way to the influence of Greek philosophical interpretation found in Philo and later in

---

[30]M. Simon, *Versus Israel: A Study of the Relations Between Christians and Jews in the Roman Empire (135–425)*, trans. H. McKeating (Oxford: Oxford University Press, 1986), 65. Simon says Jewish Christians ascribed the disaster to "Israel's sinful rejection of Jesus the Messiah." They did not, though, believe this was the "wholesale condemnation of the people." Because of the disaster, "they felt all the more keenly their obligation to deliver the Christian message to their brethren and convert them to the Christian hope" (66).

[31]Richardson, *Israel in the Apostolic Church*, 203.

[32]L. M. McDonald, "Anti-Judaism in the Early Church Fathers," in *Anti-Semitism and Early Christianity: Issues of Polemic and Faith*, ed. C. A. Evans and D. A. Hagner (Minneapolis: Fortress, 1993), 230.

[33]House, "The Church's Appropriation of Israel's Blessings," 97. See also J. Pelikan, *The Emergence of the Catholic Tradition (100–600)*, vol. 1 of *The Christian Tradition: A History of the Development of Doctrine* (Chicago: University of Chicago Press, 1971), 19; Simon, *Versus Israel*, 69.

[34]Justin, *Dialogue with Trypho* 29, *ANF* 1:209.

Hermes and Justin Martyr. By the time of the brilliant Alexandrian theologian Origen, allegory was readily used to move beyond the literal sense of the text.[35]

Pelikan points out that "spiritual exegesis" was applied to the OT Scriptures by the early church.[36] As a result, "there was no early Christian who simultaneously acknowledged the doctrinal authority of the Old Testament and interpreted it literally."[37] While this may be an overstatement, it does reinforce that there was a tendency to interpret OT texts nonliterally. Tertullian, for example, allegorically interpreted Gen 25:21–23 and its statement that "the older will serve the younger." For him, this was evidence that national Israel would become subservient to the church:

> Accordingly, since the people or nation of the Jews is anterior in time, and "greater" through the grace of primary favor in the Law, whereas ours is understood to be "less" in the age of times, as having in the last era of the world attained the knowledge of divine mercy: beyond doubt, through the edict of divine utterance, the prior and "greater" people—that is, the Jewish—must necessarily serve the "less" and the "less" people—that is, the Christian—overcome the "greater."[38]

The third factor relating to hermeneutics was the church's perception that it was the genuine continuation of the OT faith. As House says, "Church fathers saw Christians as the proper inheritors of the Old Testament faith, and saw proof for this in the teachings of Christ when he said, 'Therefore, I tell you, the kingdom of God will be taken from you and given to a nation producing the *fruits* of it' (Matt. 21:43)."[39] In his debate with Celsus, Origen declared, "Our Lord, seeing the conduct of the Jews not to be at all in keeping with the teaching of the prophets, inculcated by a parable that the kingdom of God would be taken from them, and given to the converts from heathenism."[40]

The church also believed it had inherited the covenants of Israel. This was the view of the *Epistle of Barnabas*: "I further beg of you . . . take

---

[35]House, "The Church's Appropriation of Israel's Blessings," 98; See also H. Küng, *Judaism: Between Yesterday and Tomorrow*, trans. J. Bowden (New York: Crossroad, 1992), 152.

[36]Pelikan, *The Emergence of the Catholic Tradition (100–600)*, 81.

[37]Ibid. Virkler observes, "The allegorical method as practiced by the church fathers often neglected completely the author's intended meaning." H. Virkler, *Hermeneutics: Principles and Processes of Biblical Interpretation* (Grand Rapids: Baker, 1981), 59.

[38]Tertullian, *An Answer to the Jews* 1, ANF 3:151.

[39]House, "The Church's Appropriation of Israel's Blessings," 99. Emphasis in original.

[40]Origen, *Against Celsus* 2.5, ANF 4:431.

heed now to yourselves, and not to be like some, adding largely to your sins, and saying, 'The covenant is both theirs [Jews] and ours [Christians].' But they finally lost it."[41]

Together these three developments contributed to the idea that the church was the new Israel.

---

[41]*The Epistle of Barnabas* 4, *ANF* 1:138.

Chapter 4

Supersessionism in the Patristic Era

The doctrine of supersessionism was held by many Christians in the patristic era. Yet theologians of this era mostly held to a moderate supersessionism in which the church was the new Israel, although a "last days" conversion of Israel was expected. Thus, the doctrine of Israel during this period included the concepts of rejection and hope. This is important since many works often detail the early church's supersessionist views but often do not emphasize their equally clear belief that Israel would be saved in the latter days.

THE REJECTION OF ISRAEL

As Jewish animosity toward Christians continued and it became increasingly clear that the Jews would not believe in Christ, many Christians of the early church began to view the Jews as their enemies. Pelikan points out that "virtually every major Christian writer of the first five centuries either composed a treatise in opposition to Judaism or made this issue a dominant theme in a treatise devoted to some other subject."[1] Siker, too, writes that "Christians increasingly [began] to see non-Christian Jews not as potential converts but as opponents to the gospel."[2]

During the patristic era,[3] it became increasingly common for church leaders to stereotype the Jews as Christ killers. Melito of Sardis (c. AD 150) stated, "The King of Israel slain with Israel's right hand! Alas for the new wickedness of the new murder."[4] Ignatius (c. AD 36–108) wrote that

---

[1] J. Pelikan, *The Emergence of the Catholic Tradition (100–600)*, vol. 1 of *The Christian Tradition: A History of the Development of Doctrine* (Chicago: University of Chicago Press, 1971), 15. McDonald adds, "Under such titles as *Adversus Judaeos* and *Altercatio cum Judaeo*, the early church fathers produced many harsh polemical writings against the Jewish people." L.M. McDonald, "Anti-Judaism in the Early Church Fathers," in *Anti-Semitism and Early Christianity: Issues of Polemic and Faith*, ed. C. A. Evans and D. A. Hagner (Minneapolis: Fortress, 1993), 215.

[2] J. S. Siker, *Disinheriting the Jews: Abraham in Early Christian Controversy* (Louisville, KY: Westminster/John Knox, 1991), 94; See Justin, *Dialogue with Trypho* 11, *ANF* 1:199–200.

[3] By "Patristic Era" I am referring to the period of AD 100–430.

[4] Melito, *ANF* 8:757. Melito also stated, "God has suffered from the right hand of Israel" (8:760).

Jesus Christ suffered "at the hands of the Christ-killing Jews."[5] As these quotations show, some Christian fathers blamed the crucifixion of Christ on the Jews as a people. Wylen summarizes this trend: "As Christians abandoned the mission to their fellow Jews and proselytized among the Gentiles they shifted blame for the crucifixion of Jesus from the Romans to the Jews—not just some Jews but the Jewish people as a whole. The Jews were branded as deicides—killers of God. This accusation became a deep source of hatred against the Jews."[6]

In addition to its anti-Jewish stance, the predominately Gentile church continued its insistence that the Jews had been rejected by God and that the church was now the true Israel. For example, the *Epistle of Barnabas* stated that the new covenant was never intended for Israel. Instead, it was for the church—the true inheritor of the promise through Christ: "But He [Jesus] was manifested, in order that they [Israelites] might be perfected in their iniquities, and that we, being the constituted heirs through Him, might receive the testament of the Lord Jesus."[7] Summarizing the supersessionist approach of the *Epistle of Barnabas*, Diprose writes, "The writing, as a whole, manifests the latent presupposition that the Church, the true heir of the promises, occupies the place that Israel had always been unworthy of occupying."[8]

Declarations about Israel's rejection existed in the statements of some early church fathers. Irenaeus (130–200) wrote, "For inasmuch as the former [the Jews] have rejected the Son of God, and cast Him out of the vineyard when they slew Him, God has justly rejected them, and given to the Gentiles outside the vineyard the fruits of its cultivation."[9] Clement of Alexandria (c. 195) claimed that Israel "denied the Lord" and thus "forfeited the place of the true Israel."[10] Tertullian (c. 197) declared, "Israel has been divorced."[11] Cyprian (c. 250), too, promoted a supersessionist

---

[5]Ignatius, *Epistle to the Magnesians* 11, *ANF* 1:64.

[6]S. M. Wylen, *The Jews in the Time of Jesus* (Mahwah, NJ: Paulist Press, 1996), 191.

[7]*The Epistle of Barnabas* 14, *ANF* 1:146. Horbury says that the anti-Judaistic tone and supersessionist approach to Israel's covenants in this work can be linked to the author's fear of Christian assimilation to the Jews during this time. See W. Horbury, "Jewish-Christian Relations in Barnabas and Justin Martyr," in *Jews and Christians*, ed. J. D. G. Dunn (Grand Rapids: Eerdmans, 1999), 323–27.

[8]R. E. Diprose, *Israel in the Development of Christian Thought* (Rome: Istituto Biblico Evangelico Italiano, 2000), 78.

[9]Irenaeus, *Against Heresies* 36.2, *ANF* 1:515. While Irenaeus made a strong statement of punitive supersessionism here, Soulen asserts that Irenaeus also held to a form of economic supersessionism: "In sum, Irenaeus sees God's history with Israel as an episode within the larger story whereby God prepares a fallen humanity for the incarnation." K. Soulen, *The God of Israel and Christian Theology* (Minneapolis: Fortress, 1996), 46.

[10]Clement, *The Instructor* 2.8, *ANF* 2:256.

[11]Tertullian, *An Answer to the Jews* 1, *ANF* 3:152.

approach when he wrote, "I have endeavoured to show that the Jews, according to what had before been foretold, had departed from God, and had lost God's favour, which had been given them in past time, and had been promised them for the future; while the Christians had succeeded to their place, deserving well of the Lord by faith, and coming out of all nations and from the whole world."[12]

He also declared, "We Christians, when we pray, say Our Father; because He has begun to be ours, and has ceased to be the Father of the Jews, who have forsaken Him."[13] Lactantius (c. fourth century) expressed his supersessionist views when he stated, "But it is plain that the house of Judah does not signify the Jews, whom He casts off, but us, who have been called by Him out of the Gentiles, and have by adoption succeeded to their place, and are called sons of the Jews."[14]

Justin Martyr (c. AD 100–165)

As the last section showed, statements in support of supersessionism were common in the patristic era. Particularly significant during this period, though, were the influences of three men: Justin, Origen, and Augustine.

Justin is important in the history of supersessionism because he was the first Christian writer to explicitly identify the church as "Israel."[15] Justin declared, "For the true spiritual Israel, and descendants of Judah, Jacob, Isaac, and Abraham . . . are we who have been led to God through this crucified Christ."[16] He also said, "Since then God blesses this people [i.e., Christians], and calls them Israel, and declares them to be His inheritance, how is it that you [Jews] repent not of the deception you practise on yourselves, as if you alone were the Israel?"[17] Justin also announced that "we, who have been quarried out from the bowels of Christ, are the true Israelite race."[18] For Siker, "Justin is a transitional figure"[19] in the development of supersessionism. Justin does not mark the beginning of supersessionism, but he does openly advocate

---

[12]Cyprian, *Three Books of Testimonies Against the Jews, ANF* 5:507.

[13]Cyprian, *On the Lord's Prayer, ANF* 5:450. "For the vineyard of the Lord of hosts was the house of Israel; but Christ, when teaching and showing that the people of the Gentiles should succeed them, and that by the merit of faith we should subsequently attain to the place which the Jews had lost" (*ANF* 5:361).

[14]Lactantius, *The Divine Institutes* 4.20, *ANF* 7:123.

[15]Justin, *Dialogue with Trypho* 11, *ANF* 1:200. See also 1:261, 267. P. Richardson has observed that the first explicit identification of the church as "Israel" was made by Justin Martyr in AD 160. See P. Richardson, *Israel in the Apostolic Church* (Cambridge: Cambridge University Press, 1969), 1.

[16]Justin, *Dialogue with Trypho* 11, *ANF* 1:200.

[17]Ibid., 1:261. He also says, "Those who were selected out of every nation have obeyed His will through Christ . . . must be Jacob and Israel" (1:265).

[18]Justin, *Dialogue with Trypho* 135, *ANF* 1:267.

[19]Siker, *Disinheriting the Jews*, 15.

a replacement approach concerning Israel and the church that had been form-ing for nearly a century: "Justin marks the end of an era, the culmination of a process in formative Christianity that had begun much earlier."[20]

Justin's hermeneutical approach to the OT was also important in the devel-opment of supersessionism. He reapplied OT promises so that the church, not Israel, was viewed as the beneficiary of its promised blessings. Justin declared to Trypho, "And along with Abraham we [Christians] shall inherit the holy land, when we shall receive the inheritance for an endless eternity, being chil-dren of Abraham through the like faith. . . . Accordingly, He promises to him a nation of similar faith, God fearing, righteous . . . but it is not you, 'in whom is no faith.'"[21] Siker adds, "According to Justin, the patriarchal promises do not apply to the Jews; rather, God has transferred these promises to the Christians and . . . to Gentile Christians in particular."[22]

Origen (c. AD 185–254)

The influential theologian Origen taught that Israel was rejected by God and that the church was the new Israel. Concerning Israel's rejection, Origen promoted a punitive supersessionist approach in which the peo-ple of Israel were forever "abandoned because of their sins."[23] He also declared, "And we say with confidence that they [Jews] will never be restored to their former condition. For they committed a crime of the most unhallowed kind, in conspiring against the Saviour of the human race in that city where they offered up to God a worship containing the symbols of mighty mysteries."[24] According to Origen, "The Jews were altogether abandoned, and possess now none of what were considered their ancient glories, so that there is no indication of any Divinity abid-ing amongst them."[25]

In addition to believing that Israel had been rejected, Origen held that the church was now the new people of God. In his debate with Celsus, for example, Origen stated, "Our Lord, seeing the conduct of the Jews not to be at all in keeping with the teaching of the prophets, inculcated by a par-able that the kingdom of God would be taken from them, and given to the converts from heathenism."[26] N. R. M. De Lange summarizes Origen's

---

[20]Ibid., 16.

[21]Justin, *Dialogue with Trypho* 119, *ANF* 1:259.

[22]Siker, *Disinheriting the Jews*, 14. Diprose asserts that Justin "adopts a typically Greek attitude" toward the characters in the Old Testament, referring to Abraham, Elijah, and Daniel's three friends as "barbarians." Diprose, *Israel in the Development of Christian Thought*, 79.

[23]Origen, *Against Celsus* 4.22, *ANF* 4:506.

[24]Ibid.

[25]Origen, *Against Celsus* 2.8, *ANF* 4:433.

[26]Origen, *Against Celsus* 2.5, *ANF* 4:431.

supersessionist perspective: "Crucial to the whole argument [of Origen] is the paradox that Jews and Gentiles suffer a reversal of roles. The historical Israelites cease to be Israelites, while the believers from the Gentiles become the New Israel. This involves a redefinition of Israel."[27]

In addition to making specific supersessionist statements, Origen helped lay a foundation for supersessionism. Diprose points out that Origen "strengthened the theoretical basis of replacement theology by grounding it in biblical exegesis."[28] This "theoretical basis" is linked to Origen's use of allegory to understand Scripture.

Origen gave Christian allegory its theoretical foundation, and he was central in making the allegorical method the Christian approach to interpreting Scripture texts regarding Israel. In his *De Principiis*, he argued for a threefold meaning of each Scripture passage.[29] While acknowledging the importance of the literal meaning at times, Origen argued that the spiritual meaning behind the literal sense was most important. For example, in reference to Jesus' statement "I was sent only to the lost sheep of the house of Israel" (Matt 15:24), Origen denied that Jesus had ethnic Israelites in view. For Origen, the title *Israel* referred to anyone who truly knows God: "We do not understand these words [Matt 15:24] as those do who savour of earthly things . . . but we understand that there exists a race of souls which is termed 'Israel,' as is indicated by the interpretation of the name itself: for Israel is interpreted to mean a 'mind,' or 'man seeing God.'"[30]

Origen also held to a distinction between *carnal* Israel and *spiritual* Israel. Carnal or physical Israel, for Origen, was never intended to inherit the promises of the OT because she was unworthy and could not understand them. At best, physical Israel functioned as a type for the spiritual Israel—the church, to whom the promises would find their complete fulfillment.[31] The result of this view, according to Diprose, was that "Origen effectively disinherits physical Israel."[32]

---

[27]N. R. M. De Lange, *Origen and the Jews: Studies in Jewish-Christian Relations in Third-Century Palestine* (Cambridge: Cambridge University Press, 1976), 80.

[28]Diprose, *Israel in the Development of Christian Thought*, 86.

[29]See Origen, *On First Principles* 4.1.11, ANF 4:359. See also "Early Christian Interpretation," in *The Oxford Companion to the Bible*, ed. B. M. Metzger and M. D. Coogan (New York: Oxford University Press, 1993), 311–12. Kaiser says Origen "championed the allegorical system of interpretation as the best way to handle most of the Old Testament." W. C. Kaiser Jr., "An Epangelical Response," in *Dispensationalism, Israel and the Church: The Search for Definition*, ed. C. A. Blaising and D. L. Bock (Grand Rapids: Zondervan, 1992), 363.

[30]Origen, *On First Principles* 4.1.22 ANF 4:371.

[31]Origen said "corporeal Israelites" [Jews] were "the type" for "spiritual Israelites" [the church]. Origen, *On First Principles* 4.21 ANF 4:370. See also Diprose, *Israel in the Development of Christian Thought*, 89.

[32]Diprose, *Israel in the Development of Christian Thought*, 89.

Augustine (AD 354–430)

Augustine's contribution to the doctrine of supersessionism is significant. James Carroll points out that Augustine's attitude toward the Jews was rooted in "assumptions of supersessionism."[33] According to Cardinal Martini, Augustine introduced a "negative element into judgment on the Jews."[34] He did so by advancing the "'theory of substitution' whereby the New Israel of the church became a substitute of ancient Israel."[35]

In line with supersessionist theology, Augustine explicitly stated that the title *Israel* belonged to the Christian church: "For if we hold with a firm heart the grace of God which hath been given us, we are Israel, the seed of Abraham. . . . Let therefore no Christian consider himself alien to the name of Israel."[36] He also said, "The Christian people then is rather Israel."[37] According to Augustine, when Gentiles believe and become part of the new covenant, their hearts are circumcised, and they become part of Israel:

> Now what the apostle attributed to Gentiles of this character, how that "they have the work of the law written in their hearts;" must be some such thing as what he says to the Corinthians: "Not in tables of stone, but in fleshly tables of the heart." For thus do they become of the house of Israel, when their uncircumcision is accounted circumcision. . . . And therefore in the house of the true Israel, in which is no guile, they are partakers of the new testament.[38]

Concerning Israel's role in the plan of God, Augustine argued that *national* Israel prefigured *spiritual* Israel—the Christian people:

> Abraham, Isaac, and Jacob three fathers, and one people. The fathers three, as it were in the beginning of the people; three fathers in whom the people was figured: and the former people itself the present people. For in the Jewish people was figured the Christian people. There a figure, here the truth; there a shadow, here the body: as the apostle says, "Now these things happened to them in a figure."[39]

---

[33]J. Carroll, *Constantine's Sword: The Church and the Jews* (Boston: Houghton Mifflin, 2001), 219.

[34]Cardinal C. M. Martini, "Christianity and Judaism, a Historical and Theological Overview," in *Jews and Christians: Exploring the Past, Present, and Future*, ed. J. H. Charlesworth (New York: Crossroad, 1990), 20.

[35]Ibid.

[36]Augustine, *On the Psalms* 114.3, *NPNF¹* 8:550.

[37]Ibid.

[38]Augustine, *On the Spirit and the Letter* 46, *NPNF¹* 5:102–3.

[39]Augustine, *On the Gospel of St. John* 11.8, *NPNF¹* 7:77. Augustine also stated, "In that people [the Jews], plainly, the future Church was much more evidently prefigured." Augustine, *On the Catechising of the Uninstructed* 19.33, *NPNF¹* 3:304. Augustine expressed a supersessionist perspective when he wrote, "But when they [the Jews] killed Him, then though they knew it not, they prepared a Supper for us." Augustine, *Sermons on New Testament Lessons*, Sermon 62, *NPNF¹* 6:447.

For the most part, Augustine's supersessionist views were not original. In fact, they were mostly consistent with the patristic tradition that preceded him. Augustine's most original contribution regarding Israel and the church, however, can be found in his reasons for Israel's continued existence. During Augustine's time, the existence of the Jews and Judaism posed an apologetic problem for the church. If the church was the new Israel, for what purpose did Jews of the other Israel exist?

Augustine offered an answer for this perceived dilemma. For him the Jews functioned primarily as witnesses. They were witnesses to the faith preached by the prophets, witnesses of divine judgment, and witnesses of the validity of Christianity. He wrote, "But the Jews who slew Him . . . are thus by their own Scriptures a testimony to us that we have not forged the prophecies about Christ."[40] The Jews, according to Augustine Augustine, shielded Christians from accusations that Christians invented OT prophecies that pointed to Jesus. Thus, the existence of non-Christian Jews was not a problem but an essential testimony to the truth of Christianity.

Hood views Augustine's contribution in this area as "ingenious" because it "provided a foundation for tolerating Jews within a Christian society."[41] Augustine's contention that the Jews were witnesses to Christianity became especially important when the crusades began and the church began to persecute heretics. Hood asserts that Augustine's views "shielded the Jews of western Europe from the full force of Christendom's coercive powers."[42]

Although devoting much of his attention to matters such as free will, original sin, and predestination, Augustine's views on the Jews and Judaism carried great weight for many years. In fact, Hood asserts that Augustine's ideas on these matters "dominated the medieval debate."[43] This was so "despite the fact that Judaism and the Jews are not major themes in Augustine's voluminous writings."[44] Yet, because Augustine's writings in the medieval era were so revered, his thoughts on any topic, no matter how sparse, were considered important.

---

[40] Augustine, *The City of God* 18.46, *NPNF¹* 2:389.

[41] J. Y. B. Hood, *Aquinas and the Jews* (Philadelphia: University of Pennsylvania Press, 1995), 12. Carroll states, "It is not too much to say that, at this juncture, Christianity 'permitted' Judaism to endure because of Augustine." Carroll, *Constantine's Sword*, 218. See also J. Cohen, "Introduction," in *Essential Papers on Judaism and Christianity in Conflict: From Late Antiquity to the Reformation*, ed. J. Cohen (New York: New York University Press, 1991), 13–14.

[42] Hood, *Aquinas and the Jews*, 13.

[43] Ibid., 10.

[44] Ibid.

THE HOPE FOR ISRAEL

As shown by the quotations above, some theologians of the patristic era viewed the church as the new or true Israel. However, this supersessionist belief was a moderate one in that many of the early theologians also believed in a coming salvation of the nation Israel that was in accord with OT prophecies and Paul's words regarding Israel in Romans 11.

Fahey, in reference to a list from Father Lemamn, lists the theologians through the twelfth century who believed "that the Jews will be converted." This list includes Tertullian, Origen, St. Hillary, St. Ambrose, St. Chrysostom, St. Jerome, St. Cyril of Alexandria, St. Prosper of Aquitaine, Cassiodorus, Preniasius, St. Gregory the Great, St. Isidore, Venerable Bede, St. Anselm, St. Damian, and St. Bernard.[45] In fact, Fahey points out that the view that "the Jews will be converted . . . towards the end of the world can be proved from the texts of the Fathers, century by century."[46]

This salvation of the Jews, as expected by the early church theologians, was not merely a trickle of believing Jews throughout history but a dramatic eschatological event that took place with the prophesied comings of Elijah, Antichrist, and Jesus. For the early theologians, the salvation of Israel would be a spectacular last-days occurrence.

Justin Martyr
For example, Justin held that the tribes of Israel would be gathered and restored in accord with what the prophet Zechariah predicted:

> And what the people of the Jews shall say and do, when they see Him coming in glory, has been thus predicted by Zechariah the prophet: "I will command the four winds to gather the scattered children; I will command the north wind to bring them, and the south wind, that it keep not back. And then in Jerusalem there shall be great lamentation, not the lamentation of mouths or of lips, but the lamentation of the heart; and they shall rend not their garments, but their hearts. Tribe by tribe they shall mourn, and then they shall look on Him whom they have pierced; and they shall say, Why, O Lord, hast Thou made us to err from Thy way? The glory which our fathers blessed, has for us been turned into shame."[47]

In regard to this comment by Justin, Hauser states, "Justin also links the Jews with the second advent of Christ. It will be at this time that Christ

---

[45]D. Fahey, *The Kingship of Christ and the Conversion of the Jewish Nation* (Kimmage, Dublin: Holy Ghost Missionary College, 1953), 7.

[46]Ibid.

[47]Justin, *First Apology* 52, *ANF* 1:180.

will gather the nation Israel and the Jews shall look on him and repent tribe by tribe."[48] Significantly, Significantly, Justin not only held to a future hope for the literal tribes of Israel but also did so on the basis of OT promises to the nation—in this case, Zechariah. For Justin, the hope for Israel presented in the OT was alive.

Tertullian

Tertullian discussed the future blessings and salvation of Israel when he said, "He [God] will favour with His acceptance and blessing the circumcision also, even the race of Abraham, which by and by is to acknowledge Him."[49] He also urged Christians eagerly to anticipate and rejoice over the coming restoration of Israel: "For it will be fitting for the Christian to rejoice, and not to grieve, at the restoration of Israel, if it be true, (as it is), that the whole of our hope is intimately united with the remaining expectation of Israel."[50]

Origen

Surprisingly, Origen, the primary promoter of Christian allegorical interpretation, also affirmed a future salvation of the nation Israel. As Cohen has observed, "He [Origen] affirms Paul's commitment to—and confidence in—the ultimate salvation of the Jews."[51] This belief was linked to "the glorious forecast of [Romans] 11:25–26."[52] For example, in his comments on the Song of Songs, Origen mentions "two callings of Israel." In between these two callings is God's call of the church. But after the call of the church, Israel will experience salvation: "For the Church was called between the two callings of Israel; that is to say, first Israel was called, and afterwards when Israel had stumbled and fallen, the Church of the Gentiles was called. 'But when the fullness of the Gentiles has come in, then will all Israel, having been called again, be saved.'"[53]

According to Cohen, "Origen does appear to assume that the Jewish people as a whole will regain their status as a community of God's faithful, that all Jews will ultimately be saved."[54] This is true even though Israel, for

---

[48]C. A. Hauser Jr., "The Eschatology of the Church Fathers" (Ph.D. diss., Grace Theological Seminary, 1961), 112.

[49]Tertullian, *Against Marcion* 5.9, *ANF* 3:448.

[50]Tertullian, *On Modesty* 8, *ANF* 4:82.

[51]J. Cohen, "The Mystery of Israel's Salvation: Romans 11:25–26 in Patristic and Medieval Exegesis," *HTR* 98 (2005): 256.

[52]Ibid.

[53]Origen, *The Song of Songs*, in *ACW*, ed. J. Quasten and J. C. Plumpe (Westminster, MD: Newman Press, 1957), 26:252.

[54]Cohen, "The Mystery of Israel's Salvation," 263.

a time, has rejected Christ. As Cohen points out, "Despite the Jews' rejection of Jesus and his apostles, the potential for restoration and renewal remains inherent within them."[55]

Origen's belief in a salvation of Israel can also be seen in his *Commentary on the Epistle to the Romans*:

> Now indeed, until all the Gentiles come to salvation the riches of God are concentrated in the multitude of believers, but as long as Israel remains in its unbelief it will not be possible to say that the fullness of the Lord's portion has been attained. The people of Israel are still missing from the complete picture. But when the fullness of the Gentiles has come in and Israel comes to salvation at the end of time, then it will be the people which, although it existed long ago, will come at the last and complete the fullness of the Lord's portion and inheritance.[56]

A belief in a future salvation of the Jews was also held by several others. Cyril of Jerusalem (c. 315–386), when discussing events regarding "the end of the world drawing near," discussed the coming of the Antichrist and his *temporary* deception of the Jews. For him, the Antichrist will deceive "the Jews by the lying signs and wonders of his magical deceit, until they believe he is the expected Christ."[57] Thus, for Cyril, the coming Antichrist would deceive the Jews for a time until they believed in Jesus.

Chrysostom (349–407), who often made harsh statements against the Jews, still believed in a future salvation of the Jews. He linked the coming salvation of the Jews with the coming of Elijah:

> To show therefore that [Elijah] the Tishbite comes before that other [second] advent . . . He said this. . . . And what is this reason? That when He is come, He may persuade the Jews to believe in Christ, and that they may not all utterly perish at His coming. Wherefore He too, guiding them on to that remembrance, saith, "And he shall restore all things"; that is, shall correct the unbelief of the Jews that are then in being.[58]

According to Chrysostom, the coming of Elijah means "the conversion of the Jews."[59]

---

[55]Ibid., 260.

[56]Origen, *Commentary on the Epistle to the Romans*, ACCS (Downers Grove, IL: InterVarsity, 1998), 6:291.

[57]Cyril of Jerusalem, *Catechetical Lectures*, in W. A. Jurgens, *The Faith of the Early Fathers* (Collegeville, MN: Liturgical Press, 1970), 1:356–57.

[58]John Chrysostom, *The Gospel of Matthew* 57, NPNF¹ 10:352.

[59]Ibid., 353.

Chrysostom also taught that Romans 11 holds future significance for the nation Israel. In reference to Rom 11:27 and the statement "For this is my covenant with them, when I will take away their sins," Chrysostom declared, "If then this hath been promised, but has never yet happened in their case, nor have they ever enjoyed the remission of sins by baptism, certainly it will come to pass."[60]

Augustine

Some of the strongest statements affirming the salvation of Israel come from Augustine. As Cohen points out, "Augustine speaks of the ultimate salvation of the Jewish people, ostensibly as a whole."[61] Like Chrysostom, Augustine, in his *City of God*, linked the salvation of the Jews with the coming of Elijah:

> It is a familiar theme in the conversation and heart of the faithful, that in the last days before the judgment the Jews shall believe in the true Christ, that is, our Christ, by means of this great and admirable prophet Elias who shall expound the law to them. . . . When, therefore, he is come, he shall give a spiritual explanation of the law which the Jews at present understand carnally, and shall thus "turn the heart of the father to the son," that is, the heart of the fathers to the children.[62]

Significantly, Augustine mentions that his view concerning the salvation of the Jews was "familiar" to believers of his day. Thus, his belief in the salvation of the Jews went beyond just his own personal view. This perspective was common for those of his generation.

Augustine also adopted a literal approach to Zech 12:10 in regard to the salvation of Israel. In doing so, he shows that at least some OT prophecies still had continuing relevance in regard to the salvation of Israel:

> "And they shall look upon me because they have insulted me, and they shall mourn for Him as if for one very dear (or beloved), and shall be in bitterness for Him as for an only-begotten." For in that day the Jews— those of them, at least, who shall receive the spirit of grace and mercy—when they see Him coming in His majesty, and recognize that it is He whom they, in the person of their parents, insulted when He came before in His humiliation, shall repent of insulting Him in His passion.[63]

---

[60]John Chrysostom, *The Epistle to the Romans* 19, *NPNF¹* 11:493.

[61]Cohen, "The Mystery of Israel's Salvation," 275.

[62]Augustine, *The City of God* 29, *NPNF¹* 2:448.

[63]Ibid., *NPNF¹* 2:450.

Augustine also offered a chronology of end-time events. In connection with the coming of Elijah and other events, the nation of the Jews will be saved: "And at or in connection with that judgment the following events shall come to pass, as we have learned: Elias the Tishbite shall come; the Jews shall believe; Antichrist shall persecute; Christ shall judge; the dead shall rise; the good and the wicked shall be separated; the world shall be burned and renewed."[64]

In addition, Augustine also took a literal view of the prophecy of Hos 3:5: "But let us hear what he adds: 'And afterward shall the children of Israel return, and seek the Lord their God, and David their king, and shall be amazed at the Lord and at His goodness in the latter days.' Nothing is clearer than this prophecy."[65] He also believed that the people of Israel would be saved in accord with what Paul taught in Romans 11: "That, forasmuch as in that humble coming [first advent] 'blindness that happened in part unto Israel, that the fullness of the Gentiles might enter in' [Rom 11:25], in that other should happen what follows, 'and so all Israel should be saved' [Rom 11:26]."[66]

This salvation of Israel is linked with the removal of Israel's captivity: "For the Jews, as it is here, 'Who shall give salvation to Israel out of Sion?' 'When the Lord shall turn away the captivity of His people, Jacob shall rejoice, and Israel shall be glad.'"[67] Augustine also argued that the church had not permanently supplanted the Jews:

> What! have we supplanted the Jews? No, but we are said to be their supplanters, for that for our sakes they were supplanted. If they had not been blinded, Christ would not have been crucified; His precious Blood would not be shed; if that Blood had not been shed, the world would not have been redeemed. Because then their blindness hath profited us, therefore hath the elder brother been supplanted by the younger, and the younger is called the Supplanter. But how long shall this be?[68]

He then answers the question, "But how long shall this be?" Israel has been supplanted to bring blessings to the church, but this time of being supplanted will come to an end: "The time will come, the end of the world

---

[64]Augustine, *The City of God* 20.30, *NPNF¹* 2:451. Augustine states that we cannot know with certainty the exact order of the events although "my opinion, however, is, that they will happen in the order in which I have related them."

[65]Ibid., 18.28, *NPNF¹* 2:375–76.

[66]Augustine, *On the Psalms*, Psalm 15, *NPNF¹* 8:47.

[67]Ibid.

[68]Augustine, *Sermons on New Testament Lessons*, Sermon 72, *NPNF¹* 6:472.

will come, and all Israel shall believe; not they who now are, but their children who shall then be."[69]

Like Augustine, Jerome (347–420) believed in a future salvation of the Jews. He said, "When the Jews receive the faith at the end of the world, they will find themselves in dazzling light, as if Our Lord were returning to them from Egypt."[70]

St. Prosper of Aquitaine (c. 390–455) argued that Israel's current state of blindness is being used by God for the salvation of the Gentiles. But after this, Israel will be saved:

> As we have already said above, it is not given to any human study or genius to explore the decree and design according to which God . . . *hath concluded all in unbelief, that He may have mercy on all.* . . . He delayed for centuries, while He was educating Israel, to enlighten the countless peoples of infidels; and now He allows that same Israel to go blind till the universality of the Gentiles enter the fold. He allows so many thousands of this people to be born and die to be lost, when only those whom the end of the world will find alive will attain salvation.[71]

This idea of Israel's salvation after the time of Gentile blessing is also found in the following statement of St. Prosper of Aquitaine:

> But He has shown His mercy for all men in a far more extraordinary manner when the Son of God became the Son of man. . . . Since then the glory of the race of Israel shines not in one people only . . . The promised heritage falls no longer to the sons of the flesh, but to the sons of the promise. The great parsimony in bestowing grace which in the past ages befell all other nations, is now the lot of the Jewish people. Yet, when the fulness of the Gentiles will have come in, then a flood of the same waters of grace is promised for their dry hearts. . . . When the Apostle Paul stopped in his knowledge and discussion of this problem and gave way to utter astonishment, who would be so presumptuous as to believe that he could try and explain it rather than admire it in silence?[72]

Ambrose (c. 340–397) makes a connection between Miriam's conflict with Moses and Paul's declaration in Romans 11 that Israel would be saved:

---

[69]Ibid.

[70]Jerome, *Commentary on St. Matthew*, 2, quoted in D. Fahey, *The Kingship of Christ and the Conversion of the Jewish Nation* (Kimmage, Dublin: Holy Ghost Missionary College, 1953), 108.

[71]Prosper of Aquitaine, *The Call of All Nations* 1.21, in *ACW* 14:69. Emphasis in original.

[72]Ibid., in *ACW* 14:103.

This murmuring refers to the type of the Synagogue, which is ignorant of the mystery of . . . the Church gathered out of the nations, and murmurs with daily reproaches, and envies that people through whose faith itself also shall be delivered from the leprosy of its unbelief, according to what we read that: "blindness in part has happened unto Israel, until the fulness of the Gentiles be come in, and so all Israel shall be saved."[73]

In his commentary on Rom 11:26, Theodoret of Cyrus (393–457), like Augustine, stated that the Jews would believe in connection with the coming of Elijah in the end time: "And he [Paul] urges them not to despair of the salvation of the other Jews; for when the Gentiles have received the message, even they, the Jews, will believe, when the excellent Elijah comes, bringing to them the doctrine of faith. For even the Lord said this in the sacred gospels: 'Elijah is coming, and he will restore all things.'"[74] According to Weaver, this hope for a salvation of Israel in relation to the coming of Elijah "is not an isolated reading but rather part of a larger, widespread . . . expectation in Christianity."[75]

Others, too, affirmed a future for Israel. In regard to Rom 11:26, St. Cyril of Alexandria (378–444) stated with confidence that Israel would be saved after the calling of the Gentiles: "Although it was rejected, Israel will also be saved eventually, a hope which Paul confirms. . . . For indeed, Israel will be saved in its own time and will be called at the end, after the calling of the Gentiles."[76]

Cyril offers one of the more extended discussions on the future salvation of Israel in his *Commentary on Genesis*. For him the salvation of Israel is something that cannot be doubted by the readers of Scripture: "At the end of time our Lord Jesus Christ will be reconciled with Israel, his ancient persecutor, just as Jacob kissed Esau after his return from Haran. No one who listens to the words of holy Scripture can actually doubt that with the passing of time Israel also will have to be received again into the love of Christ through faith."[77] Cyril then quotes Hos 3:4–5 for proof of this belief and then says,

While Christ, the Savior of us all, gathers believers from the nations, Israel is deserted, since it has no law to elect its leaders, and it cannot offer

---

[73] Ambrose, *Letters*, Letter 63, 57, *NPNF*², 10:464–65.

[74] Theodoret of Cyrus, *Commentaries on the Epistles of Saint Paul*, trans. J. A. Weaver, *Theodoret of Cyrus on Romans 11:26: Recovering and Early Christian Redivivus Tradition* (New York: Peter Lang, 2007), 15.

[75] Weaver, *Theodoret of Cyrus on Romans 11:26*, 150.

[76] Cyril of Alexandria, *Explanation of the Letter to the Romans*, PG 74:849. See ACCS 6.298–99.

[77] Cyril of Alexandria, *Commentary on Genesis*, PG 69:261, trans. from ACCS 1:225.

to the divine altar the sacrifices prescribed by the laws. It therefore awaits Christ's return from his action of converting the nations, so that he may receive it as well and unite it with the law of his love to the others. See how Jacob, who rejoiced in the generation of his children and in his numerous herds of sheep, came back from Haran and received again Esau into his friendship. In time Israel itself will be converted after the calling of the nations and will admire these riches in Christ.[78]

Cyril also held that Matt 23:38–39 had relevance to the coming salvation of Israel. In reference to Jesus' statement to unbelieving Israel that "you will never see Me again until you say, 'Blessed is He who comes in the name of the Lord,'" Cyril said, "That which has been spoken possesses an interpretation that comes through the vision of faith. For when 'the fullness of the nations comes in' and they believe in Christ, then the Jews who believe after these things see the beauty of the divine nature of Christ."[79]

Writing in the last third of the fourth century, Ambrosiaster stated, "However seriously the Jews may have sinned by rejecting the gift of God . . . nevertheless, because they are the children of good people, whose privileges and many benefits from God they have received, they will be received with joy when they return to the faith, because God's love for them is stirred up by the memory of their ancestors."[80]

Slightly outside the patristic era, Cassiodorus (c. 485–585) linked the salvation of Israel with Psalm 103. Commenting on verse 9, "He will not always be angry, nor will he be wroth for ever," he declared, "This verse can be applied also to the Jewish people, who we know are to be converted at the world's end. On this Paul says: *Blindness in part has happened in Israel, that the fullness of the Gentiles should come in, and so all Israel should be saved.*"[81] When Cassiodorus states "we know," it appears that this belief in a future salvation of Israel is something that was common during his day. It does not appear that he is presenting a novel idea.

In sum, the early church adopted a moderate form of supersessionism in regard to Israel and the church. The church believed that the nation Israel had been rejected by God because of its disobedience and rejection of Christ. This rejection appeared to be confirmed by the destructions of Jerusalem in AD 70 and 135. The early church held that the church was now the new Israel and that the Scriptures, covenants, and promises given to Israel were now primarily the possession of the Christian church.

---

[78]Ibid.

[79]Cyril of Alexandria, *Fragment* 264, ACCS 1b.185.

[80]Ambrosiaster, *Commentary on Paul's Epistles*, ACCS 6:299.

[81]Cassiodorus, *Explanation of the Psalms, Ancient Christian Writers*, ed. W. J. Burghardt and T. C. Lawler (New York: Paulist, 1991), 53:22–23.

Yet there was a consensus among the theologians of this era that the nation Israel would be converted in the last days in connection with the promises of the OT prophets and Paul's words in Romans 11. According to some, this salvation was to be accompanied by a repossession of Israel's land by the tribes of Israel. Thus, the early church's doctrine of Israel included the element of hope. Thus, while we rightly note the early church's adoption of a moderate supersessionism, we must not neglect the fact that it also believed in a future salvation of Israel based on OT and NT passages.

Chapter 5

Supersessionism in the Medieval Era

In the period between the sixth and twelfth centuries, little doctrinal development occurred in relation to supersessionism. Like the patristic era before it, supersessionism in the medieval period was well accepted. In fact, Hood observes that "the supersession theory" was one of the primary "givens" among Christian theologians of the medieval era.[1] There was, like in the patristic era, a dualistic view concerning the fate of the Jews during this time. Medieval Christians held that the Jews would eventually accept Christ and be saved, but they also saw the Jews as dangerous infidels who had been rejected and punished by God.[2]

MEDIEVAL ART

The medieval church's perspective concerning the Jews and Judaism is evident in the art of the period. Several twelfth- and thirteenth-century images found in Christian cathedrals testify to the dominant supersessionism of the era.[3] For example, at the south entrance of the Strasbourg Cathedral in France stand two female statues. One represents *Ecclesia* (the church) while the other symbolizes *Synagoga* (the synagogue). *Ecclesia* stands triumphant with a crown on her head and a royal robe draped across her shoulders. Head up, her gaze is confident, and her posture is noble. The staff and chalice in her hands represent her divine authority. *Synagoga*, however, is looking down, and a veil covers her eyes. The staff she carries in her right hand is broken, and the Torah she holds in her left hand appears ready to slip. *Synagoga* stands defeated.

---

[1] J. Y. B. Hood, *Aquinas and the Jews* (Philadelphia: University of Pennsylvania Press, 1995), 3. The other two were "the belief that the Old Testament was rife with prefigurative 'types' of Christ and the Church, and the notion that the Jews *in toto* were guilty for killing Jesus" (3).

[2] Ibid., xii.

[3] See G. Zinn, "History and Interpretation: 'Hebrew Truth,' Judaism, and the Victorine Exegetical Tradition," in *Jews and Christians: Exploring the Past, Present, and Future*, ed. J. H. Charlesworth (New York: Crossroad, 1990), 103–4.

A similar scene is found at Reims Cathedral where one sculpture represents a triumphant and crowned *Ecclesia* while another shows a defeated and blindfolded *Synagoga*. A sculpture of fallen Synagogue also exists at Notre Dame de Paris. Depicted as a woman, Synagogue is blindfolded. Her torso is slumping, and her crown is shattered. The staff in her left hand is broken while the five books of Torah are about to slip from her right hand. Zinn states that this image is "horrifyingly anti-Jewish" and "one of the most shocking portrayals of Judaism in European cathedrals."[4]

These artistic representations give visible testimony to how the medieval Christian church viewed itself in relation to Israel. The church is viewed as triumphant while Israel is represented as defeated and rejected.[5]

Thomas Aquinas (1224–1274)

Thomas Aquinas viewed the Jews and Judaism like the majority of Christians of his era. He did not alter the traditional understandings of the Jews and Israel in any significant way. Instead, Aquinas's contributions lie elsewhere. Aquinas, as Hood observes, "served as a major conduit of the traditional Christian view of the Jews for some seven hundred years."[6]

For Aquinas, the Jews were important because of their role in history. He accepted Augustine's theory that the Jews pointed to the validity of the Christian faith and the fulfillment of OT prophecies. Aquinas also believed in a future conversion of the Jews as a group based on his interpretation of Rom 11:25–26:

> It is possible to designate an end, because it seems evident that the blindness of the Jews will remain until the fullness of the Gentiles has come into faith. And this is in accord with what he says about the future healing of the Jews, when he says at that time, certainly when the fullness of the

---

[4]Zinn, "History and Interpretation," Illus. 7, n.p. Another image of supersessionism is found at the Erfurt Cathedral in Thuringia, Germany, with a wood carving at the choir of benches. The carving depicts two riders. One is on a horse while the other sits on a pig. *Ecclesia*, who sits on the horse, carries a shield with the Christian symbol of a fish. Her lance penetrates Synagogue, the rider of the pig. The message is clear—victory belongs to *Ecclesia*.

[5]One exception to the negative portrayals of the Jews and Judaism can be found in a twelfth-century stained-glass window in the Church of the Abbey of St. Denis near Paris. The window shows Christ standing between two figures representing *Synagoga* and *Ecclesia*. He crowns *Ecclesia* while lifting a veil from the face of *Synagoga*. Unlike the imagery at Reims and Strassbourg, though, *Synagoga* is not pictured as defeated. The tablets of the Law are held firmly in her left hand, and her staff is not broken.

[6]Hood, *Aquinas and the Jews*, xii.

Gentiles will be reached, all Israel will be saved. Not every individual, but all Jews in a general sense.[7]

To summarize, an examination of medieval art and the views of Thomas Aquinas reveals that supersessionism was dominant in the medieval period. Most saw Israel and the Jews as being rejected by God. This belief, though, was coupled with the idea that ethnic Jews would someday experience a conversion to the Christian faith.

---

[7]"Potest etiam designare terminum, quia videlicet usque tunc caecitas Iudaeorum durabit, quousque plenitudo Gentium ad fidem intrabit. Et huic concordat quod intra subdit de futuro remedio Iudaeorum, cum dicit et tunc, scilicet cum plenitudo Gentium intraverit, omnis Israel salvus fiet, nonparticulariter sicut modo, sed universaliter omnes." T. Aquinas, *Sancti Thomae de Aquino Super Epistolam B. Pauli ad Romanos lectura*, 11.4, http://www.unav.es/filosofia/alarcon/cro05.html, accessed January 26, 2004.

Chapter 6

Supersessionism in the Reformation Era

Although old ideas were being challenged during the Reformation era, there was no unified stance regarding supersessionism. Some important theologians of this time promoted this position while others appeared to reject parts or all of it. This summary of supersessionism in the Reformation era begins with the two leading Reformers, Martin Luther and John Calvin.

MARTIN LUTHER (1483–1546)

Martin Luther's views concerning the Jews and Judaism have been the subject of much debate. According to Hillerbrand, "There is scholarly agreement that the early Luther spoke thoughtfully and positively about Jews."[1] Luther prayed for the Jews and called for their friendly treatment.[2] He said, "We ought, therefore, not to treat the Jews in so unkindly a spirit, for there are future Christians among them, and they are turning every day."[3] Luther also held to a special distinction for the Jews in God's plan: "Moreover, they alone, and not we Gentiles, have this promise, that there shall always be Christians among Abraham's seed, who acknowledge the blessed Seed."[4]

With his 1523 work "That Jesus Christ Was Born a Jew," Luther appeared optimistic that many Jews would convert to Christianity. His hope was that "many of them will become genuine Christians and turn again to the faith of their fathers, the prophets and patriarchs."[5] Hans Küng

---

[1]H. J. Hillerbrand, "Martin Luther and the Jews," in *Jews and Christians: Exploring the Past, Present, and Future*, ed. J. H. Charlesworth (New York: Crossroad, 1990), 129.

[2]See M. Luther, "That Jesus Christ Was Born a Jew," *LW* 45:199–229; *WA* 11:314–36.

[3]M. Luther, "The Magnificat," *LW* 21:354–55; *WA* 7:600. See M. U. Edwards Jr., "Against the Jews," in *Essential Papers on Judaism and Christianity in Conflict: From Late Antiquity to the Reformation*, ed. J. Cohen (New York: New York University Press, 1991), 352.

[4]*LW* 21:355; *WA* 7:600–601.

[5]*LW* 45:200; *WA* 11:315.

points out that with the dawning of the Reformation, Luther believed "a new last age had dawned for the Jews as well."[6]

Luther's attitude toward the Jews changed dramatically, though, in his later years. As Hillerbrand writes, "From the end of the 1530s onward . . . a different tone can be discerned in Luther's writings. There is less optimism about the possibility of Jewish conversion."[7] This decreasing optimism concerning Jewish conversion may have stimulated much of Luther's harsh rhetoric toward the Jews.[8]

Luther's strongest statements against the Jews are found in his 1543 tract "Concerning the Jews and Their Lies." He referred to the Jews as a "miserable and accursed people."[9] Luther's intolerance toward the Jews is also evident in the following statement: "What shall we Christians do with this rejected and condemned people, the Jews? Since they live among us, we dare not tolerate their conduct, now that we are aware of their lying and reviling and blaspheming."[10]

In addition to his anti-Semitic rhetoric, Luther also made statements consistent with a punitive replacement view toward Israel. He viewed the destruction of Jerusalem and the temple in AD 70 as evidence of God's permanent rejection of the Jews: "'Listen, Jew, are you aware that Jerusalem and your sovereignty, together with your temple and priesthood, have been destroyed for over 1,460 years?' . . . This work of wrath is proof that the Jews, surely rejected by God, are no longer his people, and neither is he any longer their God."[11]

In reference to the promise of Abraham's descendants being a "great nation," Luther said, "Therefore the Jews have lost this promise, no matter how much they boast of their father Abraham. . . . They are no longer the people of God."[12]

Luther also argued that the designations *Israel* and *Jew* had undergone a transformation. True Israelites, according to him, were those who now accepted the new covenant:

---

[6]H. Küng, *Judaism: Between Yesterday and Tomorrow*, trans. J. Bowden (New York: Crossroad, 1992), 181.

[7]Hillerbrand, "Martin Luther and the Jews," 130.

[8]Hillerbrand also says, "I do believe that there is a change over time in Luther. And the change has to do, first of all, with a clear diminishing of his interest in or optimism about Jewish conversion." Ibid., 147. See also B. Lohse, *Martin Luther's Theology: Its Historical and Systematic Development*, trans. R. A. Harrisville (Minneapolis: Fortress, 1999), 342.

[9]*LW* 47:137; *WA* 53:417.

[10]*LW* 47:268; *WA* 53:522.

[11]*LW* 47:138–39; *WA* 53:418.

[12]*LW* 3:113; *WA* 42:629.

> The Jews make a point of the name Israel and claim that they alone are Israel and we are Gentiles. Now this is true so far as the first part of the prophecy and the old covenant of Moses are concerned. . . . But according to the second part of the prophecy and the new covenant, the Jews are no longer Israel, for all things are to be new, and Israel must become new. Those alone are the true Israel who have accepted the new covenant, which was established and begun at Jerusalem.[13]

Luther also said, "Thus all the Gentiles who are Christians are the true Israelites and new Jews, born of Christ, the noblest Jew."[14]

Summarizing Luther's later supersessionist views concerning Israel and the Jews, Hillerbrand states, "There is no more promise for Israel. God is silent. Israel experiences the silence of God, which is his wrath. . . . In his later writings Luther appears to have abandoned the notion of the permanence of Israel's election."[15]

JOHN CALVIN (1509–1564)

John Calvin shared the anti-Jewish prejudices of his day, but his approach toward the Jews and Israel was more moderate than Luther's. He did not resort to harsh language, nor did he advocate the use of violence against the Jews.[16] According to VanGemeren, Calvin did not have "a clearly defined position on Israel."[17]

As a result, there has been some confusion and disagreement concerning what Calvin actually believed about Israel. VanGemeren notes that "some have seen the utter rejection of Israel in Calvin's writings, whereas others have also viewed the hope for national Israel."[18] Engel,

---

[13]*LW* 35:287–88; *WA, DB* 11?:400.

[14]*LW* 35:288; *WA, DB* 11?:400.

[15]Hillerbrand, "Martin Luther and the Jews," 136.

[16]"Yet, despite the great obstinacy with which they continue to wage war against the gospel, we must not despise them, while we consider that, for the sake of the promise, God's blessing still rests among them." J. Calvin, *Institutes of the Christian Religion*, LCC 2, ed. J. T. McNeill, trans. F. Battles, no. 21 (Philadelphia: Westminster, 1960), 1337.

[17]W. VanGemeren, "Israel as the Hermeneutical Crux in the Interpretation of Prophecy (II)," *WTJ* 46 (1984): 254.

[18]W. VanGemeren, "Israel as the Hermeneutical Crux in the Interpretation of Prophecy," *WTJ* 45, no. 1 (1983): 142. For example, C. Williamson states that Calvin strongly believed that God's covenant with Israel was "unconditional, unbreakable, and gracious," but he also asserts that Calvin "makes statements exactly opposing the above." C. M. Williamson, *A Guest in the House of Israel: Post-Holocaust Church Theology* (Louisville, KY: Westerminster/John Knox, 1993), 131. VanGemeren and I. Murray appear to disagree on this issue. VanGemeren argues that Calvin believed in a restoration of national Israel. See VanGemeren, "Israel as the Hermeneutical Crux in the Interpretation of Prophecy (II)," 290. I. H. Murray, on the other hand, states that "neither Luther nor Calvin saw a future general conversion of the Jews promised in Scripture." I. H. Murray, *The Puritan Hope: Revival and the Interpretation of Prophecy* (Carlisle, PA: Banner of Truth, 1991), 41.

too, asserts that Calvin's views on the Jews and Judaism are "maddeningly complex."[19]

Calvin, at times, made statements consistent with a replacement view. He interpreted the "all Israel" who will be saved in Rom 11:26 as the church composed of both believing Jews and Gentiles: "When the Gentiles have come in, the Jews will at the same time return from their defection to the obedience of faith. The salvation of the whole Israel of God, which must be drawn from both, will thus be completed, and yet in such a way that the Jews, as the first born in the family of God, may obtain the first place."[20]

He also held the view that the "Israel of God" in Gal 6:16 refers to "all believers, whether Jews or Gentiles, who were united into one church."[21] Calvin, thus, believed that the church was the new Israel. As Engel points out, much of Calvin's language "supports traditional Christian supersessionism."[22] At times, though, Calvin made statements that seem to indicate he believed in a future for the Jews in the plan of God. In his commentary on Isa 59:20, he wrote,

> Paul quotes this passage, (Rom. xi. 26,) in order to shew that there is still some remaining hope among the Jews; although from their unconquerable obstinacy it might be inferred that they were altogether cast off and doomed to eternal death. But because God is continually mindful of his covenant, and "his gifts and calling are without repentance," (Rom. xi. 29) Paul justly concludes that it is impossible that they shall not at length be collected along with the Gentiles that out of both "there may be one fold" under Christ. (John x. 16).[23]

Noting Calvin's remarks in the above statement, VanGemeren declares, "Calvin in his Isaiah commentary goes on record in favor of a national restoration of Israel to the covenant."[24] Williamson's study of Calvin has led him to assert that "Calvin denies supersessionism."[25] He also says,

---

[19]M. P. Engel, "Calvin and the Jews: A Textual Puzzle," *PSB* Supplementary Issue, no. 1 (1990): 123. This variance of opinion may be because Calvin did not write a specific work about the Jews.

[20]J. Calvin, *The Epistles of Paul the Apostle to the Romans and to the Thessalonians*, ed. D. W. Torrance and T. F. Torrance, trans. R. Mackenzie (Grand Rapids: Eerdmans, 1961), 255.

[21]J. Calvin, "Commentaries on the Epistles of Paul to the Galatians and Ephesians," in *Calvin's Commentaries*, trans. W. Pringle (Edinburgh: Calvin Translation Society, 1844–56; repr., Grand Rapids: Baker, 1999), 21:186.

[22]Engel, "Calvin and the Jews," 120.

[23]J. Calvin, "Commentary on the Book of the Prophet Isaiah," in *Calvin's Commentaries*, 8:269.

[24]VanGemeren, "Israel as the Hermeneutical Crux in the Interpretation of Prophecy," 290.

[25]Williamson, *A Guest in the House of Israel*, 132.

"Calvin meant that Christians may not expropriate for themselves promises made to the people Israel."[26]

Was Calvin a supersessionist? Part of the confusion on this matter may result from the different emphases Calvin had about the Jews. Holwerda points out that Calvin made two important assertions regarding the Jews and Israel. First, Calvin believed that the church was the new Israel.[27] But second, Calvin held to some form of a future conversion of the Jews. As Holwerda states, "Thus, based on Israel's election, Calvin continued to hold to a future conversion of Jewish Israel."[28]

The conclusion here is that Calvin held to a moderate form of supersessionism. For him, the church was the new Israel, but a future conversion of the Jews into the church was also to be expected. As Holwerda states, "While Calvin teaches a future conversion of Jewish Israel, he interprets 'all Israel' as referring to both Jewish and Gentile believers."[29]

According to Holwerda, some of Calvin's followers followed Calvin's emphasis that the church was the new Israel but excluded his beliefs concerning a future for the Jews. He states, "Within that emphasis [the church being the new Israel], moreover, it became possible for some of Calvin's followers to develop a theology of election that no longer left room for any significant use of 'election' with regard to Jewish Israel."[30]

OTHER REFORMERS

Although Luther and Calvin were the primary figures during the Reformation period, they were not the only Reformers to make significant statements concerning Israel and the church. Melanchthon (1497–1560) viewed all true believers since Adam and Eve to be part of the church.[31] He also appears to have adopted a punitive supersessionist approach to national Israel. He said, "God adorned his Church in Israel with Elijah and the other prophets. In all kingdoms it has been known. However, like the Jews, many have scorned God and have entirely lost the teaching of the gospel through their own evil and ingratitude."[32]

On the other hand, the editors of the *Geneva Bible* had a more positive view of Israel's future. The comment on Rom 11:26 from the 1581 version

---

[26]Ibid.

[27]See D. E. Holwerda, *Jesus & Israel: One Covenant or Two*? (Grand Rapids: Eerdmans, 1995), 3–4.

[28]Ibid., 3.

[29]Ibid., 4, n. 7.

[30]Ibid., 4.

[31]P. Melanchthon, *Melanchthon on Christian Doctrine: Loci Communes 1555*, ed. and trans. C. L. Manschreck (New York: Oxford University Press, 1965), xlvi–xlvii.

[32]Ibid., 191; see also 73.

states, "He [Paul] sheweth that the time shall come that the whole nation of the Jewes, though not every one particularly, shall be joyned to the Church of Christ."[33]

According to Hsia, "No single view of Jews and Judaism" characterized those who were part of the Radical Reformation.[34] Simons (c. 1496–1561), while holding that the church consists of all true believers of all ages going back to Adam and Eve,[35] affirmed a future for national Israel:

> The Jews despised this King Christ and therefore they were blinded. Yet they shall return and come to Christ, their King David, as Paul testifies, saying: Blindness in part is happened to Israel, until the fullness of the Gentiles be come in. And so all Israel shall be saved, as it is written: There shall come out of Zion the deliverer, and shall turn away the ungodliness from Jacob. For this is my covenant with them, when I shall take away their sins. Isa. 59:20. Since Israel is yet to be converted unto Christ, it follows incontrovertibly that the King David, whom Israel shall seek, can be none other than Christ.[36]

Although supersessionism was well accepted in the seventeenth century, two groups appear to have believed in a salvation or restoration of the Jews—the English Puritans and the Dutch Reformed theologians. In his study of the Puritans of the seventeenth century, Murray notes that "belief in a future conversion of the Jews became commonplace among the English Puritans."[37] He mentions some who believed this:

> This same belief concerning the future of the Jews is to be found very widely in seventeenth-century Puritan literature. It appears in the works of such well-known Puritans as John Owen, Thomas Manton and John Flavel. . . . It is also handled in a rich array of commentaries, both folios and quartos—David Dickson on the Psalms, George Hutcheson on the Minor Prophets, Jeremiah Burroughs on Hosea, William Greenhill on Ezekiel, Elnathan Parr on Romans and James Durham on Revelation: a list which could be greatly extended.[38]

In his 1669 work *The Mystery of Israel's Salvation Explained and Applied*, Mather expressed belief in a conversion of the tribes of Israel:

---

[33]*Geneva Bible* (London: n.p., 1581).

[34]R. P. Hsia, "Jews," in *The Oxford Encyclopedia of the Reformation*, ed. H. J. Hillerbrand (New York: Oxford University Press, 1996), 2:344.

[35]M. Simons, *The Complete Works of Menno Simons*, ed. J. Christian Wenger; trans. L. Verduin (Scottsdale, PA: Herald, 1956), 734–35, 742.

[36]Ibid., 38.

[37]Murray, *The Puritan Hope*, 43.

[38]Ibid., 44.

"That there shall be a general conversion of the Tribes of Israel is a truth which in some measure hath been known and believed in all ages of the Church of God, since the Apostle's days."[39] He also declared, "There is indeed a fullness of the Gentiles, which shall be after the conversion of the Jews, Psal. 98.3,4 . . . in which fullness, the saved Tribes of Israel, shall be very instrumental."[40] Sibbes, too, in his book *The Bruised Reed*, declared a future for the Jews:

> The Jews are not yet come in under Christ's banner; but God hath persuaded Japhet to come into the tents of Shem, will persuade Shem to come into the tents of Japhet, Gen. Ix. 27. The "fulness of the Gentiles is not yet come in," Rom. Xi. 25, but Christ, that hath the "utmost parts of the earth given him for his possession," Ps. Ii. 8, will gather all the sheep his Father hath given him into one fold. . . . The faithful Jews rejoiced to think of the calling of the Gentiles; and why should not we joy to think of the calling of the Jews?[41]

Matar points out that the idea of "the Restoration of the Jews to Palestine" was held in English Protestant thought immediately following the Reformation.[42] Three ideas were behind this belief: (1) the Turko-Catholic threat to Protestant Christendom, (2) Puritan millennial speculations, and (3) England's perceived moral responsibility to the Jews.[43] For some, "the Jews' Restoration to Palestine would inaugurate England's messianic age."[44]

In a similar way as the English Puritans, Van Den Berg claims that most theologians in the Netherlands affirmed a future for Israel: "For . . . virtually all Dutch theologians of the seventeenth century, 'the whole of Israel' indicated the fullness of the people of Israel 'according to the flesh': in other words, the fullness of the Jewish people. This meant that there was a basis for an expectation of a future conversion of the Jews—an expectation which was shared by a large majority of Dutch theologians."[45]

---

[39]I. Mather, *The Mystery of Israel's Salvation Explained and Applied* (London: n.p., 1669), c.

[40]Ibid., 2.

[41]*The Complete Works of Richard Sibbes*, ed. A. B. Grosart (Edinburgh: Nichol, 1862), 1:99.

[42]N. I. Matar, "The Idea of the Restoration of the Jews in English Protestant Thought, 1661–1701," *HTR* 78, nos. 1–2 (1985): 115.

[43]Ibid.

[44]Ibid.

[45]J. Van Den Berg, "Appendix III: The Eschatological Expectation of Seventeenth-Century Dutch Protestantism with Regard to the Jewish People," in *Puritan Eschatology: 1600–1660*, ed. P. Toon (Cambridge: James Clarke, 1970), 140. According to Van Den Berg, theologians who affirmed a future salvation and/or restoration of Israel include the following: S. Maresius (1599–1673), S. Episcopius (1583–1643), J. Batalerius (1593–1672), G. Voetius (1589–1676), J. Hoornbeek (1617–1666), A. Essenius (1618–1677), J. Coccejus (1603–1669), H. Groenewegen (1640–1692), H. Witsius (1636–1708), and W. à Brakel (1635–1711) (137–53).

Serrarius (1600–1699) of Amsterdam also expressed belief in both a conversion of the Jews and a restoration of Israel when he said, "The time of the Conversion of the Jews and the restoring of the Kingdom of Israel (of which the Prophets are full) . . . is at hand."[46]

---

[46]P. Serrarius, *An Awakening Warning to the Wofull World* (Amstrodam [sic]: n.p., 1662), 27. See also 29.

Chapter 7

Supersessionism in the Modern Era

The modern era[1] has witnessed a variety of opinions regarding supersessionism. The supersessionist view has remained popular and is held by many. Yet some theologians and churches of this era reject some or all elements of supersessionism. In this chapter, I will look at the influence of key theologians and events of the modern era that have had a significant relationship to the doctrine of supersessionism.

IMMANUEL KANT (1724–1804)

Immanuel Kant contributed to the church's understanding of supersessionism by promoting a form of structural supersessionism in which the Jewishness of Jesus was downplayed and the Hebrew Scriptures were not viewed as contributing to a proper understanding of God's purposes with His creation.

In his 1793 work *Religion Within the Limits of Reason Alone*,[2] Kant attempted to show the essence of true moral religion. In doing so, he argued that certain matters are eternal and enduring while others need to be discarded as useless. Kant affirmed those parts of Christianity that taught moral law or moral experience. He rejected, however, those elements that he believed hindered Christianity's role as a vehicle for moral religion.[3] This included Christianity's Jewish elements.

Kant, for example, rejected the belief that Christianity had a direct relationship to Judaism and the Jewish people. He stated, "The Jewish faith stands in no essential connection whatever, *i.e.*, in no unity of concepts, with this ecclesiastical faith whose history we wish to consider, though the

---

[1]By "modern era" I am referring generally to the time period from the eighteenth century through the present time.

[2]I. Kant, *Religion Within the Limits of Reason Alone*, trans. T. M. Greene and H. H. Hudson (New York: Harper Torchbooks, 1960).

[3]See K. Soulen, *The God of Israel and Christian Theology* (Minneapolis: Fortress, 1996), 64.

Jewish immediately preceded this (the Christian) church and provided the physical occasion for its establishment."[4]

As a result, Kant had little regard for the OT or Jewish aspects of the Bible. For him, Christianity fell short of moral religion whenever it maintained elements of Jewish belief. These Jewish elements, therefore, needed to be removed. As Soulen summarizes,

> Kant has put his finger on the critical fault line that runs through the center of the standard model of Christian theology: the line that divides the standard model's creaturely-universal foreground from its Israelite background. By identifying this fault line and exploiting it, Kant hits upon a strategy for adapting Christian doctrine to the modern age and its canons of rationality: Christian doctrine simply *is* the story of the triumph of creaturely-universal spirit over historical-particular flesh. This triumph, paradigmatically achieved in the church's supersessionism of the Jewish people, is for Kant the enduring spiritual content of Christianity. Purifying Christian doctrine of its residual Jewishness is therefore no distortion of the Christian faith but the necessary expression of its basic genius.[5]

FRIEDRICH SCHLEIERMACHER (1768–1834)

Schleiermacher also contributed to the doctrine of supersessionism. In his work *The Christian Faith*, Schleiermacher put forth a scheme to retain the elements of Christianity that he believed were consistent with moral religion while removing those elements that he considered "heretical" or inconsistent with true religion.[6] He did this in two major ways.

First, like Kant, Schleiermacher denied any significant connection between OT Judaism and Christianity. He declared, "Christianity cannot in any wise be regarded as a remodeling or a renewal and continuation of Judaism."[7] In taking this approach, Schleiermacher removed the connection between the Hebrew Scriptures and Christianity. For him, the OT should not be considered an authority for Christian theology: "Hence the Old Testament

---

[4]Kant, *Religion Within the Limits of Reason Alone*, 116. Kant even denied that Judaism was a religion: "Judaism is really not a religion at all but merely a union of a number of people who, since they belonged to a particular stock, formed themselves into a commonwealth under purely political laws, and not into a church" (116).

[5]Soulen, *The God of Israel and Christian Theology*, 67–68. Emphasis in original.

[6]"In order to build up a system of doctrine, it is necessary first to eliminate from the total mass of dogmatic material everything that is heretical, and to retain only what is ecclesiastical." F. Schleiermacher, *The Christian Faith*, ed. H. R. Mackintosh and J. S. Stewart (Edinburgh: T&T Clark, 1999), 95. This is an English translation of *Der christliche Glaube nach den Grundsätzen der evangelischen Kirch im Zusammemhang dargestellt*, 2nd. ed. (Berlin: n.p., 1830).

[7]Schleiermacher, *The Christian Faith*, 61.

appears simply as a superfluous authority for Dogmatics."[8] Concerning the OT, Schleiermacher declared, "Whatever is most definitely Jewish has least value."[9] In taking this view, he adopted a form of structural supersessionism in which the Hebrew Scriptures were not considered a factor in the determination of how God presently engages His creation.

Second, Schleiermacher also adopted a "Scotist"[10] or "Christocentric" approach to Christian doctrine in which everything is viewed as being related to the redemption accomplished by Jesus.[11] This Scotist perspective of Schleiermacher helped remove Israelite elements from the Christian faith. As Soulen writes, "His [Schleiermacher's] reconstruction of Christian doctrine epitomizes the process whereby the truth of Christian faith comes to be articulated solely in terms of Jesus Christ's significance for the creaturely-universal dimension of human existence, while the Israelite dimension of Christian faith is cut away altogether."[12]

Both Kant and Schleiermacher were significant to the doctrine of supersessionism because they de-emphasized the Jewishness of Jesus and God's relationship with Israel. As Soulen explains,

> Key to this whole development [of Kant and Schleiermacher] is the rosy confidence that the Christian conception of God can be coherently maintained in separation from the God of Israel. So long as Christians identified the Creator with the God of Israel, it could not occur to them to seek to expel the Jewish dimension of Christian faith in the name of the creaturely-universal. But once this identification was denied, Christians inevitably experienced the Jewish aspects of Christianity as foreign and unassimilable.[13]

KARL BARTH (1886–1968)

Barth's significant impact on theology in the twentieth century extended to the areas of Israel and the church.[14] His views on these subjects were

---

[8]Ibid., 115. Schleiermacher also suggested that the Old Testament be treated as an "appendix" to the New Testament (611).

[9]Ibid., 62.

[10]According to Soulen, "A Scotist account . . . holds that God's work as Consummator is oriented from the very beginning toward the incarnation." Soulen, *The God of Israel and Christian Theology*, 74.

[11]"Christianity is a monotheistic faith, belonging to the teleological type of religion, and is essentially distinguished from other such faiths by the fact that in it everything is related to the redemption accomplished by Jesus of Nazareth." Schleiermacher, *The Christian Faith*, 52.

[12]Soulen, *The God of Israel and Christian Theology*, 68. Soulen also says, "Christocentrism represents Schleiermacher's strategy for maintaining the doctrinal integrity of Christian theology after its internal reference to the God of Israel has been wholly cut away" (77).

[13]Ibid., 78–79.

[14]"The theology of Karl Barth has had a remarkable impact on subsequent thinking about the relationship of Church and Israel." D. E. Holwerda, *Jesus & Israel: One Covenant or Two?* (Grand Rapids: Eerdmans, 1995), 11.

related to his position on election. Barth saw an essential connection between Israel and the church that was based on the Elect One, Jesus Christ. According to Barth, there is one elect community of God. This community in its form as Israel represents divine judgment; in its form as the church, it represents divine mercy:

> The election of grace as the election of Jesus Christ, is simultaneously the eternal election of the one community of God by the existence of which Jesus Christ is to be attested to the whole world and the whole world summoned to faith in Jesus Christ. This one community of God in its form as Israel has to serve the representation of the divine judgment, in its form as the Church the representation of the divine mercy. In its form as Israel it is determined for hearing, and in its form as the Church for believing the promise sent forth to man. To the one elected community of God is given in the one case its passing, and in the other its coming form.[15]

For Barth, Israel is representative of those who reject their own election while the church consists of those who live in light of their election. As he states, "Israel is the people of the Jews which resists its election; the Church is the gathering of Jews and Gentiles called on the ground of its election."[16] Summarizing Barth's view, Holwerda observes, "Jesus Christ is the Elect One, but what is elected in Christ is a community with a two-fold form, Israel and the Church."[17]

Like Augustine, Barth believed that Israel's existence and unbelief functioned as a sign. Israel's unbelief exemplified the sorry state of humanity in its rebellion against God.[18] In contrast to some theologians such as Kant and Schleiermacher, though, Barth placed a high importance on Israel's role in the history of redemption. As Wyschogrod states, "Because he reads Scripture obediently, [Barth] becomes aware of the centrality of Israel in God's relation with man and with the very message that Christianity proclaims to the world."[19]

---

[15]K. Barth, *CD* II/2, 195.

[16]Ibid., 199.

[17]Holwerda, *Jesus and Israel*, 11.

[18]See Barth, *CD* II/2, 195. Johnson says that "Barth seems far more optimistic than Augustine about the ultimate salvation of the Jews." J. J. Johnson, "A New Testament Understanding of the Jewish Rejection of Jesus: Four Theologians on the Salvation of Israel," *JETS* 43 (June 2000): 237, n. 39.

[19]M. Wyschogrod, "Why Was and Is the Theology of Karl Barth of Interest to a Jewish Theologian?" in *Footnotes to a Theology: The Karl Barth Barth Colloquium of 1972*, ed. M. Rumscheidt (Waterloo, ON: Corporation for the Publication of Academic Studies in Religion in Canada, 1974), 111. Soulen writes that Barth critiqued and revised Schleiermacher's "extreme Israel-forgetfulness." Soulen, *The God of Israel and Christian Theology*, 83.

Barth's views on supersessionism can be summarized in two assertions. First, he rejected punitive supersessionism in which national Israel is viewed as being permanently rejected because of its disobedience. As Johnson states, "For Barth, the Jews were, are, and will remain the chosen people of God—nothing can alter this divinely ordained fact."[20] In his *Dogmatics in Outline*, for example, Barth asserted that Israel's continuing existence in light of ongoing persecutions is the only "visible and tangible" evidence of God's existence.[21]

Second, Barth affirmed a form of economic supersessionism in which Israel's unique role came to an end with the death and resurrection of Christ.[22] He stated,

> The new Israel . . . is not (like the old Israel) a "nation," a natural society . . . but a people gathered solely by the preaching of the Word and the free election and calling of the Spirit. The first Israel, constituted on the basis of physical descent from Abraham, has fulfilled its mission now that the Savior of the world has sprung from it and its Messiah has appeared. Its members can only accept this fact with gratitude, and in confirmation of their own deepest election and calling attach themselves to the people of this Savior, their own King, whose members the Gentiles are now called to be as well. Its mission as a natural community has now run its course and cannot be continued or repeated.[23]

Summarizing Barth's economic supersessionism, Soulen writes, "Christ's death and resurrection bring Israel's career as a natural people to an end. Thereafter Israel's sole legitimate destiny is to be taken up into the church, the new and true Israel, where the significance of its identity as a carnal people is permanently transcended."[24]

Barth's economic supersessionism is also connected to his Christology in which all human history, including Israel's history, is viewed as culminating in Jesus Christ.[25] With Barth's Christocentric emphasis, God's covenant with Israel is fulfilled in Jesus. Thus, Israel's distinct role comes to an end. Its place is now taken by the church. For Barth, as Soulen points

---

[20]Johnson, "A New Testament Understanding of the Jewish Rejection of Jesus," 236.

[21]K. Barth, *Dogmatics in Outline*, trans. G. T. Thompson (London: SCM, 1949), 75.

[22]"Karl Barth's theology offers a classic example of the view that holds fast to economic supersessionism while rejecting punitive supersessionism." Soulen, *The God of Israel and Christian Theology*, 180, n. 5.

[23]Barth, *CD* III/2, 584.

[24]Soulen, *The God of Israel and Christian Theology*, 91. According to Barth, "Israel as the passing form of the community makes room for the Church as its coming form." Barth, *CD* II/2, 201. Barth also explicitly identifies the church as "the new Israel" (*CD* III/2, 584).

[25]See Barth, *CD* III/3, 180–81; III/2, 582.

out, "the church supersedes Israel as a community of witness by testifying to God's covenant in its definitive christological form."[26]

By rejecting punitive supersessionism and affirming economic supersessionism, Barth promoted a more positive view of the Jewish people[27] than did either Kant or Schleiermacher. Although still promoting a form of supersessionism, Barth expressed both a love and respect for the Jewish people. As Peter Ochs writes, Barth's "dialectical and ambivalent theology of Judaism displays to the modern reader the classical sources of both Christian supersessionism and Christian love of the people of Israel."[28]

THE HOLOCAUST AND THE MODERN STATE OF ISRAEL

Perspectives concerning supersessionism have been seriously affected by two twentieth-century developments—the Holocaust and the establishment of the modern state of Israel. These events have pushed questions and issues concerning Israel and the church to the forefront of Christian theology.[29]

More than any other event, the Holocaust has been the most significant factor in the church's reevaluation of supersessionism. According to Borowsky, "Within Christendom since the time of Hitler, there has existed a widespread reaction of shock and soul-searching concerning the Holocaust."[30] Ochs asserts that Christian reflections on the Jews and Judaism after the Holocaust "have generated theological questions of fundamental significance."[31] These questions include the following: (1) "What are Christians to make of the persistence of the Jewish people?" (2) "Is the

---

[26]Soulen, *The God of Israel and Christian Theology*, 91.

[27]Johnson writes, "Despite many charges to the contrary, Barth was not anti-Semitic. He insisted on the validity of the Jews' designation as the chosen people, he strongly supported the state of Israel, and he went as far as to say that 'antisemitism is sin against the Holy Ghost.'" Johnson, "A New Testament Understanding of the Jewish Rejection of Jesus," 236.

[28]P. Ochs, "Judaism and Christian Theology," in *The Modern Theologians*, ed. D. F. Ford (Malden, MA: Blackwell, 1997), 608.

[29]"Since the tragic events of the *Shoah* and the birth of the modern State of Israel on May 14, 1948, the interest shown in God's ancient people has been widespread and sustained." R. E. Diprose, *Israel in the Development of Christian Thought* (Rome: Istituto Biblico Evangelico Italiano, 2000), 1.

[30]I. J. Borowsky, "Foreword," in *Jews and Christians: Exploring the Past, Present, and Future*, ed. J. H. Charlesworth (New York: Crossroad, 1990), 11. According to P. Ochs, "Christian theologies of Judaism have been stimulated, instructed, or chastened by the memory of the Holocaust—the Shoah ('Destruction, Desolation')." Ochs, "Judaism and Christian Theology," 607. Boesel says, "Overcoming the tradition of supersessionism constitutes the heart of what is commonly understood as responsible Christian response to the Holocaust." C. J. Boesel, "Respecting Difference, Risking Proclamation: Faith, Responsibility and the Tragic Dimensions of Overcoming Supersessionism" (Ph.D. diss., Emory University, 2002), 11.

[31]Ochs, "Judaism and Christian Theology," 607.

Church the new Israel?" (3) "What of Israel's sins?" (4) "What of Israel's land and state?"[32]

The answers to these questions in recent years indicate a reaction against supersessionism. Williamson states, "Post-Shoah [Destruction] theology" among contemporary theologians "criticizes the church's supersessionist ideology toward Jews and Judaism."[33]

The establishment of the state of Israel in 1948 has also raised questions concerning Israel and the doctrine of supersessionism. Ridderbos lists some of them:

> The existence of Israel once again becomes a bone of contention, this time in a theoretical and theological sense. Do the misery and suffering of Israel in the past and in the present prove that God's doom has rested and will rest upon her, as has been alleged time and again in so-called Christian theology? Or is Israel's lasting existence and, in a way, her invincibility, God's finger in history, that Israel is the object of His special providence (*providential specialissima*) and the proof of her glorious future, the future that has been beheld and foretold by Israel's own seers and prophets?[34]

Commenting on the events of the Holocaust and the establishment of the Jewish state, Soulen states, "Under the new conditions created by these events, Christian churches have begun to consider anew their relation to the God of Israel and the Israel of God in the light of the Scriptures and the gospel about Jesus."[35] This includes "revisiting the teaching of supersessionism after nearly two thousand years."[36]

CHURCHES AND DENOMINATIONS SINCE THE HOLOCAUST

Supersessionism is still held by many.[37] But since the Holocaust, there has been a strong trend away from supersessionism. As Ochs declares, "Over the last two decades, denominational assemblies have mostly done away

---

[32]Ibid.

[33]C. M. Williamson, *A Guest in the House of Israel: Post-Holocaust Church Theology* (Louisville, KY: Westminster/John Knox, 1993), 7.

[34]H. N. Ridderbos, "The Future of Israel," in *Prophecy in the Making: Messages Prepared for Jerusalem Conference on Biblical Prophecy*, ed. C. F. H. Henry (Carol Stream, IL: Creation, 1971), 316.

[35]Soulen, *The God of Israel and Christian Theology*, x.

[36]Ibid.

[37]Pannenberg points out that the "replacement thesis," which involves the verdict that the Jewish people are no longer the people of God, "is still influential today." W. Pannenberg, *Systematic Theology*, trans. G. Bromiley (Grand Rapids: Eerdmans, 1993), 3:471.

with the traditional doctrine that Israel's election has been transferred to the church."[38]

The *Nostra Aetate* ("In Our Times") of the Second Vatican Council is important in this regard. This document of the Roman Catholic Church declared that the Jews have not been rejected by God: "Although the Church is the new people of God, the Jews should not be presented as repudiated or cursed by God, as if such views followed from the holy Scriptures."[39] The Roman Catholic Church does not espouse nonsupersessionism, and the *Nostra Aetate* should not be understood as an expression of nonsupersessionism. But, as Williamson points out, the *Nostra Aetate* acted as a catalyst for other expressions of openness toward God's plans for the Jews:

> *Nostra Aetate* started things in motion in 1965 with its profession that all who believe in Christ are children of Abraham according to faith and included in God's call to Abraham to be a light to the nations, that the church of the Gentiles has been grafted onto God's well-cultivated olive tree. To call the church the 'new people of God' cannot mean that Jews are no longer the people of God.[40]

Nostra Aetate has indeed been followed by similar declarations from other churches, some of which are clearly nonsupersessionist. The 1967 Belgian Protestant Council on Relations between Christians and Jews stated, "The church's claim to be the sole, new Israel of God can in no way be based on the Bible."[41] The Joint Catholic Protestant Statement to Our Fellow Christians of 1973 declared, "The singular grace of Jesus Christ does not abrogate the covenantal relationship of God with Israel (Rom. 11:1–2). In Christ the church shares in Israel's election without superseding it."[42] In 1977, the Central Board of the Swiss Protestant Church Federation asserted, "Although the church, already in the New Testament,

---

[38]Ochs, "Judaism and Christian Theology," 618. As for individuals, Ochs observes that R. Eckardt has been "one of the most prolific contributors to the Jewish-Christian dialogue, maintaining that Christianity has not replaced Israel in the drama of human salvation" (616).

[39]W. A. Abbott, ed., "Declaration on the Relationship of the Church to Non-Christian Religions," in *The Documents of Vatican II* (New York: Guild Press, 1966), 666. "As this sacred Synod searches into the mystery of the Church, it recalls the spiritual bond linking the people of the New Covenant with Abraham's stock" (663).

[40]Williamson, *A Guest in the House of Israel*, 37.

[41]"1967 Belgian Protestant Council on Relations Between Christians and Jews," in *More Stepping Stones to Jewish-Christian Relations*, ed. H. Croner (New York: Paulist, 1985), 194.

[42]"Joint Catholic Protestant Statement to Our Fellow Christians, 1973," in *Stepping Stones to Further Jewish-Christian Relations,* ed. H. Croner (New York: Paulist, 1977), 152.

applied to herself several promises made to the Jewish people, she does not supersede the covenant people, Israel."[43]

Also in 1977, the Mennonite European Regional Conference stated, "Jesus came not to destroy the Covenant of God with the Jews, but only to affirm it in a manner that would bring the blessing of God's people to non-Jews, also."[44] In 1980, the Synod of the Evangelical Church of the Rhineland declared, "We deny that the people Israel has been rejected by God or that it has been superseded by the church."[45] The Texas Conference of Churches of 1982 stated, "We reject the position that the covenant between the Jews and God was dissolved with the coming of Christ. Our conviction is grounded in the teaching of Paul in Romans, chapters 9–11, that God's gift and call are irrevocable."[46]

In 1984, the National Conference of Brazilian Bishops declared, "St. Paul bears witness that the Jews have a zeal for God (Rom. 10:2); that God has not rejected His people (Rom. 11:1 ff). . . . Israel continues to play an important role in the history of salvation, a role which will end only in the fulfillment of the plan of God (Rom. 11:11, 15, 23)."[47] In 1987, the General Assembly of the Presbyterian Church (U.S.A.) stated, "We affirm that the church, elected in Jesus Christ, has been engrafted into the people of God established by the covenant with Abraham, Isaac and Jacob. Therefore, Christians have not replaced Jews."[48]

With the 2002 document "Reflections on Covenant and Mission," Catholic bishops from the United States declared, "Thus, while the Catholic Church regards the saving act of Christ as central to the process of human salvation for all, it also acknowledges that Jews already dwell in a saving covenant with God."[49]

---

[43]"1977 Central Board of the Swiss Protestant Church Federation," in *The Theology of the Churches and the Jewish People: Statements by the World Council of Churches and Its Member Churches*, ed. A. Brockway, P. van Buren, R. Rendtorff, and S. Schoon (Geneva: WCC Publications, 1988), 84–85.

[44]"1977 Mennonite European Regional Conference," in *More Stepping Stones to Jewish-Christian Relations*, 205.

[45]"Synod of the Evangelical Church of the Rhineland, 1980," in *The Theology of the Churches and the Jewish People*, 94.

[46]"1982 Texas Conference of Churches," in *More Stepping Stones to Jewish-Christian Relations*, 186.

[47]"1984 National Conference of Brazilian Bishops," in *More Stepping Stones to Jewish-Christian Relations*, 152.

[48]"Statement of the 1987 General Assembly of the Presbyterian Church (U.S.A.)," in *The Theology of the Churches and the Jewish People*, 115.

[49]Consultation of the National Council of Synagogues and the Bishops Committee for Ecumenical and Interreligious Affairs, USCCB, "Reflections on Covenant and Mission," August 22, 2002, http://www.bc.edu/bc_org/research/cjl/Documents/ncs_usccb120802.htm, accessed January 6, 2003. According to this document, "John Paul II has explicitly taught that Jews are 'the people of God of the Old Covenant, never revoked by God,' 'the present-day people of the covenant concluded with Moses,' and 'partners in a covenant of eternal love which was never revoked.'"

Commenting on the various declarations from the Christian denominations, Waxman observes, "The assertion that God repudiated the Jews and elected a new Israel in their place is put aside. Paul's statement in Romans that God has not repudiated His covenant with the Jewish people is emphasized."[50] As a result, supersessionism's grip on the Christian church as a whole has been lessened significantly. In fact, it is doubtful whether the supersessionist approach is anymore the dominant view. As Holwerda points out, "The traditional view that the Christian Church has superseded Jewish Israel, which no longer has a role in God's plan of redemption, is no longer dominant. Even though no consensus has developed on how to evaluate the present position and future role of Jewish Israel, the negative tones prominent in the Church's traditional view have been greatly muted."[51]

DISPENSATIONALISM

Dispensational theology, a movement with Calvinist roots[52] that came to fruition in the nineteenth century with the teachings of John Nelson Darby, has had a significant impact on how many American Christians viewed Israel and the church. Dispensationalism is strongly nonsupersessionist in its theology. For example, Ryrie, a primary leader within the dispensational movement, lists belief in a distinction between Israel and the church as one of the three essentials of dispensationalism.[53] Dispensationalists also hold that national Israel will be restored in a future dispensation. As Blaising, who also is a dispensationalist, states, "One of the most well-known features of the dispensational tradition is the belief in a future for national Israel."[54] This "future" includes belief in a "national restoration" of Israel.[55] In addition to Ryrie and Blaising, other dispensational theologians who have

---

[50]M. Waxman, "The Dialogue, Touching New Bases?" in *More Stepping Stones to Jewish-Christian Relations*, 25.

[51]Holwerda, *Jesus and Israel*, 11.

[52]G. M. Marsden says, "Dispensationalism was essentially Reformed in its nineteenth-century origins and had in later nineteenth-century America spread most among revival-oriented Calvinists." G. M. Marsden, "Introduction: Reformed and American," in *Reformed Theology in America: A History of Its Modern Development*, 2nd ed., ed. G. M. Marsden (Grand Rapids: Baker, 1997), 8.

[53]See C. C. Ryrie, *Dispensationalism* (Chicago: Moody, 1995), 38. The other two essentials, which make up the *sine qua non* of dispensationalism, according to Ryrie, include belief in a literal interpretation of Scripture and belief that the underlying purpose of God in the world is the glory of God (40).

[54]C. A. Blaising and D. L. Bock, *Progressive Dispensationalism: An Up-to-Date Handbook of Contemporary Dispensational Thought* (Wheaton, IL: Baker, 1993), 21.

[55]Ibid. Blaising and Bock state that dispensationalism has taken three forms in its history: classical, revised, and progressive. However, all dispensational theologians, regardless of which category of dispensationalism they fit into, have asserted belief in a future restoration of national Israel (see 9–56).

promoted nonsupersessionism include Walvoord, Pentecost, McClain, Saucy, and Bock.[56]

Dispensationalism and its nonsupersessionist views have become popular in the United States. Dispensationalists had a significant influence on the Bible Conference movement of the early twentieth century.[57] C. I. Scofield, with the writing and distribution of his *Scofield Reference Bible*,[58] put a dispensational study Bible into the hands of thousands of Christians. According to Blaising, through the Bible conferences and *Scofield Reference Bible*, "dispensationalism came to characterize the views and beliefs of a large constituency of American evangelicalism scattered throughout mainstream Protestantism."[59]

In addition, many educational institutions have promoted dispensational theology to some degree. The foremost promoter of dispensationalism has been Dallas Theological Seminary. Other schools that have promoted dispensationalism to some degree include Grace Theological Seminary, Grand Rapids Baptist Seminary, Western Seminary, Talbot School of Theology, Philadelphia College of the Bible, Denver Seminary, The Master's Seminary, and Moody Bible Institute.

Many popular Christian radio teachers in the past century have promoted dispensational views. Some of these radio personalities include: Fuller, M. R. DeHaan and Richard DeHaan, Epp, Wiersbe, Kroll, McGee, Swindoll, Rogers, Stanley, Falwell, and MacArthur. Dispensationalists have also had a strong influence on mission agencies and parachurch ministries like Central American Mission, Navigators, Campus Crusade for Christ, and Youth for Christ.[60]

Through schools, churches, denominations, literature, broadcast media, and parachurch organizations, dispensationalism has asserted a strong influence on the theological beliefs of American Christians. As Blaising puts it, "Dispensationalism has expanded to become one of the most common expressions of evangelical Christianity."[61]

---

[56]J. F. Walvoord, *The Millennial Kingdom* (Grand Rapids: Zondervan, 1959); J. D. Pentecost, *Things to Come: A Study in Biblical Eschatology* (Grand Rapids: Zondervan, 1958); A. J. McClain, *The Greatness of the Kingdom: An Inductive Study of the Kingdom of God* (Winona Lake, IN: BMH, 1959); R. L. Saucy, *The Case for Progressive Dispensationalism: The Interface Between Dispensational and Nondispensational Theology* (Grand Rapids: Zondervan, 1993); Blaising and Bock, *Progressive Dispensationalism*.

[57]Blaising and Bock, *Progressive Dispensationalism*, 10.

[58]*Scofield Reference Bible* (New York: Oxford University Press, 1909).

[59]Blaising and Bock, *Progressive Dispensationalism*, 11. Blaising says the influence of dispensationalism "was especially concentrated in Presbyterian, Baptist, and Congregationalist circles" (11).

[60]Ibid., 13.

[61]Ibid.

HISTORICAL JESUS RESEARCH

In recent years, some biblical scholars have argued that the mission of the historical Jesus must be understood within the context of his vision for a restored Israel. As Blaising states, "Many Biblical scholars working in historical Jesus research share the view that the teaching and mission of Jesus can only be understood in terms of Jesus' vision for the restoration of Israel."[62] For example, Sanders says, "What we know with almost complete assurance . . . is that *Jesus is to be positively connected with the hope for Jewish restoration*."[63] Meier argues, "It is within this context of restoration eschatology that Jesus' prophetic proclamation and the institution of the Twelve must be understood. . . . He addresses himself squarely to the people of Israel."[64] Meier argues that older conceptions of Jesus as just a spiritual teacher must be replaced with "an approach to Jesus that anchors his religious genius in a national vision for Israel."[65] According to McKnight, "Jesus' hope was not so much the 'Church' as the restoration of the twelve tribes (cf. Matt. 8:11–12; 10:23; and 19:28), the fulfillment of the promises of Moses to national Israel, and the hope of God's kingdom (focused on and through Israel) on earth."[66]

The recent consensus that Jesus' mission was directly related to the restoration of national Israel has significant implications for the doctrine of supersessionism. In fact, Blaising believes it threatens the very existence of the supersessionist view: "As Biblical scholarship makes ever more clear that Jesus and Paul taught a future for national Israel in the eschatological plan of God, the legitimacy of a supersessionist reading of Scripture grows ever more dim to the point of vanishing altogether."[67]

---

[62]C. A. Blaising, "The Future of Israel as a Theological Question," *JETS* 44 (2001): 438. McKnight adds, "Contemporary scholarship is nearly united in the view that Jesus' vision concerned Israel as a nation and not a new religion. He wanted to consummate God's promises to Israel, and he saw this taking place in the land of Israel." S. McKnight, *A New Vision for Israel: The Teachings of Jesus in National Context* (Grand Rapids: Eerdmans, 1999), 6.

[63]E. P. Sanders, *Jesus and Judaism* (Philadelphia: Fortress, 1985), 118. Emphasis in original. Sanders categorizes how certain it is that Jesus believed various things. In the category of "certain or virtually certain," Sanders declares that "Jesus shared the world-view that I have called 'Jewish restoration eschatology'" (326). The category of "certain or virtually certain" was the highest category of certainty in Sanders's work (326–27). McKnight says Jesus' vision "centered on the restoration of the Jewish nation and on the fulfillment of the covenants that God had made with the nation." McKnight, *A New Vision for Israel*, 10.

[64]J. P. Meier, *A Marginal Jew: Rethinking the Historical Jesus*, ABRL (New York: Doubleday, 2001), 152.

[65]McKnight, *A New Vision for Israel*, 9–10.

[66]Ibid., 10–11.

[67]Blaising, "The Future of Israel as a Theological Question," 439.

SUMMARY OF SUPERSESSIONISM IN CHURCH HISTORY

The doctrine of supersessionism has deep roots in church history. Several factors converged that contributed to the early church's understanding that the church had replaced Israel in God's plan. These factors were (1) the increasing Gentile composition of the early church, (2) the church's perception of the destructions of Jerusalem in AD 70 and 135, and (3) a hermeneutical approach to Scripture that allowed the church to appropriate Israel's promises to itself.

The patristic period was dominated by a punitive supersessionist view in which Israel was viewed as being rejected by God because of its disobedience. In addition, the church, consisting mostly of Gentiles, was viewed as being the new Israel. Justin became the first church father explicitly to identify the church as Israel. Origen, with his allegorical approach to Scripture, laid a hermeneutical foundation in which OT promises to Israel were transferred spiritually to the church. Augustine gave a rationale for the existence of the Jews, arguing that they were a testimony to the validity of the Bible and Christianity. Yet while affirming supersessionism, the church of this time also believed in a future salvation of Israel based on OT texts and Romans 11.

The medieval era carried on with the established view that the church had permanently replaced Israel in God's plan, although belief in a future conversion of the Jews was also widespread. The art of the period reflected the common belief of supersessionism. Aquinas accepted the established supersessionist view although his views on Romans 11 led him to believe in a future conversion of the Jews.

The Reformation period was a time of mixed views concerning supersessionism. Luther, in his later years, promoted a strong punitive supersessionist approach to Israel and the church. Calvin espoused a mild form of supersessionism in which the church was viewed as Israel, but there was also to be a conversion of the Jews. English Puritans and theologians in the Netherlands took a positive view toward a coming salvation of the Jews.

The modern era saw mixed perspectives concerning supersessionism. Kant and Schleiermacher promoted a form of structural supersessionism in which Jesus' Jewishness was downplayed and the Hebrew Scriptures were largely ignored. Barth, while rejecting punitive supersessionism, promoted a form of economic supersessionism in which national Israel's special role as the people of God expired with the coming of Christ.

Recent events such as the Holocaust and the establishment of the modern state of Israel in 1948 caused many to reexamine the doctrine of supersessionism and ponder again God's relationship to Israel. The rise of dispensationalism has led many American Christians to reject a supersessionist view. In addition, recent research on the historical Jesus has concluded that Jesus' mission was directly in regard to a restored national Israel. As a result, the last century has seen a large-scale reaction against supersessionism with many churches and denominations formally rejecting the supersessionist view.

One can rightly ask the question, "Does supersessionism have the weight of church history on its side?" The answer depends largely on how one looks at history. Certainly, from the time of Justin through most of the nineteenth century, supersessionism has been the majority position. So in this sense supersessionism has the weight of church history on its side. On the other hand, the last century has witnessed a strong reaction against supersessionism. As a result, many denominations and churches have declared their rejection of supersessionism. This trend away from supersessionism has been so great that some, like Blaising, have speculated that supersessionism is on the verge of "vanishing altogether."[68] Although it is difficult to see supersessionism disappearing from the theological landscape, it does appear unlikely that supersessionism will regain its dominant status anytime soon. Thus, recent history is on the side of nonsupersessionism.

---

[68]Ibid.

Part 3

Supersessionism and Hermeneutics

Chapter 8

The Hermeneutics of Supersessionism

This chapter will focus on presenting the hermeneutics of supersessionism, those principles of interpretation that allegedly support the claim that the church is the new Israel that supersedes national Israel as the people of God. Doing such an examination is important since the hermeneutical foundation of a theological perspective has an important influence on how people who hold that perspective approach and interpret biblical texts. LaRondelle correctly observes that "correct biblical principles of interpretation are ultimately far more crucial than the exegesis of isolated texts and words, not only because such principles affect and guide all exegesis, but also because they determine how false exegesis and misinterpretation can be corrected."[1]

The doctrine of supersessionism is largely controlled by three interrelated beliefs: (1) belief in the interpretive priority of the NT over the OT,[2] (2) belief in nonliteral fulfillments of OT texts regarding Israel,[3] and (3) belief that national Israel is a type of the NT church.[4] Our focus in this chapter is to explain the supersessionist perspective on these three

---

[1]H. K. LaRondelle, *The Israel of God in Prophecy: Principles of Prophetic Interpretation* (Berrien Springs, MI: Andrews University Press, 1983), 1.

[2]See G. E. Ladd, "Historic Premillennialism," in *The Meaning of the Millennium: Four Views*, ed. R. G. Clouse (Downers Grove, IL: InterVarsity, 1977), 20; LaRondelle, *The Israel of God in Prophecy*, 3; A. A. Hoekema, "Amillennialism," in *The Meaning of the Millennium*, 55; L. Berkhof, *Systematic Theology* (Grand Rapids: Eerdmans, 1941; repr. 1991), 699; B. K. Waltke, "Kingdom Promises as Spiritual," in *Continuity and Discontinuity: Perspectives on the Relationship Between the Old and New Testaments*, ed. J. S. Feinberg (Wheaton, IL: Crossway, 1988), 264; R. B. Strimple, "Amillennialism," in *Three Views on the Millennium and Beyond*, ed. D. L. Bock (Grand Rapids: Zondervan, 1999), 99–100.

[3]See Hoekema, "Amillennialism," 172; Berkhof, *Systematic Theology*, 713; Ladd, "Historic Premillennialism," 24; LaRondelle, *The Israel of God in Prophecy*, 107; A. Richardson, *An Introduction to the Theology of the New Testament* (New York: Harper & Row, 1958), 270; W. G. Kümmel, *The Theology of the New Testament*, trans. J. E. Steely (Nashville: Abingdon, 1973), 211; O. P. Robertson, "Hermeneutics of Continuity," in *Continuity and Discontinuity*, 107; F. F. Bruce, *Commentary on the Book of Acts*, NICNT (Grand Rapids: Eerdmans, 1970), 310; R. O. Zorn, *Christ Triumphant: Biblical Perspectives on His Church and Kingdom* (Carlisle, PA: Banner of Truth, 1997), 5; J. A. Fitzmeyer, *The Acts of the Apostles*, AB 31 (New York: Doubleday, 1998), 250.

assertions. The chapters immediately after will critique these beliefs and then offer what I believe to be a better approach.

INTERPRETIVE PRIORITY OF THE NEW TESTAMENT

One important hermeneutical issue in the debate over supersessionism concerns the relationship between the Old and New Testaments. Just how do these two Testaments relate to each other, and how should their relationship influence our understanding of Israel and the church? In particular, how should the connection between the Testaments influence how we understand texts that speak about Israel's identity and function in the plan of God? Can one rightly use a grammatical-historical-literary approach to OT passages? Or should the student interpret the OT primarily through the lens of the NT?[5]

A common belief among supersessionists is that the NT has interpretive priority over the OT. Supersessionists often argue that the proper starting point for understanding OT texts, including their prophecies and promises related to Israel, is not the OT but the NT. Thus, the NT is the interpreter or reinterpreter of the Hebrew Scriptures. For example, LaRondelle, who has offered an extensive hermeneutical presentation and defense of the supersessionist view, affirms that "the New Testament is the authorized and authoritative interpreter of the Old Testament."[6] Others agree. Sizer states that "Jesus and the apostles reinterpreted the Old Testament."[7] Riddlebarger says, "Eschatological themes [in the OT] are reinterpreted in the New Testament."[8]

---

[4]See Strimple, "Amillennialism," 85–86; Waltke, "Kingdom Promises as Spiritual," 282; LaRondelle, *The Israel of God in Prophecy*, 45; G. Von Rad, "Typological Interpretation of the Old Testament," in *A Guide to Contemporary Hermeneutics: Major Trends in Biblical Interpretation*, ed. D. K. McKim, trans. J. Bright (Grand Rapids: Eerdmans, 1986), 28–46; E. E. Ellis, "How the New Testament Uses the Old," in *New Testament Interpretation: Essays on Principles and Methods*, ed. I. H. Marshall (Grand Rapids: Eerdmans, 1977), 210; L. Goppelt, *Typos: The Typological Interpretation of the Old Testament in the New*, trans. D. H. Madvig (Grand Rapids: Eerdmans, 1982), 140–51; M. W. Karlberg, "The Significance of Israel in Biblical Typology," *JETS* 31 (1988): 259; W. G. C. Murdoch, "Interpretation of Symbols, Types, Allegories, and Parables," in *A Symposium on Biblical Hermeneutics*, ed. G. M. Hyde (Washington, DC: The Review and Herald Publishing Association, 1974), 215; W. E. Cox, *Amillennialism Today* (Phillipsburg, NJ: P&R, 1966), 45–46.

[5]J. Feinberg has identified this as the key issue between dispensationalists who are nonsupersessionists and nondispensationalists who are often supersessionists. "Nondispensationalists begin with NT teaching as having priority and then go back to the OT. Dispensationalists often begin with the OT, but wherever they begin they demand that the OT be taken on its own terms rather than reinterpreted in the light of the NT." J. S. Feinberg, "Systems of Discontinuity," in *Continuity and Discontinuity*, 75. See also Ladd, "Historic Premillennialism," 28.

[6]LaRondelle, *The Israel of God in Prophecy*, 3.

[7]S. Sizer, *Zion's Christian Soldiers: The Bible, Israel and the Church* (Nottingham, England: InterVarsity, 2008), 36.

[8]K. Riddlebarger, *A Case for Amillennialism: Understanding the End Times* (Grand Rapids: Baker, 2003), 37.

With this assumption of NT priority, supersessionists argue that the NT writers sometimes introduced change, alteration, or reinterpretation to the original meaning of OT texts, including those that speak of national Israel's restoration. This is the view of George Ladd: "The fact is that the New Testament frequently interprets Old Testament prophecies in a way *not suggested by the Old Testament context*."[9] Responding in agreement to Ladd's statement, Hoekema writes, "I agree with him that the Old Testament must be interpreted in light of the New Testament and that a totally and exclusively literal interpretation of Old Testament prophecy is not justified."[10] The result of this approach, as Ladd has argued, is that physical promises to Israel are reinterpreted and find their spiritual fulfillment in the church:

> The Old Testament must be interpreted by the New Testament. In principle it is quite possible that the prophecies addressed originally to literal Israel describing physical blessings have their fulfillment exclusively in the spiritual blessings enjoyed by the church. It is also possible that the Old Testament expectation of a kingdom on earth could be reinterpreted by the New Testament altogether of blessings in the spiritual realm.[11]

As a result of this view concerning priority of the NT, OT texts that speak of Israel's restoration should not be understood literally. They should be read in light of the NT. As Berkhof states, "It is very doubtful, however, whether Scripture warrants the expectation that Israel will finally be reestablished as a nation, and will as a nation turn to the Lord. Some Old Testament prophecies seem to predict this, but these should be read in light of the New Testament."[12] With his view that "the New interprets the Old,"[13] Waltke holds that "the kingdom promises are comprehensively fulfilled in the church, not in restored national Israel."[14]

Some supersessionists have argued that NT reinterpretations of OT promises to Israel are not violations of God's promises. The reason is that God is now offering something that greatly transcends the original promises of the OT. To illustrate this perspective, Strimple offers a hypothetical example of a young man getting ready to enter college. In appreciation for his good work, the boy's father promises him some "wheels" for his upcoming birthday so the boy will have transportation.[15] The son is happy

---

[9]Ladd, "Historic Premillennialism," 20. Emphasis in original. He also says, "Old Testament prophecies must be interpreted in the light of the New Testament to find their deeper meaning" (23).

[10]Hoekema, "Amillennialism," 55.

[11]G. E. Ladd, "Revelation 20 and the Millennium," *RevExp* 57 (1960): 167.

[12]Berkhof, *Systematic Theology*, 699.

[13]Waltke, "Kingdom Promises as Spiritual," 264.

[14]Ibid., 263.

because he thinks his father is going to buy him a motorbike. On the morning of the son's birthday, though, the son hurries outside to find a $200,000 Ferrari instead of a motorbike. Strimple points out that the boy's reaction is not "You have robbed me of my hope!" The boy is overjoyed that the father's promise is fulfilled in a way that is far greater than the boy anticipated. Strimple likens this to how spiritual blessings in Christ relate to the OT promises. According to Strimple, "With regard to the reality of our spiritual blessings in Christ, the fulfillment by God's grace . . . far transcends the terms in which the promise has been revealed."[16]

Supersessionists usually are not opposed to studying OT prophecies about Israel in their original contexts. To them, however, the student of the Bible must not stop with simply reading the OT texts apart from the NT. Nor should the student of Scripture use the NT simply to substantiate one's findings in the OT.[17] He or she must also turn to the NT to see if any alterations or expansions have been introduced to the OT passages by the NT writers. As Wright explains,

> It is agreed that in the case of an Old Testament passage, one must examine and expound it in relation to the revelation of God to Israel both before and after its own period. Then the interpreter should turn to the New Testament in order to view the passage in that perspective. In this procedure the Old Testament passage may receive limitation and correction, and it may also disclose in the light of the New Testament a new and more profound significance, unknown to the original writer.[18]

This concept of NT priority, in our view, lies at the heart of the supersessionist hermeneutic. This approach allows supersessionists to see the church as the replacement or fulfillment of the nation Israel.

NONLITERAL FULFILLMENTS OF OLD TESTAMENT PROPHECIES

Closely related to the supersessionist view of NT priority over the OT is the belief that the NT indicates that there are nonliteral fulfillments of OT

---

[15]Strimple, "Amillennialism," 99–100.

[16]Ibid., 100.

[17]For example, Waltke chastised B. Ware, a nonsupersessionist, and his article "The New Covenant and the People(s) of God" for placing too much emphasis on the new covenant text in Jer 31:31–34 and not enough on Heb 8:8–13. According to Waltke, "Ware begs the issue by starting with the Old and uses the book of Hebrews selectively to substantiate his interpretation." B. K. Waltke, "A Response," in *Dispensationalism, Israel and the Church: The Search for Definition*, ed. C. A. Blaising and D. L. Bock (Grand Rapids: Zondervan, 1992), 351. For Ware's article, see B. A. Ware, "The New Covenant and the People(s) of God," in *Dispensationalism, Israel and the Church*, 68–97.

[18]G. E. Wright, "The Problem of Archaizing Ourselves," *Int* 3 (1949): 457.

promises, prophecies, and covenants related to Israel.

A straightforward or plain reading of certain OT passages, apart from other hermeneutical considerations, seems to predict a future restoration for national Israel. Amos 9:11–15, for instance, tells of a day in which God will restore Israel to her land. Zecheriah 14:16 speaks of a time when Jerusalem will be the place where the kings of the nations come to pay homage to the Lord. Joel 3:17–18 predicts a time when the mountains of Israel "will drip with sweet wine" and the hills "will flow with milk."[19] Together the restoration texts in the OT appear to predict a time when Israel will fully possess its land and have a special place of service among the nations.

The fact that the OT predicts a restoration of the nation Israel is hard to deny. But how do supersessionists deal with this predicted restoration of Israel? They argue that these OT texts that speak of a restoration of Israel have been fulfilled in nonliteral or other-than-literal ways. Hoekema, for instance, asserts that while "many Old Testament prophecies are indeed to be interpreted literally, many others are to be interpreted in a nonliteral way."[20] Likewise, Berkhof states that "the books of the [OT] prophets themselves already contain indications that point to a spiritual fulfillment."[21]

Many supersessionists believe they have a solid scriptural basis for holding to a nonliteral fulfillment of certain OT prophecies that teach a restoration of national Israel. They point to a series of texts in which some NT writers appear to apply OT prophetic texts regarding Israel's restoration in nonliteral ways to the NT church. Three important texts in this regard are Acts 2:16–21; Acts 15:15–18; and Rom 9:24–26.

Acts 2:16–21

One text sometimes used to support the idea of nonliteral fulfillment of some OT promises with the church is Acts 2:16–21. In this passage, Peter quotes Joel 2:28–32, a text that speaks of national Israel's restoration. But Peter not only quotes it on the day of Pentecost but also says that Joel's prophecy was being fulfilled:

> On the contrary, this is what was spoken through the prophet Joel: And it will be in the last days, says God, that I will pour out My Spirit on all humanity; then your sons and your daughters will prophesy, your young

---

[19]Other restoration texts include Isa 2:1–4; 32:18; Ezek 36:22–36; and Zech 10:8–12.
[20]Hoekema, "Amillennialism," 172.
[21]Berkhof, *Systematic Theology*, 713.

men will see visions, and your old men will dream dreams. I will even pour out My Spirit on My male and female slaves in those days, and they will prophesy. I will display wonders in the heaven above and signs on the earth below: blood and fire and a cloud of smoke. The sun will be turned to darkness, and the moon to blood, before the great and remarkable day of the Lord comes; then whoever calls on the name of the Lord will be saved. (Acts 2:16–21)

What is the significance of Peter's quotation of Joel? According to Raymond O. Zorn, "Pentecost is therefore merely a new aspect of Christ's continuing reign . . . by which Old Testament prophecy concerning the messianic age is fulfilled (Acts 2:16–21)."[22] Commenting on Peter's use of Joel, Fitzmeyer also states, "Thus God's people will take a new shape under the guidance of the Spirit; Israel itself will be reconstituted."[23]

Acts 15:15–18

Another text used by supersessionists to show that some OT texts are fulfilled in nonliteral ways with the church is Acts 15:15–18. At the Jerusalem Council, as described in Acts 15, James promoted the message that God was "taking from among the Gentiles a people for His name" (Acts 15:14). To support this, he cited Amos 9:11–12:

And the words of the prophets agree with this, as it is written: After these things I will return and will rebuild David's tent, which has fallen down. I will rebuild its ruins and will set it up again, so that those who are left of mankind may seek the Lord— even all the Gentiles who are called by My name, says the Lord who does these things, which have been known from long ago. (Acts 15:15–18)

The Amos text, which refers to the restoration of national Israel, is viewed by James as somehow relating to God's work among the Gentiles. What, then, is the significance of James's quotation of Amos 9:11–12? Hoekema argues that the Amos passage "is being fulfilled right now, as Gentiles are being gathered into the community of God's people."[24] To him, this is "a clear example in the Bible itself of a figurative, nonliteral

---

[22]Zorn, *Christ Triumphant*, 5.
[23]Fitzmeyer, *The Acts of the Apostles*, AB 31, 250.

interpretation of an Old Testament passage dealing with the restoration of Israel."[25]

Bruce also views Acts 15 as evidence that members of the church were being identified as "Israel": "James's application of the prophecy finds the fulfillment of its first part (the rebuilding of the tabernacle of David) in the resurrection and exaltation of Christ, the Son of David, and the reconstitution of His disciples as the new Israel, and the fulfilment of its second part in the presence of believing Gentiles as well as believing Jews in the Church."[26]

Wall makes a similar point concerning the fulfillment of Amos's prophecy: "Amos's promise of a rebuilt 'tent of David' is fulfilled by this Davidic Messiah; and the prospect of Israel's eschatological purification and the conversion of 'all other peoples' have been transferred to him."[27]

Romans 9:24–26

Another NT text in which promises to national Israel are referred is Rom 9:24–26. In discussing the calling of the Gentiles, Paul quotes Hos 2:23 and 1:10:

> On us whom He also called, not only from the Jews but also from the Gentiles? As He also says in Hosea:

> I will call "Not-My-People," "My-People," and she who is "Unloved," Beloved." And it will be in the place where they were told, you are not My people, there they will be called sons of the living God.

Ladd believes that Rom 9:24–26 is evidence that the Christian church fulfills promises made to national Israel. He states, "Paul deliberately takes these two prophecies about the future salvation of Israel and applies them to the church. The church consisting of Jews and Gentiles has become the people of God. The prophecies of Hosea are fulfilled in the Christian church."[28] LaRondelle, too, makes a similar point when he writes, "He [Paul] joins Peter in citing Hosea's prophecy of Israel's

---

[24] A. A. Hoekema, *The Bible and the Future* (Grand Rapids: Eerdmans, 1979), 210.

[25] Ibid. See also O. P. Robertson, "Hermeneutics of Continuity," in *Continuity and Discontinuity*, 107.

[26] F. F. Bruce, *Commentary on the Book of Acts*, 310. See also I. H. Marshall, *Acts*, TNTC 5 (Grand Rapids: Eerdmans, 1980; repr., 1989), 252.

[27] R. W. Wall, "The Acts of the Apostles," *NIB* 10 (Nashville: Abingdon, 2002), 219.

restoration, in order to affirm its fulfillment in the universal Church of Christ (see Romans 9:24–26)."[29] According to Richardson, the prophecy in Hosea means that "God had raised up a new Israel and made with her a new covenant, because the old Israel had failed to keep the promise."[30]

TYPOLOGICAL INTERPRETATION

Many theologians, whether they hold to supersessionism or not, believe in the existence of OT types[31] that prefigure and point to greater corresponding NT antitypes. Many, for example, believe that the OT sacrifices prefigured Jesus Christ's ultimate sacrifice on the cross. Thus, belief in biblical types alone does not make one a supersessionist. Supersessionists, however, often argue for the validity of what can be called *typological interpretation*.[32]

Typological interpretation is a hermeneutical approach that attempts to understand the connection between the OT and NT based on the type-antitype relationships found in the two Testaments.[33] According to Ramm, "typological interpretation" is "the interpretation of the Old Testament based on the fundamental theological unity of the two Testaments whereby something in the Old shadows, prefigures, adumbrates something in the New."[34] Goppelt points out that "the typological method" has "been part of the church's exegesis and hermeneutics from the very beginning."[35] Typological interpretation is about more than just understanding that there are types in Scripture; it is an interpretive approach that views the

---

[28]Ladd, "Historic Premillennialism," 24.

[29]LaRondelle, *The Israel of God in Prophecy*, 107. See also M. H. Woudstra, "Israel and the Church: A Case for Continuity," in *Continuity and Discontinuity*, 236.

[30]A. Richardson, *An Introduction to the Theology of the New Testament*, 270. See also Kümmel, *The Theology of the New Testament*, 211.

[31]According to Virkler, a type is a "preordained representative relationship which certain persons, events, and institutions bear to corresponding persons, events, and institutions occurring at a later time in salvation history." H. A. Virkler, *Hermeneutics: Principles and Processes of Biblical Interpretation* (Grand Rapids: Baker, 1981), 184. Eichrodt refers to typology as "objectivized prophecy." W. Eichrodt, "Is Typological Exegesis an Appropriate Method?" in *Essays on Old Testament Hermeneutics*, ed. C. Westermann, trans. J. Barr (Richmond, VA: John Knox, 1969), 229.

[32]Typological interpretation is also called typological "method" or "exegesis." For more on this approach in relation to Israel and the church, see Goppelt, *Typos*, 140–51; D. L. Baker, *Two Testaments: One Bible* (Downers Grove, IL: InterVarsity, 1976), 114; G. W. H. Lampe and K. J. Woollcombe, *Essays on Typology* (London: SCM, 1957), 9–38; and E. E. Ellis, *Paul's Use of the Old Testament* (Edinburgh: Oliver & Boyd, 1957), 126–35. See especially Von Rad, "Typological Interpretation of the Old Testament," 28–46.

[33]According to Ellis, "Typological interpretation expresses most clearly 'the basic attitude of primitive Christianity toward the Old Testament.'" Ellis, "How the New Testament Uses the Old," 210.

[34]B. Ramm, *Protestant Biblical Interpretation* (Grand Rapids: Baker, 1970), 223.

relationship of the Testaments as being primarily typological. Thus, the OT is viewed as being a Testament of types, pictures, and shadows that gives way to the NT with its superior antitypes.

Those who hold to typological interpretation usually view the Christ event as being the complete fulfillment of the OT. They, as Glenny observes, believe that "all biblical history moves forward toward Christ and his work of redemption and is fulfilled in Christ and the Church."[36] With typological interpretation, as LaRondelle states, the relationship between OT types and NT antitypes is that of "eschatological completion."[37] Once the greater NT antitype is revealed, the OT type is completed and transcended by the greater reality.

What are some of these OT types that allegedly find "eschatological completion" in the NT? According to Strimple, the concepts of the land of Canaan, the city of Jerusalem, the temple, the sacrifices, the throne of David, and even the people of Israel were all "typological images" that found fulfillment in Jesus Christ.[38] Now that the reality, Jesus Christ, has been introduced, "the shadow passes away," never to be restored again.[39] Waltke, too, asserts that many OT symbols have found a spiritual fulfillment in Christ: "With the transformation of Christ's body from an earthly physical body to a heavenly spiritual body, and with his ascension from the earthly realism to the heavenly Jerusalem with its heavenly throne and the outpouring of his Holy Spirit, the earthly material symbols were done away and the spiritual reality portrayed by the symbols superseded the shadows."[40] This perspective leads Waltke to conclude that "prophecies about Israel's future kingdom that pertain to the church age, which began with Pentecost, find a spiritual fulfillment."[41]

---

[35]Goppelt, *Typos*, 4. For example, in his epistle, Clement said, "Moreover, they gave her [Rahab] a sign to this effect, that she should hang forth from her house a scarlet thread. And thus, they made it manifest that redemption should flow through the blood of the Lord to all them that believe and hope in God. Ye see, beloved, that there was not only faith, but prophecy, in this woman." Clement, *The First Epistle of Clement* 12, *ANF* 1:8.

[36]W. E. Glenny, "Typology: A Summary of the Present Evangelical Discussion," *JETS* 40 (1997): 629. Glenny is not a supersessionist.

[37]LaRondelle, *The Israel of God in Prophecy*, 45. According to Ellis, "The rationale of NT typological exegesis is not only the 'continuity of God's purpose throughout the history of His Covenant,' but also His Lordship in molding and using history to reveal and illumine His purpose." Ellis, *Paul's Use of the Old Testament*, 127–28.

[38]Strimple, "Amillennialism," 85–86.

[39]Ibid., 86.

[40]Waltke, "Kingdom Promises as Spiritual," 282.

[41]Ibid.

Essential to typological interpretation, then, is the belief that the grammatical-historical-literary approach to OT texts is not sufficient by itself to understand fully what God is communicating in these passages. According to LaRondelle, "More than a historical-grammatical exegesis of isolated parts of Scripture is needed."[42] Instead, the "immediate and wider theological contexts" must take priority.[43] This means reading "the Hebrew Scriptures in the light of the New Testament as a whole."[44] Supersessionists, who stress the importance of typological interpretation, claim that OT texts must be understood within a larger theological framework. As Gerhard Von Rad declares, "Typological interpretation will thus in a fundamental way leave the historical self-understanding of the Old Testament texts in question behind, and go beyond it. It sees in the Old Testament facts something in preparation, something sketching itself out, of which the Old Testament witness is not itself aware, because it lies quite beyond its purview."[45] Goppelt, too, states that there is more to understanding OT texts than just gathering facts from the grammatical-historical method: "The typological use of the OT in the NT has always provided an example of a more profound interpretation of the OT and has motivated the search for a meaning that goes beyond the literal grammatical-historical explanation."[46]

What, though, is the specific connection between typological interpretation and supersessionism? Supersessionists often argue that a type-antitype relationship exists between national Israel in the OT and the church in the NT. Origen, for example, stated that "corporeal Israelites" (Jews) were "the type" for "spiritual Israelites" (the church).[47] Augustine, too, believed that national Israel prefigured the Christian church: "For in the Jewish people was figured the Christian people. There a figure, here the truth; there a shadow, here the body."[48]

According to Goppelt, whenever metaphors used for Israel in the OT are applied to Jesus' disciples, "it is an allusion to the fact that they, as the new people of God, are related typologically to the old people of God."[49] That is why, for example, Goppelt gives great significance to Jesus' calling of the 12 apostles, which has obvious parallels to the 12 tribes of Israel

---

[42]LaRondelle, *The Israel of God in Prophecy*, 7.

[43]Ibid.

[44]Ibid., 19.

[45]Von Rad, "Typological Interpretation of the Old Testament," 43.

[46]Goppelt, *Typos*, 7.

[47]Origen, *On First Principles* 4.21, *ANF* 4:370.

[48]Augustine, *On the Gospel of St. John* 11.8, *NPNF¹* 7:77. Augustine also stated, "In that people [the Jews], plainly, the future Church was much more evidently prefigured." Augustine, *On the Catechising of the Uninstructed* 19.33, *NPNF¹* 3:304.

mentioned in the OT. Goppelt believes that Jesus' calling of the 12 apostles shows a typological connection between the old people of God (Israel) and the new people of God (the church):

> The flock that Jesus gathers from Israel is not the nucleus of the people of the Old Covenant; it is a new people who are not related to the old people by natural descent, but are related to them in redemptive history and in a typological way. This is expressed most clearly in the call of the twelve, where it is stated, "He appointed twelve that they might be with him and that he might send them out to preach." . . . The number twelve is clearly an allusion to the twelve tribes of Israel. . . . Jesus creates the new people of God in that he, like God, calls from the crowd the twelve who follow him in continuous fellowship and he sends them forth to gather the twelve tribes. They are the representatives of and the active nucleus for the formation of the twelve new tribes.[50]

For some, this typological connection between Israel and the church means that national Israel functioned as a type of the NT church. And like other types that pass away in significance when the greater reality or antitype comes, Israel's special role as a nation in God's plan has also come to an end. That role has been superseded by the greater reality and antitype—the church.[51] Waltke, for example, believes "the apostles taught that the type of national Israel and its law as a means of governing the nation were done away finally and permanently."[52]

Karlberg, too, has directly addressed what he believes is the type-antitype relationship between Israel and the church. Arguing against a future restoration of national Israel based on typological interpretation, he writes, "If one grants that national Israel in OT revelation was truly a type of the eternal kingdom of Christ, then it seems that, according to the canons of Biblical typology, national Israel can no longer retain any independent status whatever."[53]

According to Karlberg, Israel's special place in the plan of God has been transferred to the Christian church, which is now "the true people of

---

[49]Goppelt, *Typos*, 109.

[50]Ibid., 108. R. E. Menninger points argues that Matthew's use of the terms "kingdom of heaven," "church," and "twelve" is evidence that the church is "the new Israel." R. E. Menninger, "The Relationship Between Israel and the Church in the Gospel of Matthew" (Ph.D. diss., Fuller Theological Seminary, 1991). Flew asserts that Jesus' choice of 12 was "deliberate" and thus "the community to be gathered was that of a new Israel." R. N. Flew, *Jesus and His Church: A Study of the Idea of the Ecclesia in the New Testament* (London: Epworth, 1938; repr., 1956), 38.

[51]See LaRondelle, *The Israel of God in Prophecy*, 40. Goppelt writes, "Israel's salvation in its perfected form now belongs to the people of Christ (cf. Rom 9:4f.; Eph 2:12,19). Consequently, there is a typological relationship between the people of God in the Old and New Testaments that reveals to the NT people of God the nature of their salvation." Goppelt, *Typos*, 142.

[52]Waltke, "Kingdom Promises as Spiritual," 279.

[53]Karlberg, "The Significance of Israel in Biblical Typology," 259.

God with the privileges, the responsibilities, and the destiny of Israel."[54] This belief that national Israel is a type of the church means that OT prophecies and promises given to Israel find their typological fulfillment in the church. This rules out a literal fulfillment of these promises with national Israel.[55] Karlberg claims his view is consistent with historic Reformed theology, which views national Israel as having served "a symbolic and typological purpose in redemptive history."[56] Cox has gone even further than Karlberg, stating that the belief that national Israel was a type of the church has been the historic view of the church: "The historic Christian teaching holds that national Israel was a type or forerunner of the church, and that the church replaced Israel on the Day of Pentecost."[57]

According to adherents of typological interpretation, the church, which is identified with the ultimate Israelite, Jesus Christ, fulfills Israel's mission and inherits the covenants and promises made with Israel in the OT. As LaRondelle asserts, "The Church, as the eschatological Israel, with its new covenant in the blood of Christ, is the fulfillment of God's plan with ancient Israel."[58] Murdoch also offers a concise summary of what it means for the church to be the fulfillment of Israel:

> Israel was God's chosen people in the OT era. They were called to do a special work, but failed in their commission. In the NT God called another people, who were free from ethnic restrictions. Their faith and commitment centered in Christ. The OT promises are now fulfilled to them who are Jews inwardly (see Rom 2:29). The commission to take the gospel to all the world will be fulfilled by them. The church (spiritual Israel) consists now of those who will proclaim Heaven's last message of mercy to the world.[59]

In sum, the hermeneutical foundation of supersessionism consists of three main pillars—NT priority over the OT, nonliteral fulfillments of OT prophecies, and typological interpretation in which the OT is viewed primarily as a testament of types, shadows, and pictures that prefigure greater NT realities. I will now critique these three hermeneutical beliefs.

---

[54]Ibid., 263.

[55]Summarizing this view of supersessionists, Glenny states, "Since the Church has replaced Israel in God's program, specific and direct prophecies made to Israel are only fulfilled typologically in the Church—that is, there will be no application of even direct OT prophecies to ethnic, national Israel in the future. . . . Such a fulfillment to Israel would require a move backward in God's program of salvation history and is not necessary since some OT prophecies for Israel are applied to the Church in the NT." Glenny, "Typology," 631–32.

[56]M. W. Karlberg, "Legitimate Discontinuities Between the Testaments," *JETS* 28 (1985): 16.

[57]Cox, *Amillennialism Today*, 45–46.

[58]LaRondelle, *The Israel of God in Prophecy*, 40.

[59]Murdoch, "Interpretation of Symbols, Types, Allegories, and Parables," 215.

Chapter 9

Evaluating the Hermeneutics
of Supersessionism

As mentioned in the last chapter, the three hermeneutical assumptions of supersessionism are (1) the interpretive priority of the NT over the OT, (2) the belief in a nonliteral fulfillment of OT texts originally addressed to Israel, and (3) a view of typology that sees national Israel as a type of the church. In this chapter, I am going to analyze these hermeneutical assumptions. I will argue that the hermeneutical beliefs of supersessionism are not accurate and have led to erroneous views regarding Israel and the church.

Before doing this, though, some comments need to be made regarding the topic of hermeneutics in regard to Israel and the church. As many have noted, the hermeneutical issue of how the NT uses the OT is a difficult and complex topic.[1] Questions in this area include: Are *sensus plenior* and additional meanings given to OT texts beyond the literal sense as determined by historical-grammatical-literary hermeneutics? What is the relationship of typology to the Testaments? Do NT authors pay close attention to the contexts of OT texts? Are NT authors operating according to interpretive principles associated with Second-Temple Judaism?[2] Are the interpretive principles of the NT authors something we should adopt in our interpretation of the OT?

These topics are complex, and a full treatment of them is beyond the purposes of this work. Yet some fair observations can be made in regard to hermeneutics as they relate to the Israel-church issue. Two extremes need to be avoided. The first is assuming that the NT always deals with the OT in a straightforward, literal manner. Clearly Matthew's quotation of Hos 11:1 in Matt 2:15—"out of Egypt I called My Son"—is not a literal rendering of Hos 11:1. The Hosea passage refers to the historical event of Israel's exodus from Egypt, while Matthew is relating Hos 11:1 to Jesus. Matthew's

---

[1] For a helpful treatment of this issue see *Three Views on the New Testament Use of the Old Testament*, ed. K. Berding and J. Lunde (Grand Rapids: Zondervan, 2007).

[2] This includes midrash, pesher, and allegory.

interpretation of Hos 11:1 is not contrary to the literal meaning of Hos 11:1, but this use of Hosea also goes beyond a literal meaning in the sense that Hosea was probably not thinking of Christ when he wrote what he did. This appears to be a case of "literal plus typological" connection. Hosea 11:1 refers to the historical exodus of Israel from Egypt while Matthew makes a typological connection between Israel and Christ. Thus, there is a sense in which Hos 11:1 refers to the actual historical event of the exodus from Egypt *and* typologically points forward to Christ, the ultimate Israelite who is everything God intended Israel to be. Nevertheless, as Hos 11:1 and Matt 2:15 show, it appears that the NT writers sometimes apply OT passages to Jesus in a Christological manner that goes beyond a simple literal or plain interpretation.[3]

The second extreme is concluding that since NT writers sometimes quote or appeal to OT passages in nonliteral or less than literal ways, then we should not expect any literal fulfillment of OT promises and covenants to Israel. This approach, in our view, is to fall off the other side of the log. While the NT sometimes uses the OT in less than literal ways, many times it quotes the OT quite literally. Matthew 2:15 may use Hos 11:1 in a way beyond the literal, but Matt 3:5–6 declares that Mic 5:2 was literally fulfilled with Jesus' being born in Bethlehem. According to Matt 21:4–5, the Zech 9:9 prophecy of the King's coming to Zion humbly on a donkey was literally fulfilled. Thus, while the NT uses the OT at times in different ways, and perhaps at times in accord with some of the interpretive principles associated with Second-Temple Judaism, it often still quotes the OT in literal ways. So although this issue is complex, I do not accept that *if* the NT writers sometimes used the OT in nonliteral ways or adopted interpretive principles consistent with Second-Temple Judaism that this means historical-grammatical hermeneutics is out the window or not satisfactory for understanding the OT. If a *pesher* or other Second-Temple Judaism principle is used, I believe this is in addition to and supplemental to the authorial intent of the OT authors. As will be argued later, the claims of nonliteral interpretations of certain passages by supersessionists is not always accurate.

NEW TESTAMENT PRIORITY

The supersessionist view of NT priority[4] is beset with serious problems. In fact, this approach introduces more problems than it solves. Before

---

[3]Also see the treatment of these texts in M. Rydelnik, *The Messianic Hope: Is the Hebrew Bible Really Messianic?* NACSBT (Nashville: B&H, 2010), 203–8.

[4]Those who espouse the supersessionist view on this matter include H. K. LaRondelle, *The Israel of God in Prophecy: Principles of Prophetic Interpretation* (Berrien Springs, MI: Andrews University Press, 1983), 3; G. E. Ladd, "Historic Premillennialism," in *The Meaning of the Millennium: Four Views*, ed. R. G. Clouse (Downers Grove, IL: InterVarsity, 1977), 20–21.

explaining why the supersessionist hermeneutic is not satisfactory, though, some important clarifications need to be made. Nonsupersessionists, too, acknowledge that there is a sense in which the NT has priority over the OT, but their understanding of this concept is quite different from that of supersessionists. This difference needs to be explained.

First, nonsupersessionists acknowledge the concept of progressive revelation in which God gives inspired revelation that adds to, clarifies, and expands on revelations previously given. They believe that the NT is a more complete revelation than the OT and offers information and insight not found in the OT. For example, the NT gives us much more detail concerning the fates of the saved and the lost than the OT does. What is revealed about heaven and hell in the NT does not contradict what was in the OT, but it adds to previous revelation.

Second, nonsupersessionists acknowledge the authority of the NT to cancel temporary commands, covenants, or institutions in the OT. For example, Leviticus 11 established various food laws for the nation Israel. These food restrictions have clearly been revoked by the NT (see Mark 7:19). So today we are no longer bound by the food laws of Leviticus 11. What about the Mosaic law? The NT clearly states that the Christian is no longer under Mosaic law (see Rom 10:4; Gal 5:18). So then, Mosaic law as a unit is not binding on the Christian today. Also, the NT is clear that a change in priesthood priority has occurred and that Jesus Christ is the final sacrifice for sins (see Hebrews 9). So nonsupersessionists believe the NT, at times, revokes practices and institutions that were in effect in the OT era.

In addition, nonsupersessionists acknowledge the right of the NT to add applications and referents to OT revelation. Clearly, there are times when NT writers use and apply the OT in ways that were unforeseen by the OT writers (see Matt 2:15 and Hos 11:1). This is not disputed. But must we conclude that the NT meaning becomes the OT meaning? Not necessarily. The NT could be making analogies or drawing on principles. Or the NT may be adding new referents to OT promises, prophecies, and covenants but not at the expense of the original referent.

For example, if an OT promise or covenant is given to Israel in the OT and the NT includes Gentiles or the church in that promise or covenant, then perhaps a new referent to the OT promise or covenant may have been added. In this case, there may be two referents to an OT promise—the first referent is Israel while the second referent is the Gentiles, the church, or both. The fact that an OT promise or covenant is applied/fulfilled with the church does not mean that the original referent—Israel—is no longer related to the promise or covenant. Thus, at times there are both-and constructs.

The new covenant, for instance, is clearly related to the church. Jesus inaugurated the new covenant with His death (see Luke 22:20), and Paul indicated that Christians are "ministers of a new covenant" (2 Cor 3:6). But Paul clearly states in Rom 11:26–27 that the new covenant will be fulfilled with Israel. In 11:26, Paul says "all Israel will be saved" and then links this promise with Isa 59:21 in Rom 11:27: "And this will be My covenant with them, when I take away their sins". This "covenant" of Isa 59:21 is the new covenant. Isaiah 59:21 says, "My Spirit who is on you [Israel]". So Paul clearly links Israel's salvation and the coming of the Redeemer with a new covenant passage for Israel in the OT. Thus, the new covenant is in effect for the church now and will be fulfilled with Israel in the future. This is a both-and situation.

Finally, nonsupersessionists understand that there are divine correspondences or even typological connections between the Testaments. For example, there is a correspondence between Adam and Jesus Christ (see Romans 5). There is a connection between the Levitical priesthood and the priesthood of Jesus Christ as Hebrews indicates. There is a connection between the Passover and the death of Christ (see 1 Cor 5:7). Those who reject supersessionism believe in types and their significance.

As the points above show, there is a real sense in which nonsupersessionists believe in a form of "New Testament priority." Nonsupersessionists, though, disagree strongly with the supersessionist understanding of NT priority. For supersessionists, NT priority means that the NT must be the interpretive lens for understanding OT passages. Thus, the primary meaning of an OT passage is found not in the OT passages themselves but in the alleged NT interpretations or reinterpretations of those texts. To understand the primary meaning of an OT text, one should not go to that OT text itself; instead, one must go to the NT and read the OT passage through the lens of the NT.

What makes this approach of supersessionists so significant is that it does not allow for OT passages to be the reference points for their own meanings anymore. This approach also removes the necessity of historical-grammatical-literary hermeneutics for understanding the OT. The implications of this are immense. If correct, over two-thirds of the Bible, the entire OT, is not to be approached in a straightforward manner that takes into account the authorial intent of the OT authors as determined by historical-grammatical-literary hermeneutics. Thus, when a Christian reads books like Jeremiah or Zechariah, the meaning is not found in these books. He or she must view the books of Jeremiah and Zechariah through the lens of the NT.

I have concerns about this view of NT priority. This unfounded "structural supersessionism" ties the hands of the older Testament and does not let it speak to the issues it addresses. While acknowledging varied uses of the OT in the NT, it has not been established that the apostles and the NT writers viewed their sayings and writings as replacing the original meanings of the OT authors.

Certainly, the NT writers understood that the last days and the messianic era had begun in some way and that they were ministers of a new covenant. They also showed how Jesus was the fulfillment of OT prophecy and how what was going on was related to Him. Thus, there is a Christological focus with the NT writers. But did the NT authors believe their writings overrode the original authorial intent of the OT writers? This is highly debatable. Certainly, there is no statement in the NT that the original authorial intent of the OT writers had been superseded by the NT writers. Barry Horner expresses rightful concern on this issue when he states, "Our concern is now the hermeneutical principle that imposes the NT revelation of Jesus Christ on the OT in such a way that the new covenant (upper layer) has become the controlling hermeneutic whereby the old covenant (lower layer) is christologically reinterpreted."[5]

NT use of the OT is a complex topic. We also know that the NT writers used OT passages in a variety of ways. I am not convinced, though, that the NT writers transferred or reinterpreted the meaning of OT passages. As Feinberg rightly observes, "No NT writer claims his new understanding of the OT passage cancels the meaning of the OT passage in its own context or that the new application is the only meaning of the OT passage. The NT writer merely offers a different application of an OT passage than the OT might have foreseen; he is not claiming the OT understanding is now irrelevant."[6]

Supersessionists often appeal to Acts 2/Joel 2; Acts 15/Amos 9; Hebrews 8/ Jeremiah 31; and other passages to show that the NT writers redirected, transferred, or reinterpreted the original OT promises. But as will be discussed later, it is highly questionable whether these passages actually support the idea that the original OT meanings have been altered or entirely fulfilled in ways not predicted by the OT authors.

---

[5] B. E. Horner, *Future Israel: Why Christian Anti-Judaism Must Be Challenged*, NACSBT (Nashville: B&H Academic, 2007), 179.

[6] J. Feinberg, "Systems of Discontinuity," in *Continuity and Discontinuity: Perspectives on the Relationship Between the Old and New Testaments*, ed. J. S. Feinberg (Wheaton, IL: Crossway, 1988), 77.

While supersessionists may argue that some passages show that the OT expectation for Israel has been entirely fulfilled in a different manner, their arguments are far from convincing and do not account for other possible explanations. Perhaps the NT writers are appealing to principles and analogies found in the OT without stressing a full and final fulfillment. Perhaps they are including other referents in a partial fulfillment of OT passages (i.e. Gentiles) but not doing so in such a way that excludes a fulfillment with the nation Israel. Is this an unreasonable expectation in light of the fact that there are two comings of Jesus? Should we not expect already/not yet and partial fulfillment constructs in light of this? Thus, new applications of OT passages or new referents do not mean the original meaning has been jettisoned.

The "interpret the Old through the New" approach in our view is too broad and sweeping. It is simplistic and does not do justice to the nuances found in the relationship between the Testaments. Plus it does not properly take into account the many OT quotations and allusions that can be taken literally. The supersessionist approach defangs the OT and does not allow the Hebrew Scriptures to speak to the issues they address such as God's plans for the nation Israel. It also does not take into account partial fulfillment and multiple referent constructs that are found in Scripture. On the other hand, I prefer an approach that recognizes the authority of the NT and its right to revoke things in the OT and add referents to OT promises in ways unforeseen by the OT authors. Yet it allows the OT texts to retain their integrity as revelation by paying heed to the original authorial intent of the OT authors.

Second, the supersessionist view of NT priority brings into doubt the integrity of the OT texts. If the NT reinterprets the OT or seriously modifies or transcends its promises and covenants, one may rightly wonder in what sense the OT revelations were actually revelations in good faith to the original readers of the promises.[7] As Turner explains, "If NT reinterpretation reverses, cancels, or seriously modifies OT promises to Israel, one wonders how to define the word 'progressive.' God's faithfulness to His promises to Israel must also be explained."[8] Turner also points out that the supersessionist approach comes close to violating NT statements that

---

[7]In response to G. Ladd's declaration that the NT reinterprets the OT, P. Feinberg asks some relevant questions: "If Ladd is correct that the NT reinterprets the OT, his hermeneutic does raise some serious questions. How can the integrity of the OT text be maintained? In what sense can the OT really be called a *revelation* in its original meaning?" P. Feinberg, "Hermeneutics of Discontinuity," in *Continuity and Discontinuity*, 116. Emphasis in original.

[8]D. L. Turner, "The Continuity of Scripture and Eschatology: Key Hermeneutical Issues," *GTJ* 6 (1985): 281.

uphold the truth claims of the OT: "It appears exceedingly doubtful that the NT reinterprets the OT. . . . This comes perilously close to conflicting with such NT passages as Matt 5:18 and John 10:35b."[9]

Kaiser correctly points out that Christians "misjudge the revelation of God if we have a theory of interpretation which says the most recent revelation of God is to be preferred or substituted for that which came earlier."[10] He also argues that the assertion that the NT must be the guide for interpreting the OT comes dangerously close to the idea that there is a canon within the canon. He asks, "But why would a rule be imposed on the revelation of God that demands that the OT passages may not become the basis for giving primary direction on any doctrines or truths that have relevancy for NT times? This is only to argue in the end for a canon within a canon."[11]

In addition, we must not lose sight of the fact that the OT promises, prophecies, and covenants were given to specific audiences at certain times in history. Thus, these revelations had relevance for the original audiences. This is easy to forget for those of us living thousands of years after the OT was completed. But we have to remember that the content of these revelations mattered to the original audiences. When God revealed Himself to the authors and audiences of the OT revelations, He revealed truths to them as well. The original writers and audiences of the OT revelations understood God to be promising literal spiritual and physical blessings to a future generation of ethnic Israel. Do we have the right to say, "We know that you were led to believe that God would do these things for the nation Israel, but now with the coming of the NT revelation, we know better—these are just pictures of greater spiritual realities for the church"? In the nineteenth century, Peters addressed this issue of the original hearers of the prophecies when he stated, "If no restoration [of Israel] was intended; if all was to be understood typically, or spiritually, or conditionally, then surely the language was most eminently calculated to deceive the hearers."[12]

If God is true and does not lie, how do we explain that He clearly promised certain things to a certain people but then fulfills these promises in a different manner than what He communicated? To say that God's ultimate

---

[9]Ibid., 282.

[10]W. C. Kaiser Jr., "The Land of Israel and the Future Return (Zechariah 10:6–12)," in *Israel, the Land and the People: An Evangelical Affirmation of God's Promises*, ed. H. W. House (Grand Rapids: Kregel, 1998), 222.

[11]Ibid., 219.

[12]G. N. H. Peters, *The Theocratic Kingdom of Our Lord Jesus, the Christ as Covenanted in the Old Testament* (New York: Funk & Wagnalls, 1884; repr., Grand Rapids: Kregel, 1988), 2:51.

fulfillment in the NT era is greater than what was promised in the OT does not escape this problem.

Third, the supersessionist approach to Testament priority also does not adequately account for OT texts that explicitly promise the perpetuity of Israel as a nation. Jeremiah 31:35–37, for example, declares that Israel's status as a *nation* before God can never be canceled and is as sure as the continuation of the universe.[13] Since the NT is viewed as the starting point and the lens through which the OT is understood, texts like Jer 31:35–37, which explicitly declare the perpetuity of national Israel's place in God's plan, are not given the proper weight they deserve.[14]

Fourth, another weakness of the supersessionist understanding of Testament priority is that the NT explicitly upholds many aspects of Israel's expectation as revealed in the OT. It teaches and reaffirms the OT expectations concerning a future for national Israel. Texts such as Matt 19:28; Luke 22:30; and Acts 1:6 reaffirm the OT expectation of a future for national Israel. Thus, it is difficult to accept that the NT transcends the OT promises and prophecies of a future for Israel when a cluster of NT texts reaffirms the original OT expectations for Israel.

Horner is correct when he states that "the hermeneutic of reinterpretation and transference is illegitimate, which takes the adapted quotation of the OT in the NT to be justification for nullifying the literal interpretation of that same OT passage."[15] This is the case because "it not only ignores a fundamental, Hebrew, hermeneutical frame of reference, but it also brings about a serious distortion of meaning, especially where the eschatological message of the Prophets is concerned."[16] Thus, I find the supersessionist understanding of NT priority to be lacking.

In the previous chapter, I referred to Strimple's analogy of a son who was promised wheels for his birthday by his father. The son to his great surprise and joy sees a $200,000 Ferrari when he was expecting much less. This illustration supposedly parallels what God was doing when He made certain physical promises to national Israel and then transcends this hope

---

[13]Verses 35–36 of this passage read, "This is what the Lord says: The One who gives the sun for light by day, the fixed order of moon and stars for light by night, who stirs up the sea and makes its waves roar—Yahweh of Hosts is His name: If this fixed order departs from My presence—this is the Lord's declaration—then also Israel's descendants will cease to be a nation before Me forever." In this poem made up of two sayings (vv. 35–36 and 37), the Lord declares what E. W. Nicholson has called "the impossibility of Israel being forsaken forever by God." E. W. Nicholson, *The Book of the Prophet Jeremiah: Chapters 26–52* (Cambridge, UK: Cambridge University Press, 1975), 72.

[14]See W. C. Kaiser Jr., "Evidence from Jeremiah," in *A Case for Premillennialism*, ed. D. K. Campbell and J. L. Townsend (Chicago: Moody, 1992), 113.

[15]Horner, *Future Israel*, 185.

[16]Ibid.

in a much greater way with blessings for the church, which is the new Israel. This analogy, though, is not satisfactory. With Strimple's analogy, the son who receives the Ferrari is the same son to whom the wheels were promised. But this is not really the case with the supersessionist view. According to supersessionism, the nation Israel is promised certain blessings, but in reality, these blessings are given to another group, the church, an entity that is not national Israel.

To pick up on Strimple's analogy, the supersessionist view is best illustrated by the following: In order to celebrate the good work of his son who is going to college, the father promises his son some wheels. On the son's birthday, the father reveals the presence of a recently adopted son to whom a $200,000 Ferrari is given. The father then turns to the first son and declares, "I am sorry, but my true son is this adopted son who represents everything our family name stands for." The first son says, "But Father you made a promise to me. I don't mind if out of your wealth you give great gifts to this new adopted member of the family, but giving blessings to this new son does not mean you fulfilled what you promised me."

NONLITERAL FULFILLMENTS

The supersessionist belief of NT priority over the OT is closely linked to the belief that there are nonliteral fulfillments of OT passages. Earlier it was pointed out that the NT sometimes quotes the OT in ways that go beyond a literal understanding. Yet I think supersessionists have overstated the case for nonliteral understandings of OT passages that speak of a future for Israel.

James's use of Amos 9 in Acts 15 is primary evidence offered by supersessionists to show a nonliteral fulfillment of an OT text.[17] With it a restoration passage from Amos 9 is quoted in regard to the Gentile salvation that was taking place in the early church. This allegedly shows that the original prediction in Amos 9 was being entirely fulfilled in a nonliteral way.[18]

While acknowledging difficult interpretive challenges with this passage, I do not believe that Acts 15:13–18 is an example of a nonliteral fulfillment of an OT passage. There is an initial application/fulfillment of the Amos 9:11–15 prophecy with believing Gentiles today, but this in

---

[17]In his chapter "Hermeneutics of Continuity," O. Palmer devotes his entire discussion to showing a supersessionist understanding of Acts 15/Amos 9 (see *Continuity and Discontinuity*, 89–108.). See also K. Riddlebarger, *A Case for Amillennialism: Understanding the End Times* (Grand Rapids: Baker, 2003), 39.

[18]Robertson, "Hermeneutics of Continuity," 107.

no way rules out a future final fulfillment with the nation Israel when Jesus returns.

In regard to Acts 15 and Amos 9, James does not explicitly say that the salvation of Gentiles "fulfills" the Amos 9 prophecy. He states that what is taking place in his day "agree(s)" with what the OT prophets had predicted about the Gentiles (Acts 15:15). Thus, a case could be made that James is not claiming a fulfillment of the Amos 9 passage but is pointing to a principle found in the OT that applies to the current situation in Acts 15. What is this principle? James could be appealing to a general principle found in the OT "prophets" that Gentiles would someday be saved without becoming Jews and keeping the Mosaic law.[19] Thus, James might be arguing that since the OT prophets predicted a future day in which Gentiles would be saved without becoming Jews, Gentiles who are being saved presently should not be coerced into Judaism. This is a possible interpretation.

Yet while acknowledging the possibility of this view, I believe another interpretation is preferable. That there is some initial application/fulfillment of the Amos 9 prophecy in the church is difficult to avoid. When James says, "And with this the words of the prophets agree," the word "this" refers back to Acts 15:14 and the Gentile inclusion that Simeon witnessed. Thus, something is going on presently that is related to what Amos predicted. The inclusion of Gentiles into the people of God without becoming Jews is being fulfilled or applied. Yet while this part of Amos's prophecy that relates to Gentile salvation is being fulfilled/applied, I see no reason to believe that the restoration of the Davidic kingdom to Israel was being fulfilled with the events of Acts 15. Why do I say this? The answer is found in the context of the passage and the specific issue being addressed.

The primary issue in Acts 15 is soteriological. It is the salvation of the Gentiles and whether they need to be circumcised and converted to Judaism. Eschatology and Israel's place in the plan of God are not the primary issues here, certainly not as they are in Romans 11, where Paul specifically addresses Israel's future. This is not to say that what James is talking about is unrelated to the issue of Israel's restoration, but it should be understood that the restoration of Israel was not the primary topic at hand. Inclusion of Gentiles in the messianic plan without having to keep the Mosaic law is the main issue here. This is important because supersessionists want us to believe the OT expectation for Israel has been altered and reinterpreted with the events of Acts 15, but is this not too much to conclude from a

---

[19]According to H. Heater Jr., "We do not have here a citation of Amos, but of a theological idea derived from the OT concerning a time when Gentiles will be included in God's program for Israel." H. Heater Jr., "Evidence from Joel and Amos," in *A Case for Premillennialism*, ed. D. K. Campbell and J. L. Townsend (Chicago: Moody, 1992), 156.

passage that is not directly addressing the restoration of Israel? Jesus had already told the disciples that the restoration of the kingdom to Israel was not going to take place soon (see Acts 1:6–7; cf. 3:19–21). Supersessionists are asking us to accept too much from too little evidence.

The point James appears to be making is that the Jews should not require Gentiles to be circumcised and become Jews because in the OT messianic texts it was predicted that Gentiles would become saved without becoming Jews. As Marshall states, "God is making a people out of the nations and nothing in the text suggests that they are to become Jews in order to become God's people. So there are no entrance 'conditions' to be imposed upon them."[20]

Thus, what we probably have here is a case of *initial fulfillment* of Amos 9. There is a real sense in which Gentile inclusion in salvation corresponds with what was predicted in the OT. But as Bock points out, "Initial fulfillment is not exhausted fulfillment."[21] The salvation of the Gentiles that Amos predicted is being fulfilled, but the future restoration of the Davidic kingdom to Israel is still to come (see Acts 1:6). But one could ask, "Is not the inclusion of Gentiles into the people of God evidence that the restoration of Israel is currently being fulfilled?" Not necessarily. In Rom 11:25–27, Paul explicitly declares the "mystery" that a period of Gentile salvation would precede the salvation and restoration of the nation Israel:

> "For I do not want you, brethren, to be uninformed of this mystery—so that you will not be wise in your own estimation—that a partial hardening has happened to Israel until the fullness of the Gentiles has come in; and so all Israel will be saved; just as it is written, "The Deliverer will come from Zion, He will remove ungodliness from Jacob." "This is My covenant with them, when I take away their sins."

One of the truths revealed in the NT era is that the salvation of Gentiles would precede the salvation and restoration of Israel. But the salvation of Gentiles should not be taken to mean that believing Gentiles are part of a "new Israel" or that the Davidic kingdom and restoration of Israel are fulfilled in the present age between the two comings of Christ.

Thus, Gentile salvation is not evidence that the restoration of Israel has taken place. According to Paul in Rom 11:25–27, the time period between the two comings of Christ is characterized by Gentile salvation, but when Jesus comes again, the nation Israel will be saved and restored. In our

---

[20]I. H. Marshall, *Acts*, TNTC (Grand Rapids: Eerdmans, 1980), 253. Marshall himself opts for a supersessionist position, but he is accurate on asserting the main point James is making in this passage.

[21]D. L. Bock, "Evidence from Acts," in *A Case for Premillennialism*, ed. D. K. Campbell and J. L. Townsend (Chicago: Moody, 1992), 197.

view, then, it is unjustified to assume that James reinterprets or redirects the entire OT expectation for Israel with his words in Acts 15. Heater is correct when he declares, "I would hold that the citation is merely to show that the tenor of Old Testament Scripture supports the idea of Gentiles coming to God without losing their identity. James was not ignoring the future restoration of Israel and equating the 'hut of David' with the church; he merely said that one element of what will happen in the future was happening in this day."[22]

Also, Scripture indicates that there are phases to the blessings of the Gentiles. Romans 11:12 states, "Now if their [Israel's] transgression is riches for the world and their failure is riches for Gentiles, how much more will their fulfillment be." Israel's failure means "riches for Gentiles" now, but "much more" will be in store for the Gentiles when the "fulfillment" of Israel takes place in the future (see Rom 11:26). When Israel is saved as a nation, Gentile blessings will even be greater. So then I conclude that there is a partial fulfillment of Gentiles becoming God's people as described in Acts 15:17, but there is also a sense in which Gentile blessing will be even greater when Israel is saved (see Rom 11:26). When the "tabernacle of David" is restored as Acts 15:16 states, the fulfillment of the Amos prophecy, including blessings for Gentiles, will take place.

Also, I am not convinced that in every case where an OT text is quoted in the NT that all details of that OT text are entirely being fulfilled in the present. Sometimes the broader context of an OT passage may be quoted to draw attention to a main point at hand. For example, on the day of Pentecost, Peter quotes a major passage from Joel 2 to show that the certain events of that day were being fulfilled. Events such as the pouring out of the Holy Spirit (Acts 2:17) and the nearness of salvation were being fulfilled presently in some way. Peter also mentions the Day of the Lord and the cosmic signs associated with the Day of the Lord (Acts 2:19–20). Yet the cosmic signs of the Day of the Lord were not fulfilled. The sun was not darkened, and the moon did not appear as blood. Paul places the Day of the Lord as future in 1 Thess 5:2 and 2 Thess 2:2. Peter also places the Day of the Lord as future (see 2 Pet 3:10). Clearly, the Day of the Lord is a future event even though it was mentioned in the context of a fulfillment in Acts 2. Thus, there appear to be cases of progressive fulfillment in Scripture. The Scripture has already/not yet and partial fulfillment constructs that must be taken into account.

To summarize, Acts 15 does not declare that OT passages regarding Israel are being fulfilled in nonliteral ways. In Acts 15, James quotes Amos 9 to

---

[22]Heater, "Evidence from Joel and James," 156–57.

show that God's messianic plan for Gentiles, which has been inaugurated with the coming of Jesus, includes the idea that Gentiles can be saved without becoming proselytes to Judaism. Amos and other OT prophets affirm ("agree" with) this truth. This, in no way, means that the entire OT expectation of restoration of national Israel has been changed or altered.

Acts 2 also does not redirect the OT expectation for Israel. Even if there is a fulfillment of some facets of the Joel 2 prophecy in Acts, this does not mean that the entire prophecy of Joel 2 has been fulfilled finally and perfectly. If the Day of the Lord that Joel 2 predicts is still in the future, so can the restoration of Israel, which is connected with the Day of the Lord, still be in the future. With Acts 2, the pouring out of the Holy Spirit partially fulfills the Joel 2 prophecy, but there is not enough reason to conclude that the entire prophecy of Joel 2 was fulfilled.

Finally, the claim that Paul in Rom 9:24–26 is reinterpreting passages in Hosea 1 and 2 is also not convincing. Romans 9 emphasizes God's sovereign electing purposes. While discussing the great truth that believing Gentiles are now also the people of God according to God's electing purposes, Paul quotes from Hos 2:23 and 1:10, passages originally written in reference to the disobedient northern tribes of Israel. Supersessionists often want to declare that Paul's use of Hosea must mean that the church is now the true Israel, but this understanding is far from necessary or even likely. To show that God in His sovereignty can take a disobedient people and make them His people, Paul quotes the clearest passages to highlight this principle. In this sense, God's electing purposes for Gentiles is parallel or analogous to God's choosing Israel. The main point of analogy is God's election. In this sense, there is a divine correspondence between God's calling of Israel and His calling of Gentiles.

I believe this is the best interpretation of this passage. But even if this interpretation is incorrect and Paul is claiming that Gentiles directly are fulfilling a passage originally intended for Israel, does this mean that supersessionism is automatically correct? Not necessarily. Perhaps God is adding believing Gentiles as a referent to the Hosea passages, but adding Gentiles as a referent does not mean that national Israel is no longer a referent. If God adds believing Gentiles as a referent to the Hosea passages, Israel can be a referent, too. It should be noted that in Rom 9:4, Paul already stated that Israelites are still presently related to the covenants and promises of Scripture.

Or perhaps Paul is emphasizing that the concept of the people of God has been expanded to believing Gentiles. Passages like Isa 19:24–25 and Zech 2:11 predicted that Gentiles would one day be called "people of God" without becoming "Israel." Remember that while believing Gentiles are now the people of God, two chapters later Paul will state that "God has not rejected His people [Israel] whom He foreknew" (Rom 11:2). This can be a both-and scenario. *Both* believing Gentiles *and* the nation Israel can be the people of God. This is the natural result of harmonizing Rom 9:24–26 with Rom 11:1.

The passages discussed above (Acts 2/Joel 2; Acts 15/Amos 9; Romans 9/Hosea 1–2) are challenging for all interpreters. But these passages do not come close to overturning or redirecting the multiple and explicit references to a future for national Israel found in both the OT and the NT.

TYPES AND TYPOLOGICAL INTERPRETATION

The topic of types and the study of types and their implications called typology is complex. A survey of books addressing types and typology will show that no two books agree exactly on what should be considered a type and what the implications of typology are. This should not discourage us from studying typology, but it should make us cautious when it comes to drawing implications from them.

Those who accept the authority of Scripture often agree that there are divinely intended correspondences between the Testaments, but to what extent typology applies is a more difficult issue. What is important for our purposes here is that supersessionists often claim that typology applies to the relationship between Israel and the church in such a way that the nation Israel is viewed as a type that finds its completion and fulfillment in the alleged superior antitype—the church. There is, therefore, no continuing relevance for Israel as a nation since the church is the greater antitype that fulfills what Israel was supposed to be. In a sense, national Israel is viewed as the caterpillar, and the church is the butterfly, or so it goes.

This use of typology, though, is not impressive and is not sustainable. If the nation Israel is a type that is superseded by the superior antitype, the church, then we should not expect to see any discussion in the NT concerning a future for the nation Israel. But clearly we do. Passages such as Matt 19:28; 23:39; Acts 1:6; 3:19–21; and Romans 11 speak of a future salvation and restoration of the nation Israel. Romans 11 is especially significant since Paul is writing after the church began and while Israel was currently in a state of hardened unbelief. Yet Paul links Israel's salvation with OT promises concerning Israel's future (see Rom 11:26–27). It does not appear that Paul viewed the nation Israel as a type that was forever superseded by the church.

The same can be said concerning the issue of typology and temples, a topic supersessionists say supports their understanding of the church's replacing Israel. Supersessionists are correct that the concept of temple in the NT is expanded beyond a physical structure in Jerusalem. Jesus' body is a temple according to John 2:21. The household of God made up of believing Jews and Gentiles is "a holy temple in the Lord" (Eph 2:21). The body of the Christian is a temple (see 1 Cor 3:16; 6:19). Yet multiple NT passages refer to a future literal temple in Jerusalem. In Matt 24:15, Jesus relies on Dan 9:24–27 in stating that when the abomination of desolation takes place, there will be a "standing in the holy place" that will lead to those in Judea fleeing to the mountains. This prophetic event will take place in the temple in Jerusalem. Also, 2 Thess 2:3–4 indicates that the "man of lawlessness" will take "his seat in the temple of God." This temple that belongs to God will be located in Jerusalem. Plus, Rev 11:1–2 refers to a future temple as well. Unless one takes a strong preterist approach in which these events were fulfilled in AD 70, which is hard to sustain, these events concerning the temple are still future. Thus, when it comes to the concept of temple there is an "all of the above" approach. The temple in the NT can refer to Jesus, to the church, the body of the believer, and it can refer to a future temple in Jerusalem. Context determines which sense is in mind by the biblical author.

Supersessionists often make broad sweeping generalizations about typology that do not do justice to the full picture of Scripture. They also have a tendency to see type-antitype connections that are not really there. While acknowledging the existence of types that Scripture indicates, we must not assume that everything in the OT is a type. It is best to let Scripture make the connection and put away the big broom that without warrant sweeps everything under the rug of typology.

A word about typological interpretation is also necessary. Belief in types and belief in "typological interpretation" are two different things. The former is legitimate and the latter is not. I accept that there are types, but I am much more skeptical concerning whether typological interpretation is a valid approach for understanding the Bible. A historical-grammatical-literary approach to the Bible indicates that OT types pointed toward NT antitypes. Thus, types are a real part of God's revelation. But I do not think it is valid to argue that there is the need for "typological interpretation" that is in addition to historical-grammatical interpretation. A historical-grammatical-literary approach will discover the existence of types (compare Matt 2:15 with Hos 11:1), but adoption of a hermeneutic of "typological interpretation" unnecessarily assumes

---

[23]See W. E. Glenny, "The Israelite Imagery of 1 Peter 2," in *Dispensationalism, Israel and the Church: The Search for Definition*, ed. C. A. Blaising and D. L. Bock (Grand Rapids: Zondervan, 1992), 179–82.

typological connections between the Testaments that are not warranted.

As Glenny has discussed, there may be a connection between the church and Israel in the sense that there are significant historical and theological correspondences between the two groups.[23] Clearly, "people of God" language used to describe Israel in the OT is now applied to the church (see Rom 9:24–26). This kind of connection, however, differs from the supersessionist understanding that national Israel is the lesser type that gives way to the greater reality—the church. Thus, there is not enough evidence to conclude that national Israel functioned as a type whose significance has been transcended by the church.

There are many clear OT passages that explicitly predict a future salvation and restoration of the nation Israel. The NT on several occasions reaffirms this expectation. I see nothing from the realm of types and typology that indicates that this expectation has been overturned or transferred.

Supersessionists often emphasize the typological connections found in the book of Hebrews. Hebrews indicates that Christ's priesthood is superior to that of the Levitical priesthood (see Heb 7:11–28). Hebrews also indicates that the new covenant is superior to the Mosaic covenant (see Heb 8:8–13). In Heb 12:23, there is also reference to the new Jerusalem, which is the ultimate Jerusalem. Some argue that since we see typological connections with these matters, why not view the entire OT as a type and also understand the nation Israel as a type of the church?

But does Hebrews indicate that the entire OT basically consists of types, pictures, and shadows? Not necessarily. The OT itself predicted that one day the Mosaic covenant would come to an end and be replaced by the superior new covenant (Jer 31:31–34). The Mosaic covenant by nature was a temporary and conditional covenant. Thus, a literal interpretation of the OT itself leads the Bible student to know that the Mosaic covenant was temporary and that it would be replaced by the superior new covenant. Since the primacy of the Levitical priesthood was inherently linked to the Mosaic covenant, Hebrews indicates that the Levitical priesthood gave way to the superior priesthood of Christ.

The fact that the OT itself predicts the cessation of the Mosaic covenant and the coming of the new covenant and other eschatological realities should make us pause before concluding that the OT is primarily made up of inferior typological realities. As Saucy argues,

> Recognizing that the Old Testament prophecies speak of the eschatological times and events, including the inauguration of the new covenant,

---

[24]R. L. Saucy, *The Case for Progressive Dispensationalism: The Interface Between Dispensational and Nondispensational Theology* (Grand Rapids: Zondervan, 1993), 30.

precludes our seeing all of the Old Testament as merely shadows and types that become outmoded with the coming of Christ. The fulfilled reality of the coming of Christ transcended many elements contained in the old Mosaic covenant; but this cannot be said of the promises of the new covenant and other eschatological realities.[24]

Plus, if the OT is primarily a book of types, shadows, and pictures, why do several NT passages appear to rely quite literally on many eschatological details found in the OT? Jesus' reference to the "abomination that causes desolation" in Matt 24:15 relies on a plain understanding of Dan 9:24–27. Both Peter and Paul appear to rely on the OT concept of the Day of the Lord (see 1 Thess 5:2; 2 Pet 3:10). Peter's expectation of "new heavens and a new earth" (2 Pet 3:13) appears directly reliant on what Isaiah stated in Isa 65:17 and 66:22. In several NT passages, the OT eschatological expectation is accepted. These promises are not transcended or fulfilled in some nonliteral ways. They are not considered to be typological of greater NT realities.

In regard to types and typology, there are two extremes to avoid. The first is ignoring types and acting as if they do not exist. This approach does not do justice to the typological connections mentioned in Scripture. Plus, one who does this misses out on the beauty of the divine correspondences between the Testaments. The other extreme is treating nearly everything in the OT as types, pictures, and shadows. With his response to Campbell in the late nineteenth century, Peters addressed Campbell's statement that "the Jews were the typical congregation or church of God, but Christians are the real congregation of church of God." Peters stated, "This, however, is hostile to the entire tenor of the Divine Plan as unfolded, and antagonistic to the covenants and election."[25] He is correct in his analysis. To declare that nearly everything in the OT was merely typological does not do justice to God's plans and electing purposes.

---

[25]Peters, *The Theocratic Kingdom of Our Lord Jesus, the Christ as Covenanted in the Old Testament*, 1:406.

Chapter 10

The Hermeneutics of Nonsupersessionism

So far, I have been critical of the hermeneutics of supersessionism, finding it inadequate to comprehend the biblical relationship between Israel and the church. At this point, though, I want to offer positively what I believe is the proper hermeneutical approach toward the Israel-church issue. The case for a nonsupersessionist view regarding Israel and the church includes four beliefs:

1. The starting point for understanding any passage in the Bible, including those in the OT, is the passage itself.[1]
2. Progressive revelation reveals new information, but it does not cancel unconditional promises to Israel.[2]
3. National Israel is not a type that is transcended by the church.[3]
4. Old Testament promises can have a double fulfillment or application with both Israel and the church.[4]

---

[1]Those who hold that the NT does not reinterpret the OT include the following: R. L. Saucy, *The Case for Progressive Dispensationalism: The Interface Between Dispensational and Nondispensational Theology* (Grand Rapids: Zondervan, 1993), 30; J. Feinberg, "Systems of Discontinuity," in *Continuity and Discontinuity: Perspectives on the Relationship Between the Old and New Testaments*, ed. J. S. Feinberg (Wheaton, IL: Crossway, 1988), 75; P. Feinberg, "Hermeneutics of Discontinuity," in *Continuity and Discontinuity*, 124; A. G. Fruchtenbaum, *Israelology: The Missing Link in Systematic Theology* (Tustin, CA: Ariel, 1989), 203.

[2]Those who hold that progressive revelation cannot cancel unconditional promises to Israel include the following: J. Feinberg, "Systems of Discontinuity," 76; D. L. Turner, "The Continuity of Scripture and Eschatology: Key Hermeneutical Issues," *GTJ* 6 (1985): 279; C. C. Ryrie, *Dispensationalism* (Chicago: Moody, 1995), 84; P. Feinberg, "Hermeneutics of Discontinuity," 120.

[3]Those who believe Israel is not a type that is superseded by the church include the following: J. Feinberg, "Systems of Discontinuity," 76; P. Feinberg, "Hermeneutics of Discontinuity," 124; and Saucy, *The Case for Progressive Dispensationalism*, 32.

[4]Those who believe some OT promises will have a double fulfillment with both Israel and the church include the following: P. Feinberg, "Hermeneutics of Discontinuity," 125–27; E. Sauer, *From Eternity to Eternity: An Outline of Divine Purposes* (Grand Rapids: Eerdmans, 1954), 191; K. L. Barker, "The Scope and Center of Old and New Testament Theology and Hope," in *Dispensationalism, Israel and the Church: The Search for Definition*, ed. C. A. Blaising and D. L. Bock (Grand Rapids: Zondervan, 1992), 323; D. L. Bock, "Summary Essay," in *Three Views on the Millennium and Beyond*, ed. D. L. Bock (Grand Rapids: Zondervan, 1999), 291; J. Feinberg, "Systems of Discontinuity," 77; J. H. Walton, *Covenant: God's Purpose, God's Plan* (Grand Rapids: Zondervan, 1994), 136.

THE STARTING POINT FOR INTERPRETATION IS THE PASSAGE ITSELF

This first point is straightforward. I assert that the primary meaning of any Bible passage, including those in the OT, is found in the original passage itself. As part of God's holy, inspired Word, the OT and its books are still relevant revelations and must be taken seriously and studied according to their historical-grammatical-literary contexts. This principle affirms the ongoing integrity of OT passages. Thus, the primary meanings in all passages in the Bible, both OT and NT, are found in the actual passages themselves. Scripture shines light on other Scripture, but God intends for each portion of Scripture to contribute to His revelation.

Thus, one who wants to understand what Isaiah wrote should study the passages of Isaiah in their historical-grammatical-literary contexts. One who wants to understand Jeremiah's writings should study the book of Jeremiah, and so on. I do not see enough reason to conclude that with the coming of Christ the original meanings of these passages are somehow not what they were before. Yes, NT writers will make analogies and use illustrations and applications from the OT in ways that OT writers could not have known. Yes, in the progress of history, NT writers will highlight divine correspondences and types between OT and NT persons, events, and institutions. Yes, at times the NT will offer commentary on OT passages that give us even more understanding of the OT passages. The NT may even add referents to OT prophecies. But these uses of the OT in the NT will supplement and harmonize with God's earlier revelation—not change or alter them to mean something different from what OT authors intended. God may do more than what was originally intended with these OT passages, but He will not do less.

OT texts, as understood within their historical-grammatical-literary contexts, must be the starting point for understanding God's plans for national Israel. This is the only way to maintain the integrity of the OT. As Feinberg rightly states, "The sense of any OT prediction must be determined through the application of historical-grammatical hermeneutics to that text."[5]

Feinberg observes that one key issue separating dispensationalists, who comprise a subcategory of nonsupersessionism, and nondispensationalists, who are often supersessionists,[6] is how each group approaches OT texts. He states, "Nondispensationalists [supersessionists] begin with NT teaching as having priority and then go back to the OT. Dispensationalists [nonsupersessionists] often begin with the OT, but wherever they begin they demand that the OT be taken on its own terms rather than reinterpreted in the light of the

---

[5]P. Feinberg, "Hermeneutics of Discontinuity," 123.

NT."[7] For nonsupersessionists, OT texts must be understood in their own right, and the interpreter must not be too quick to superimpose an alleged NT meaning on the OT passages. This is not a case of OT priority over the NT or interpreting the NT through the OT, but it is a call to take seriously the original intent of the OT passages.

In developing a theology of Israel, therefore, nonsupersessionists view a historical-grammatical-literary understanding of OT texts as foundational for understanding God's plans for Israel. The NT builds on OT revelation concerning the nation Israel, but the NT does not transcend or alter the original intent of the authors who penned OT promises. Blaising and Bock correctly point out that "we cannot pit Old Testament revelation against New Testament revelation in such a way that the original author's meaning is totally redefined, even if the claim is that the redefinition is a heightening."[8] It is best, therefore, to view OT promises and covenants about Israel as having continuing relevance for national Israel. As Ware states, "There can be no question that the prophets meant to communicate the promise of a national return of Israel to its land. To the extent that our hermeneutics are regulated by the principle of authorial intent, we are given ample reason to accept this literal rendering of what God, through the prophets, originally promised to his people Israel."[9]

This belief that the NT gives revelation that assumes and builds on OT revelation affects how one can respond to the charge that the NT is silent regarding national Israel's restoration and return to its land. Since the OT has already revealed God's plans on this matter, there is no need for this information to be repeated. In fact, Israel's future restoration should be assumed unless the NT explicitly states otherwise. Feinberg makes this argument:

> The fact that Israel does not have a more central position [in the New Testament] is due to the fact that the church becomes central in salvation history. But beyond that, why should something that is clearly a matter of OT revelation *have* to be *repeated* in the NT for it to have continuing validity? Should not the very opposite be the case? Should not the promises of the OT be regarded as still in effect *unless the NT states otherwise*?[10]

---

[6]Within Christian theology, most nondispensationalists are supersessionists although some exceptions do exist.

[7]J. Feinberg, "Systems of Discontinuity," 75.

[8]C. A. Blaising and D. L. Bock, "Dispensationalism, Israel and the Church: Assessment and Dialogue," in *Dispensationalism, Israel and the Church*, 391, n. 7.

[9]B. A. Ware, "The New Covenant and the People(s) of God," in *Dispensationalism, Israel and the Church*, 93.

[10]P. Feinberg, "Hermeneutics of Discontinuity," 124. Emphases in original.

Feinberg makes a similar point: "If the NT explicitly rejects an OT institution, etc., it is canceled. But if God makes a point once (the OT), why must he repeat it in the NT for it still to be true and operative? So long as he neither explicitly or implicitly rejects the OT teaching, why assume it is canceled just because the NT does not repeat it?"[11] It is not an argument from silence to claim OT promises to Israel are still in force *because God has already in the OT broken the silence and given us his thinking.*"[12]

Fruchtenbaum, too, asserts that a major OT doctrine such as the restoration of Israel cannot be disregarded simply because the NT does not explicitly repeat it: "Even if Jesus had been totally silent, that would not disprove a national restoration. It may simply mean that there was nothing to add to what was already revealed about the topic. A major Old Testament doctrine such as the national restoration of Israel cannot be dismissed simply on the basis of an argument from silence."[13]

An essential factor for understanding the meaning and significance of OT texts, including their promises to Israel, is the OT texts themselves as understood within their contexts. Thus, we should start with the OT to understand God's plans for Israel or for any other topic the OT addresses. Then we should view the NT as adding complementary information regarding this matter.

UNCONDITIONAL PROMISES ARE NOT CANCELED BY PROGRESSIVE REVELATION

In addition to emphasizing that OT passages are foundational for understanding God's plans for Israel, the unconditional nature of OT promises to Israel rules out the possibility that these promises could be fulfilled in a way that excludes national Israel. Our reasoning goes like this: Because God is true to His word and cannot lie, what He promises unconditionally to a specific people must come to pass. God may certainly add to His promises or even add other people groups to His promises, but He can never do less than what He promised. Again, God may do more than what He promised, but He cannot do less. Thus, Moo is correct when he states, "Israel still has a place in God's plan because God is faithful."[14]

Feinberg addresses this issue of the unconditional nature of certain promises for Israel and its implications for the concept of progressive revelation. As he states, "The crucial point is *how we know* whether something in the OT (especially prophecy about Israel's future) is still binding in the NT."[15] If

---

[11]J. Feinberg, "Systems of Discontinuity," 76.

[12]Ibid. Emphases in original.

[13]Fruchtenbaum, *Israelology*, 203.

[14]D. Moo, *The Epistle to the Romans*, NICNT (Grand Rapids: Eerdmans, 1996), 732.

[15]J. Feinberg, "Systems of Discontinuity," 76. Emphasis in original.

an OT promise is made unconditionally with a specific group such as Israel, then that promise must be fulfilled with that group. *Progress of revelation cannot cancel unconditional promises to Israel*: "If an OT prophecy or promise is made unconditionally to a given people and is still unfulfilled to them even in the NT era, then the prophecy must still be fulfilled to them. While a prophecy given unconditionally to Israel has a fulfillment for the church if the NT *applies* it to the church, it must also be fulfilled to Israel. Progress of revelation cannot cancel unconditional promises."[16]

Turner has also addressed how some supersessionists and nonsupersessionists have understood the relationship between the OT and NT and the implications of their views in relation to progressive revelation. In doing so, he refers to covenant theologians who are supersessionists and dispensational theologians who are nonsupersessionists. Turner argues that "covenant theologians [supersessionists] and dispensationalists [nonsupersessionists] disagree on the nature of progressive revelation."[17] He says, "Each group accuses the other of misinterpreting the NT due to alien presuppositions."[18] Turner points out that dispensationalists who are nonsupersessionists deny that the NT reinterprets OT promises to Israel. He says, "It is their contention that the NT supplies no 'reinterpretation' of OT prophecy which would cancel the OT promises to Israel of a future historical kingdom. In their view the NT use of the OT does not radically modify the OT promises to Israel."[19]

Turner rightly claims that the supersessionist understanding brings into question God's faithfulness to Israel: "If NT reinterpretation reverses, cancels, or seriously modifies OT promises to Israel, one wonders how to define the word 'progressive.' God's faithfulness to His promises to Israel must also be explained."[20] Turner also points out that the supersessionist approach comes close to violating NT statements that uphold the truth claims of the OT: "It appears exceedingly doubtful that the NT reinterprets the OT so as to evaporate the plain meaning of its promises. This comes perilously close to conflicting with such NT passages as Matt 5:18 and John 10:35b."[21]

According to Ryrie, the NT does not change the meaning of OT texts: "New revelation cannot mean contradictory revelation. Later revelation on

---

[16]Ibid. Emphasis in original.

[17]Turner, "The Continuity of Scripture and Eschatology," 280.

[18]Ibid., 280–81.

[19]Ibid., 279.

[20]Ibid., 281.

[21]Ibid., 282.

[22]Ryrie, *Dispensationalism*, 84.

a subject does not make the earlier revelation mean something different."[22] "If this were so," according to Ryrie, "God would have to be conceived of as deceiving the Old Testament prophets when He revealed to them a nationalistic kingdom, since He would have known all the time that He would completely reverse the concept in later revelation."[23] The concept of progressive revelation can be likened to a building in progress: "The superstructure does not replace the foundation."[24]

Unlike the approach of nonsupersessionists, the hermeneutical approach of supersessionists calls into question the integrity of OT passages. In response to Ladd's assertion that the NT, at times, reinterprets the OT,[25] Feinberg comments, "If Ladd is correct that the NT reinterprets the OT, his hermeneutic does raise some serious questions. How can the integrity of the OT text be maintained? In what sense can the OT really be called a *revelation* in its original meaning?"[26] Feinberg also points out that the supersessionist approach to Israel's promises has implications for the truthfulness of God. He says, "How can God be truthful and change the meaning of His promises?"[27]

To sum up, progressive revelation does not cancel unconditional promises to Israel. As Feinberg writes, "The unconditionality of the promises to Israel guarantees that the NT does not even implicitly remove those promises from Israel."[28] This may have been partly what Paul had in mind when he said that Israel is "beloved for the sake of the fathers" and that "the gifts and the calling of God are irrevocable" when discussing the future of Israel (Rom 11:28–29 NKJV).[29] Paul also ties Israel's future salvation to Israel's election (11:2,29), its relationship to the OT patriarchs (11:28), and its relationship to the new covenant (11:27). Plus, Paul states that the "covenants" and "promises" are still the possession of "Israelites" even while the people

---

[23]Ibid. G. N. H. Peters concurs, "If no restoration was intended; if all was to be understood typically, or spiritually, or conditionally, then surely the language was most eminently calculated to deceive the hearers." G. N. H. Peters, *The Theocratic Kingdom of Our Lord Jesus, the Christ as Covenanted in the Old Testament* (New York: Funk & Wagnalls, 1884; repr., Grand Rapids: Kregel, 1988), 2:51.

[24]Ryrie, *Dispensationalism*, 84.

[25]See G. E. Ladd, "Historic Premillennialism," in *The Meaning of the Millennium: Four Views*, ed. R. G. Clouse (Downers Grove, IL: InterVarsity, 1977), 21.

[26]Paul Feinberg, "Hermeneutics of Discontinuity," 116. Emphasis in original.

[27]Ibid., 120.

[28]J. Feinberg, "Systems of Discontinuity," 76.

[29]Murray writes, "'Beloved' thus means that God has not suspended or rescinded his relation to Israel as his chosen people in terms of the covenants made with the fathers. . . . God still sustains his peculiar relation of love to them, a relation that will be demonstrated and vindicated in the restoration (vss. 12, 15, 26)." J. Murray, *The Epistle to the Romans*, NICNT (Grand Rapids: Eerdmans, 1959; repr., 1997), 2:101.

of Israel are in a state of disobedience (Rom 9:4). Peter, with his speech to the Jewish leaders in Acts 3:25, affirms that they are still "sons of the prophets and of the covenant that God made with your ancestors."

Since God is true, He will not make an unconditional promise to a people group and then not fulfill that promise with that people. God's character is such that He will do what He promised.

ISRAEL IS NOT A TYPE

Anyone who undertakes an effort to understand eschatology will eventually have to deal with the issue of types and typology. These issues are often at the heart of the differences between those who see the church as the fulfillment of Israel and those who do not. This topic is complicated so I will start with some basic assertions.

First, a type is a person, thing, or institution in the OT that, by divine design, prefigures something greater in the NT. For example, Adam was a type of Jesus. Also, the primacy of the Levitical priesthood prefigured the Melchizedekian priesthood of Jesus. The presence of types shows the divine interrelationship between the OT and the NT. Typology is the study of types and their implications.

Second, both supersessionists and nonsupersessionists recognize the existence of types. So whether there are types is not the main issue since both camps agree that types exist. What is debated, though, are the implications of types in Scripture and whether the presence of types means that we must adopt an approach to the Bible called "typological interpretation." Supersessionists often argue that the presence of types means we should understand the OT as mostly a Testament of types, shadows, and pictures. For them we should approach the OT typologically. With this often comes the assertion that matters such as Israel and Israel's promised land must be viewed as types. And as types, they eventually give way to greater NT realities. Thus, Israel is understood as a type of the Christian church, and the physical land of promise is often viewed as a type of spiritual blessings Christians experience.

Nonsupersessionists, to the contrary, approach typology differently. They argue that types must be understood on a case-by-case basis. Some things in the OT are types of greater NT realities, but other things are not types. What determines a type is whether the Scripture actually connects something in the OT with something in the NT. In other words, for nonsupersessionists, the NT must explicitly make a typological connection in order for us to believe that a

---

[30]J. Feinberg, "Systems of Discontinuity," 79.

typological connection exists. As Feinberg declares, "If the NT antitype cancels the meaning of the OT type, the NT must tell us so."[30]

While accepting Adam and the primacy of the Levitical priesthood as types because Scripture makes these connections, matters such as the nation Israel and Israel's land are not types. There are two main reasons nonsupersessionists are correct for not putting Israel and Israel's land in the category of types that are transcended by greater NT antitypes.

First, nonsupersessionists do not accept the assumption that the concepts of a special nation or a land are inherently inferior or nonspiritual matters that must be transcended by greater spiritual truths. This approach is more akin to Platonism than the Bible. The spiritual blessings emphasized in the NT are not contrary to the concepts of nations and land. Second, Feinberg has rightly observed that the nature of the unconditional promises to Israel makes it highly unlikely that typology would override what God has declared concerning national Israel: "The unconditionality of the promises to Israel guarantees that the NT does not even implicitly remove those promises from Israel. Old Testament civil and ceremonial laws and institutions are shadows and are explicitly removed in the NT. But unconditional promises are not shadows, nor are the peoples to whom they are given."[31]

Feinberg's logic is sound: if God makes an unconditional and eternal promise to a specific people group, then He must fulfill His promise just as He said with that group. Thus, neither Israel nor the promises to Israel can be said to be types or shadows. As Feinberg states, "While historical-grammatical interpretation allows for symbols, types, and analogies, I see no evidence that Israel is a symbol for the church, Palestine for the New Jerusalem, *et al.*"[32]

Am I saying that there is no divine connection whatsoever between Israel and the church? Not necessarily. Saucy argues that the nation Israel is not a type in the sense that Israel has been transcended by a greater spiritual reality, the church. Yet he also points out there is a historical and theological correspondence between Israel and the church that may have typological implications. As he explains, "If a type is understood as shadow pointing forward to the reality of an antitype, then it is questionable whether Israel is a type."[33] On the other hand, if a type is viewed in terms of a correspondence between two groups, then a typological connection between Israel and the church may exist: "If a type is defined as a general historical and theological correspondence, then the many analogies

---

[31]Ibid., 76.
[32]P. Feinberg, "Hermeneutics of Discontinuity," 124.
[33]Saucy, *The Case for Progressive Dispensationalism*, 32.

between Old Testament Israel and the New Testament people of God may well be explained by seeing Israel as a type of the church. But the correspondence with God's actions among Old Testament Israel would not in this understanding of typology deny the continued existence of that nation in the future."[34]

Thus, there may be a connection between Israel and the church, but this connection is not that of the church superseding national Israel. Instead, the connection is that of a historical and theological correspondence that reveals a close relationship between Israel and the church. This typological connection between the OT and the NT, however, does not alter the original sense of the OT promises to Israel. As Turner explains, "Genuine typology and analogy between OT and NT should not be viewed as destructive to the literal fulfillment of the OT promises to Israel, but rather an indication of a greater continuity between Israel and the church."[35] Whatever relationship exists between Israel and the church, it cannot be taken to mean that Israel's significance has been transcended and superseded by the church.

Caution should be used when determining when the NT cancels an OT type. As Feinberg declares, "If the NT antitype cancels the meaning of the OT type, the NT must tell us so."[36] In the case of Israel and the church, "I do not see . . ." enough evidence to conclude that Israel is a type that is superseded by the church.

MULTIPLE FULFILLMENTS AND APPLICATIONS OF OLD TESTAMENT PROMISES

Old Testament texts that told of national Israel's restoration are related by the NT to specific events in the church age (cf. Acts 2:16–21 with Joel 2:28–32; Acts 15:15–18 with Amos 9:11–12). Some believe this is evidence that the church is the complete fulfillment of the OT promises made with Israel.

Nonsupersessionists, however, come to a different conclusion. In cases where OT texts regarding Israel are quoted in the NT, nonsupersessionists are more likely to interpret the OT passages as having a double fulfillment or application—one for the church in the present and one for national Israel in the future. As Feinberg writes, "The referent that acts as the fulfillment of an OT prediction must meet the requirements of the sense of that prediction

---

[34]Ibid., 31–32. See also W. E. Glenny, "The Israelite Imagery of 1 Peter 2," in *Dispensationalism, Israel and the Church,* 180.

[35]Turner, "The Continuity of Scripture and Eschatology," 282. See also H. Taylor, "The Continuity of the People of God in Old and New Testaments," *Scottish Bulletin of Evangelical Theology* 3 (1985): 14–15.

[36]J. Feinberg, "Systems of Discontinuity," 79.

[37]P. Feinberg, "Hermeneutics of Discontinuity," 123.

as determined by the application of historical-grammatical hermeneutics."[37] For example, with texts such as Acts 2:16–21 and Acts 15:15–18, nonsupersessionists believe that a fulfillment or application of OT prophecies is being made with the church, but they also affirm that there will be a future fulfillment with national Israel.

Feinberg, for instance, argues that Joel 2:28–32 ends up having two referents, the church and Israel. Joel 2:28–32 refers to Israel as a referent while Acts 2:16–21 indicates that the church is also a referent.[38] Likewise, Sauer views Acts 15:15–18 as telling of a present fulfillment of the Amos 9:11–12 prophecy with the church. This present fulfillment in the church, however, does not rule out a future fulfillment of the Amos prophecy with national Israel: "How shall a prior spiritual fulfillment serve to prove that a final complete fulfillment is no more to be expected? Is it not wholly incontestable that, even if these promises can have a prior spiritual fulfillment in the period of the New Testament church, the Old Testament prophets themselves, on the ground of the inspired wording of their prophecies, expected a *literal* fulfillment in a renewed Israel?"[39]

In reference to the use of Joel 2:28–32 in Acts 2:17–21 and the use of Amos 9:11–12 in Acts 15:16–17, Barker asserts that there is a present fulfillment with the church and a future fulfillment with national Israel. He states, "These propositions are not either-or but both-and."[40] Barker calls this both-and paradigm "progressive fulfillment."[41] The church, including its Gentile members, is involved with "the progressive fulfillment of the great promises in Israel's unconditional covenants," but this participation does not involve "excluding Israel in the future" from these covenants.[42]

The application or fulfillment of OT texts in the NT era is not evidence that the original meaning of the OT promises and prophecies have been jettisoned or completely transcended. This is Feinberg's point:

> NT application of the OT passage does not necessarily eliminate the passage's original meaning. No NT writer claims his new understanding of the OT passage cancels the meaning of the OT passage in its own context or that the new application is the only meaning of the OT passage. The NT writer merely offers a different application of an OT passage than the

---

[38]Ibid., 125–27.

[39]Sauer, *From Eternity to Eternity*, 191. Emphasis in original. See also Saucy, *The Case for Progressive Dispensationalism*, 78–80.

[40]Barker, "The Scope and Center of Old and New Testament Theology and Hope," 323.

[41]Ibid.

[42]Ibid., 325. Bock writes, "Other premillennialists acknowledge that the New Testament does acknowledge degrees of direct, initial Old Testament fulfillment in the church today, but because this fulfillment is 'already/not yet,' the present fulfillment complements or supplies only a piece of what is ultimately alluded to in the Old Testament." Bock, "Summary Essay," 291.

OT might have foreseen; he is not claiming the OT understanding is now irrelevant. Double fulfillment, then, is necessitated by the NT's application of the passage to the church and by maintaining the integrity of the OT's meaning, especially in view of the unconditional nature of the promises to Israel.[43]

Therefore, *expansion* of OT promises to the church does not mean that national Israel has been *excluded* from the promises. As Paul Feinberg asserts, "Where a promise or prediction is expanded or amplified, the amplification does not preclude the original addressees as a part of the referent (fulfillment) of that promise. *Expansion* does not require *exclusion*. Exclusion from any promise must be based upon some explicit or implicit statement of subsequent Scripture. Therefore, a concern for those to whom the prediction was given will always be necessary."[44] Thus, unconditional promises made to Israel are still in effect. House makes a valid point that "those who believe that the church has somehow taken over the blessings of Israel must explain the revoking of these apparently irrevocable callings of God on His people."[45]

CHRIST AND THE OLD TESTAMENT

Sometimes in the discussion of how to understand the OT an argument is made that the true meaning of the OT is not about ethnic Jews, land, and temples; it is about Jesus Christ. The implication is that the supersessionist position is more Christocentric than the nonsupersessionists who are only concerned with mundane things like nations, land, and temples while the supersessionists have the high ground of focusing on Jesus.[46] While this approach may be impressive to some, it rings hollow upon closer examination.

Nonsupersessionists, too, view themselves as Christocentric. They see Christ as the focal point of both Testaments. They affirm what the Scripture says, that "every one of God's promises is 'Yes' in Him" (2 Cor 1:20). The OT points forward to Christ and the cross, and the NT presents Jesus as the hope of the OT. Nonsupersessionists view Christ as the fulfillment of the Mosaic law (Matt 5:17). He is also the fulfillment of Israel in the sense that He is the ultimate Israelite (cf. Matt 2:15 with Hos 11:1). In addition, all the unconditional covenants—including the

---

[43]J. Feinberg, "Systems of Discontinuity," 77.

[44]P. Feinberg, "Hermeneutics of Discontinuity," 127–28. Emphases in original.

[45]House, "The Church's Appropriation of Israel's Blessings," 81.

[46]See K. Riddlebarger, *A Case for Amillennialism: Understanding the End Times* (Grand Rapids: Baker, 2003), 68–80.

Abrahamic, Davidic, and New—find their fulfillment in Him. I know of no nonsupersessionist who believes the covenants and promises of the OT can be fulfilled without Christ. Thus, Christ is the focal point of all promises, prophecies, and covenants, including those in the OT. In sum, Jesus Christ is the fulfillment of the OT.

For nonsupersessionists, however, the fact that Christ is the fulfillment of the OT does not mean that the specific details of the promises, prophecies, and covenants of the OT somehow disappear into Christ. Riddlebarger is incorrect when he claims that OT prophecies concerning Israel and kingdom "vanish in Jesus Christ, who has fulfilled them."[47] Jesus' relationship to prophecy is not that of a vanishing act. Nor should biblical prophecy be understood in some Hindu or Platonic sense in which everything is absorbed into the Absolute with no continuing relevance. If this were the case, why should we be concerned with any prophecies at all? We could simply say that all prophecy is irrelevant because it is absorbed in Jesus. But there are matters such as the final form of God's kingdom and the coming new heavens and new earth (see Isa 65:17; 66:22), which are OT concepts, that are still future from our standpoint. Jesus Himself taught the coming restoration of Israel (see Matt 19:28) and a coming abomination of desolation (see Matt 24:15). These are OT concepts. In 2 Thess 2:3–4, Paul discussed a coming desecration of the Jewish temple as predicted in Dan 9:24–27. I do not agree that the details of OT prophecy vanish into Christ. Contrary to supersessionists, nonsupersessionists affirm Christ as the center of biblical prophecy but not at the expense of the details of the prophecies.

A true Christ-honoring approach to Scripture is to understand Christ's Scripture accurately. If Christ Himself and His Word in its entirety teach a future restoration of Israel, what honor is there in declaring that we will not believe this truth because it is not Christocentric enough? It seems the Christ-honoring thing to do is to believe and accept what Christ has revealed about eschatological matters. The OT is part of Christ's revelation; as such, we need to believe it and live in light of it. Horner is correct when he states that we need "a Christocentric hermeneutic for the Hebrew Scriptures" and not "a Christocentric hermeneutic against the Hebrew Scriptures."[48]

---

[47]Ibid., 70.

[48]B. E. Horner, *Future Israel: Why Christian Anti-Judaism Must Be Challenged,* NACSBT (Nashville: B&H Academic, 2007), 195, 186.

Part 4

Supersessionism and Theological Arguments

Chapter 11

Theological Arguments
for Supersessionism

In addition to certain hermeneutical assumptions, supersessionists often appeal
to various theological arguments in support of their idea that the church permanently replaces or supersedes national Israel as the God's people. Five
primary arguments are often used to support a supersessionist view:

1. National Israel has been permanently rejected as the people of God
   (Matt 21:43).
2. Application of OT language to the church shows that the church is
   now identified as the new Israel (Gal 6:16; Rom 9:6; 2:28–29; 1 Pet
   2:9–10; Gal 3:7,29).
3. Unity of Jews and Gentiles rules out a future role or function for
   national Israel (Eph 2:11–22; Rom 11:17–24).
4. The church's relationship to the new covenant indicates that the
   church alone inherits the OT covenants originally promised to
   national Israel (Heb 8:8–13).
5. New Testament silence on the restoration of Israel is proof that
   Israel will not be restored as a nation.

Permanent Rejection of the Nation Israel (Matt 21:43)

Supersessionists agree that the nation Israel held a special status as the
"people of God" in the old covenant era. Many of them also hold, though,
that national Israel permanently forfeited this status because of its rejection
of Jesus. A verse often used to support this view of the permanent rejection
of national Israel is Matt 21:43.[1] In this verse, which Bruner calls "one of

---

[1]The following authors have expressed the idea that Matt 21:43 teaches the rejection of the
nation Israel and/or Israel's replacement by the church: J. D. Kingsbury, *Matthew: Structure,
Christology, Kingdom* (Philadelphia: Fortress, 1975), 157; R. T. France, *The Gospel According to
Matthew*, TNTC (Grand Rapids: Eerdmans, 1985; repr., 1987), 310; J. Gerstner, *Wrongly Dividing the
Word of Truth: A Critique of Dispensationalism* (Brentwood, TN: Wolgemuth & Hyatt, 1991),

the most important verses in Matthew,"[2] Jesus addressed the unbelief of the leaders of the nation Israel and announced his rejection of them because of their stubborn unbelief: "Therefore I tell you, the kingdom of God will be taken away from you and given to a nation producing its fruit."

What is the significance of Jesus' words in Matt 21:43? Supersessionists often assert that Jesus was making two major points. The first was that the nation Israel had been permanently rejected as the people of God. The second is that the "nation" to whom the kingdom would be given is the church. According to Kingsbury, "God has withdrawn his Kingdom from Israel" and has "given it to the church (21:43)."[3] France declares that Matt 21:43 is "the most explicit statement in Matthew of the view that there is to be a new people of God in place of Old Testament Israel."[4] Commenting on Matt 21:43, Gerstner states, "On the surface of it this is the end of the nation of Israel as the chosen people of God. They have been tried and found wanting."[5]

Similarly, Robertson says that Jesus' declaration "was the deathknell of the Jewish nation with their hopes of political and religious world leadership."[6] Zorn addresses what he believed to be Israel's permanent rejection and replacement by the church: "As a matter of fact, Israel having rejected its king, the kingdom of God would therefore be taken from it and be given to a nation bearing its appropriate fruits (Matt. 21:43). For this eventually Jesus made provision by the establishment of his church, the new Israel and the true people of God."[7]

190–91; A. T. Robertson, *Word Pictures in the New Testament* (Grand Rapids: Baker, 1930), 1:172; R. O. Zorn, *Christ Triumphant: Biblical Perspectives on His Church and Kingdom* (Carlisle, PA: Banner of Truth, 1997), 1:30; G. E. Ladd, *The Gospel of the Kingdom: Popular Expositions on the Kingdom of God* (Grand Rapids: Eerdmans, 1959), 114; K. Rahner, *Foundations of Christian Faith: An Introduction to the Idea of Christianity*, trans. W. V. Dych (New York: Seabury, 1978), 337; H. Ridderbos, *The Coming of the Kingdom*, trans. H. de Jongste (Philadelphia: P&R, 1962), 352–53; F. W. Beare, *The Gospel According to Matthew: A Commentary* (Oxford: Basil Blackwell, 1981), 431; H. K. LaRondelle, *The Israel of God in Prophecy: Principles of Prophetic Interpretation* (Berrien Springs, MI: Andrews University Press, 1983), 101; J. Bright, *The Kingdom of God: The Biblical Concept and Its Meaning for the Church* (Nashville: Abingdon, 1953), 226. Other texts have been used to support this idea of the permanent rejection of Israel. Diprose mentions John 8:30–59 as a possible supporting text for replacement theology. In this text Jesus stresses that the Jewish leaders were not children of Abraham but children of the devil (see 8:44). R. E. Diprose, *Israel in the Development of Christian Thought* (Rome: Istituto Biblico Evangelico Italiano, 2000), 36–38. Diprose also mentions 1 Thess 2:15–16. The latter part of verse 16 states concerning the Jews, "But wrath has come upon them to the utmost" (55). Bright mentions Matt 8:11 as being parallel to Matt 21:43. Bright, *The Kingdom of God*, 226.

[2]F. D. Bruner, *Matthew: A Commentary* (Dallas: Word, 1990), 2:770.

[3]Kingsbury, *Matthew*, 157.

[4]France, *The Gospel According to Matthew*, 310.

[5]Gerstner, *Wrongly Dividing the Word of Truth*, 190–91.

[6]Robertson, *Word Pictures in the New Testament*, 1:172.

[7]Zorn, *Christ Triumphant*, 30. See also K. A. Mathison, *Dispensationalism: Rightly Dividing the People of God* (Phillipsburg, NJ: P&R, 1995), 113.

Application of "Israel" Language to the Church

In addition to holding that the NT tells of national Israel's permanent rejection, supersessionists often point out that the NT often applies "Israel" language to the church. To them, this is further evidence that the church is now the true spiritual Israel. Key texts in this regard are Gal 6:16; Rom 9:6; Rom 2:28–29; 1 Pet 2:9–10; and Gal 3:7,29.

Galatians 6:16

Important to the supersessionist view is Gal 6:16. With this verse, the NT is believed to identify explicitly the church as Israel.[8] This verse reads, "May peace come to all those who follow this standard, and mercy to the Israel of God!"

Because of its importance in the debate over supersessionism, much debate has taken place over Gal 6:16. Köstenberger states, "Entire theological systems divide over the interpretation of this passage, which has an important bearing on the question of the relationship between Israel and the church."[9]

LaRondelle claims that this verse is "the chief witness in the New Testament in declaring that the universal Church of Christ is *the* Israel of God, *the* seed of Abraham, *the* heir to Israel's covenant promise."[10] This supersessionist view of Gal 6:16 is based on the belief that the *kai* ("and") before "Israel of God" in verse 16 should be taken in the explicative sense of "even."[11] The *kai*, it is argued, equates the "them," who are members of the church, with the "Israel of God."

---

[8]Those who interpret "Israel of God" in Gal 6:16 as a reference to the Church include the following: LaRondelle, *The Israel of God in Prophecy*, 110; J. D. G. Dunn, *The Theology of Paul's Letter to the Galatians* (Cambridge: Cambridge University Press, 1993), 100; A. A. Hoekema, *The Bible and the Future* (Grand Rapids: Eerdmans, 1979), 197; J. R. W. Stott, *The Message of Galatians: Only One Way* (Downers Grove, IL: InterVarsity, 1968), 180; M. H. Woudstra, "Israel and the Church: A Case for Continuity," in *Continuity and Discontinuity: Perspectives on the Relationship Between the Old and New Testaments*, ed. J. S. Feinberg (Wheaton, IL: Crossway, 1988), 235; H. N. Ridderbos, *The Epistle of Paul to the Churches of Galatia: The English Text with Introduction, Exposition and Notes*, trans. H. Zylstra (Grand Rapids: Eerdmans, 1953), 227; U. Luz, *Das Geschichtsverständis des Paulus* (München: Kaiser, 1968), 285; N. A. Dahl, "Der Name Israel: Zur Auslegung von Gal 6,16," *Judaica* 6 (1950): 168; G. K. Beale, "Peace and Mercy Upon the Israel of God: The Old Testament Background of Galatians 6,16b," *Biblica* 80 (1999): 205; O. P. Robertson, *The Israel of God: Yesterday, Today, and Tomorrow* (Phillipsburg, NJ: P&R, 2000), 40–41; Zorn, *Christ Triumphant*, 94; A. J. Köstenberger, "The Identity of the ΙΣΡΑΗΛ ΤΟΥ ΘΕΟΥ (Israel of God) in Galatians 6:16," *Faith and Mission* 19 (2001): 3–24; Bright, *The Kingdom of God*, 227.

[9]Köstenberger, "The Identity of the ΙΣΡΑΗΛ ΤΟΥ ΘΕΟΥ (Israel of God) in Galatians 6:16," 3.

[10]LaRondelle, *The Israel of God in Prophecy*, 110. Emphases in original. According to Dunn, this redefinition of the Israel of God in Gal 6:16 "is the most distinctive and still challenging feature of Paul's theology." Dunn, *The Theology of Paul's Letter to the Galatians*, 100.

[11]R. C. H. Lenski, *The Interpretation of Saint Paul's Epistles to the Galatians* (London: Macmillan, 1896), 224–25.

This interpretation of *kai* is found in the New International Version: "Peace and mercy to all who follow this rule, *even* to the Israel of God"[12] (emphasis added). Hoekema, who promotes a supersessionist position, agrees with this translation:

> The word *kai*, therefore, should here be rendered *even*, as the New International Version has done. When the passage is so understood, "the Israel of God" is a further description of "all who follow this rule"—that is, of all true believers, including both Jews and Gentiles, who constitute the New Testament church. Here, in other words, Paul clearly identifies the church as the true Israel. This would imply that promises which had been made to Israel during Old Testament times are fulfilled in the New Testament church.[13]

This is also the interpretation of Stott: "'All who walk by this rule' and the 'Israel of God' are not two groups, but one. The connecting particle *kai* should be translated 'even,' not 'and,' or be omitted (as in RSV). . . . Those who are in Christ today are . . . 'the Israel of God.'"[14]

If the *kai* of Gal 6:16 is to be understood as "even," as supersessionists claim, the "Israel of God" is a further description of those who "follow this standard" or "walk by this rule." Thus all believers in the church, including Gentiles, are the Israel of God. As Woudstra states, "All Christians, be they Jewish or not, are the Israel of God."[15]

Supersessionists who argue that the "Israel of God" in Gal 6:16 is a reference to the church of believing Jews *and* Gentiles often point out that the context of the book of Galatians supports this view. According to Ridderbos, "In view of what has gone before (cf. 3:29, 4:28,29) we can hardly doubt that this *Israel of God* does not refer to the empirical, national Israel as an equally authorized partner *alongside* of the believers in Christ ('they who walk by this rule'). As elsewhere (cf. Rom. 9:7), so here, Israel designates the new Israel."[16]

Since a major theme of the book of Galatians is the unity that exists between believers of different ethnic groups, it seems unlikely to supersessionists that

---

[12]The NASB, NEB, and the KJV translate the και as "and" while the RSV leaves the και untranslated.

[13]Hoekema, *The Bible and the Future*, 197. Emphasis in original. According to Hendriksen, "It is my firm belief that those many translators and interpreters are right who have decided that *kai*, as here used must be rendered *even*, or (with equal effect) must be left untranslated." W. Hendriksen, *Exposition of Galatians*, NTC (Grand Rapids: Baker, 1968), 247.

[14]Stott, *The Message of Galatians*, 180.

[15]Woudstra, "Israel and the Church," 235. See also H. Conzelmann, *An Outline of the Theology of the New Testament* (New York: Harper & Row, 1969), 255.

Paul would end his letter with a statement that separates Jews and Gentiles. Beale observes that the unity discussed in Galatians makes a reference to Christian Jews "unlikely":

> Those who have identified "the Israel of God" with the entire Galatian church (Jewish and Gentile believers) have usually done so because of the epistle's main theme of unity between believers of different ethnic groups, and especially because of the notion that the nationalistic traits distinguishing the people of God in the old age no longer hold true for the people of God in the new age. Since the dominant message is one of doing away with national distinctions among God's people (3, 7–8.26–29; 4, 26–31; 5, 2–12), it would seem unlikely that Paul would conclude the epistle by referring to those in the church according to their ethnic distinctives.[17]

Robertson claims that a reference to Christian Jews in Gal 6:16 would contradict Paul's main point in writing his letter to the Galatians:

> The phrase "Israel of God" cannot refer to the Jewish people as a community distinct from the Gentile world. . . . If the phrase "Israel of God" is understood to refer to the Jewish people, then Paul has pronounced his apostolic "peace and mercy" over a people regardless of their faith in Jesus Christ. That would flatly contradict Paul's whole argument throughout the letter to the Galatians and violate the canon he has just established.[18]

Beale believes that the OT background of Gal 6:16 offers further proof that Paul is including believing Gentiles as part of the Israel of God. He asserts that the background for Paul's statements in Gal 6:15–16 is Isaiah 54, a chapter that tells of Israel's restoration.[19] According to Beale, Paul's references to "new creation" and "peace and mercy" in Galatians were written with the contents of Isaiah 54 in mind. If this is accurate, according to Beale, "it would confirm the idea that the 'Israel of God' is a reference to the entire church and not only the Jewish Christian segment of it."[20] He states,

> Isa 54, 10 was a prophecy about the "peace" and "mercy" *Israel* would have in the coming new order after their restoration. If Paul has this verse in mind in Gal 6, 16, then he sees *all* believers in the Galatian church who experience "peace" and "mercy" to be composing end-time Israel in partial fulfillment of Isa 54, 11. Such an Old Testament background makes it unlikely that he sees two separate ethnic groups (respectively Christian

---

[16]Ridderbos, *The Epistle of Paul to the Churches of Galatia*, 227. Emphasis in original.
[17]Beale, "Peace and Mercy upon the Israel of God," 205.
[18]Robertson, *The Israel of God*, 40–41.
[19]Beale, "Peace and Mercy upon the Israel of God," 223.
[20]Ibid., 208.

Gentile and Jew) as having "peace and mercy" pronounced upon them; at the least, in view of the OT and Galatians' context, the burden of proof is on one to demonstrate that "the Israel of God" is a reference only to ethnic Jewish Christians.[21]

Romans 9:6

Along with Gal 6:16, Rom 9:6 is another passage used by supersessionists to show that the church is explicitly called Israel.[22] This verse reads, "But it is not as though the word of God has failed. For not all who are descended from Israel are Israel." Some see in the mention of "Israel" a concept of Israel that goes beyond ethnic boundaries. Thus, Paul is allegedly making a distinction between ethnic Israel and a spiritual Israel that consists of all believers including Gentiles.

This is the view of Ridderbos: "Even the distinction Paul makes within national Jerusalem between who is and who is not a 'Jew,' between 'Israel' and 'those who are of Israel' (Rom. 2:28ff.; 9:6), tends to a usage that denotes the believing gentiles as well and therefore the Christian church as such as Israel.'"[23] In reference to Rom 9:6–8, Grudem declares, "Paul here implies that the true children of Abraham, those who are in the most true sense 'Israel,' are not the nation of Israel by physical descent from Abraham but those who have believed in Christ."[24] In his comments on Rom 9:6, Robertson states, "It is those who, in addition to being related to Abraham by natural descendency, also relate to him by faith, plus those Gentiles who are ingrafted by faith, that constitute the true Israel of God."[25]

Romans 2:28–29

Whereas Gal 6:16 and Rom 9:6 are used by supersessionists to show that the church is explicitly called "Israel" in the NT, Rom 2:28–29 is often used to show that the term *Jew* has now been transferred to include Gentile

---

[21]Ibid., 217. Emphasis in original.

[22]Those who view Rom 9:6 as including believing Gentiles in the concept of "Israel" include the following: H. Ridderbos, *Paul: An Outline of His Theology*, trans. J. R. De Witt (Grand Rapids: Eerdmans, 1975), 336, n. 30; W. Grudem, *Systematic Theology: An Introduction to Biblical Doctrine* (Grand Rapids: Zondervan, 1994), 861; C. H. Dodd, *The Epistle of Paul to the Romans* (London: Hodder & Stoughton, 1932), 155; L. Goppelt, *Typos: The Typological Interpretation of the Old Testament in the New*, trans. D. H. Madvig (Grand Rapids: Eerdmans, 1982), 140; Ellis, *Paul's Use of the Old Testament*, 137; and James D. G. Dunn, *Romans 9–16*, WBC 38b (Dallas: Word, 1988), 540; LaRondelle, *The Israel of God in Prophecy*, 121; Bright, *The Kingdom of God*, 226–27. Commenting on Rom 9:6, Origen stated, "For if the judgment respecting the 'Jew inwardly' be adopted, we must understand that, as there is a 'bodily' race of Jews, so also is there a race of 'Jews inwardly.'" Origen, *On First Principles* 4.21, ANF 4:370.

[23]Ridderbos, *Paul*, 336, n. 30.

[24]Grudem, *Systematic Theology*, 861.

[25]O. P. Robertson, *The Christ of the Covenants* (Phillipsburg, NJ: P&R, 1980), 40.

members of the church.[26] The text reads, "For a person is not a Jew who is one outwardly, and [true] circumcision is not something visible in the flesh. On the contrary, a person is a Jew who is one inwardly, and circumcision is of the heart—by the Spirit, not the letter."

Here Paul is defining the essence of a true Jew. Being a true Jew is not simply a matter of being an ethnic Jew who has been circumcised. Being a true Jew also involves an inward commitment to obey God. Thus, there is a spiritual and inward dimension to being a true Jew. What is not agreed on, however, is how far Paul is taking the concept of "Jew." Is he making a declaration that all who believe in Christ, regardless of their ethnicity, are true Jews? Or is he making a distinction between ethnic Jews who have believed in Christ and ethnic Jews who have not believed?

Ridderbos says this passage teaches "a radicalizing of the concept Jew and thereby of the definition of the essence of the people of God."[27] Likewise, Stott claims that Paul is giving a "redefinition of what it means to be a Jew."[28] According to supersessionists, then, Rom 2:28–29 is evidence that the term *Jew* no longer refers exclusively to physical Jews; it has been broadened to include all believers including Gentiles.

First Peter 2:9–10

At times the NT writers applied terminology used to describe Israel in the OT to the NT church. Like OT Israel, the church is identified as God's own possession (cf. Exod 19:5 with Titus 2:14), "My people" (cf. 2 Chr 7:14 with Acts 15:14 and 2 Cor 6:16), and the "circumcision" (Phil 3:3). In addition, believing members in the church are called "a chosen race," "a royal priesthood," and "a holy nation" (1 Pet 2:9).

Disagreement exists, however, concerning the significance of these Israelite designations. Does the application of these terms to the church mean that the church is the new Israel? Those who hold a replacement view usually say that it does. To them, as Saucy points out, "this application of Israel's terminology to the church means that the New Testament writers were identifying the church as the new Israel, hence redefining the concept of Israel."[29]

---

[26]Those who view Rom 2:28–29 as including believing Gentiles in the concept of "Jew" include the following: D. Moo, *The Epistle to the Romans*, NICNT (Grand Rapids: Eerdmans, 1996), 175; Dunn, *Romans 9–16*, 125; Ridderbos, *Paul*, 334; J. Stott, *The Message of Romans: God's Good News for the World* (Downers Grove, IL: InterVarsity, 1994), 94; LaRondelle, *The Israel of God in Prophecy*, 128; Zorn, *Christ Triumphant*, 94; Bright, *The Kingdom of God*, 227.

[27]Ridderbos, *Paul*, 334.

[28]Stott, *The Message of Romans*, 94.

[29]R. L. Saucy, *The Case for Progressive Dispensationalism: The Interface Between Dispensational and Nondispensational Theology* (Grand Rapids: Zondervan, 1993), 205. Saucy is not a supersessionist.

In reference to 1 Pet 2:9–10, McKnight states, "There is no passage in the New Testament that more explicitly associates the Old Testament terms for Israel with the New Testament church than this one."[30] The text reads,

> But you are a chosen race, a royal priesthood, a holy nation, a people for His possession, so that you may proclaim the praises of the One who called you out of darkness into His marvelous light. Once you were not a people, but now you are God's people; you had not received mercy, but now you have received mercy.

The titles "chosen race," "royal priesthood," "holy nation," and "God's people" are taken from Isa 43:20 and Exod 19:5–6. These designations, used for to describe Israel in the OT, are now used by Peter to describe NT believers.

This application of "Israel" terminology to the church in 1 Pet 2:9–10 has led some to conclude that Peter is identifying the church as Israel.[31] Klooster, for example, states, "The church as the body of Christ is composed of believing Jews and Gentiles and is the new Israel, 'a chosen people, a royal priesthood, a holy nation.'"[32] Hunter and Homrighausen write, "Peter proceeds to apply title after title conferred on the old Israel to the church as the new Israel of God."[33] Grudem also believes 1 Pet 2:9 teaches a theology of replacement: "God's chosen people are no longer said to be those physically descended from Abraham, for Christians are now the true 'chosen race' (v. 9). . . . What more could be needed in order to say with assurance that the church has now become the true Israel of God."[34]

In addition to viewing the church as the new Israel, some declare that 1 Pet 2:9–10 teaches the replacement of national Israel with the church. Achtemeier writes, "The twofold description of the new community (2:5; 2:9–10) shows by

---

[30]S. McKnight, *1 Peter*, NIVAC (Grand Rapids: Zondervan, 1996), 109–10.

[31]Some who view 1 Pet 2:9–10 as teaching that the church is "Israel" include the following: F. H. Klooster, "The Biblical Method of Salvation: A Case for Continuity," in *Continuity and Discontinuity: Perspectives on the Relationship Between the Old and New Testaments*, ed. J. S. Feinberg (Wheaton, IL: Crossway, 1988), 159; W. Grudem, *1 Peter*, TNTC (Grand Rapids: Eerdmans, 1988), 113; P. H. Davids, *The First Epistle of Peter* (Grand Rapids: Eerdmans, 1990), 90–92; Woudstra, "Israel and the Church," 234; E. Best, *1 Peter*, NCB (Grand Rapids: Eerdmans, 1977), 108–09; J. N. D. Kelly, *The Epistles of Peter and Jude* (Peabody, MA: Hendrickson, 1969), 95; R. V. G. Tasker, *The Old Testament in the New Testament* (Philadelphia: Westminster, 1945), 138; R. H. Mounce, *Born Anew to a Living Hope: A Commentary on 1 and 2 Peter* (Grand Rapids: Eerdmans, 1982), 28; Bright, *The Kingdom of God*, 227; J. R. Michaels, *1 Peter*, WBC 49 (Waco, TX: Word, 1988), 107; Ridderbos, *Paul*, 332; P. J. Achtemeier, *1 Peter: A Commentary on First Peter:* (Minneapolis: Fortress, 1996), 152; I. H. Marshall, *1 Peter*, IVPNTCS (Downers Grove, IL: InterVarsity, 1991), 72–73; LaRondelle, *The Israel of God in Prophecy*, 106; Zorn, *Christ Triumphant*, 94.

[32]Klooster, "The Biblical Method of Salvation," 159.

[33]A. M. Hunter and E. G. Homrighausen, "The First Epistle of Peter," *IB* 12 (New York: Abingdon, 1957), 110.

[34]Grudem, *1 Peter*, 113.

its language that the church has now taken over the role of Israel."[35] Marshall makes a strong statement concerning the certainty of the supersessionist view of 1 Pet 2:9–10: "It is impossible to avoid the impression that Peter deliberately says that the contemporary people of Israel are no longer God's people, standing in community with his people in Old Testament times, but rather that the church is the true heir of Israel."[36]

Galatians 3:7,29

In his letter to the Galatians, Paul states that Gentile believers are now related to Abraham by faith. Through belief in Christ, they are "sons of Abraham" (Gal 3:7) and "Abraham's descendents" (Gal 3:29). For many, these designations are significant because they infer that the church is now the true Israel.[37] Since believers in the church are designated "Abraham's sons" and "Abraham's seed," they must be spiritual Jews. As Ladd states, "If Abraham is the father of a spiritual people, and if all believers are sons of Abraham, his offspring, then it follows that they are Israel, spiritually speaking."[38] Hoekema agrees with Ladd's conclusion, as his comments on Gal 3:28–29 indicate:

> What is unmistakably clear here is that all New Testament believers, all who belong to Christ, all who have been clothed with Christ (v. 27), are Abraham's seed—not in the physical sense, to be sure, but in a spiritual sense. Again we see the identification of the New Testament church as the true Israel, and of its members as the true heirs of the promise made to Abraham.[39]

One implication of Gal 3:29, according to Neil, is that the concept of Israel has now been "reconstituted."[40] The new Israel is now "the Christian Church."[41]

Supersessionists also point out that being "Abraham's seed" involves being related to the true seed of Abraham—Jesus Christ. This, too, is evidence that the church is now Israel. Commenting on Gal 3:7–9,26–27,29, Strimple states,

---

[35] Achtemeier, *1 Peter*, 152.

[36] Marshall, *1 Peter*, 72–73.

[37] The following authors assert that Gal 3:7,29 teaches that believing Gentiles are considered spiritual Jews: G. E. Ladd, "Historic Premillennialism," in *The Meaning of the Millennium: Four Views*, ed. R. G. Clouse (Downers Grove, IL: InterVarsity, 1977), 24; Hoekema, *The Bible and the Future*, 198–99; W. Neil, *The Letter of Paul to the Galatians* (Cambridge: Cambridge University Press, 1967), 62; R. B. Strimple, "Amillennialism," in *Three Views on the Millennium and Beyond*, ed. D. L. Bock (Grand Rapids: Zondervan, 1999)," 88–89; LaRondelle, *The Israel of God in Prophecy*, 108; Bright, *The Kingdom of God*, 227; B. K. Waltke, "Kingdom Promises as Spiritual," in *Continuity and Discontinuity*, 267.

[38] Ladd, "Historic Premillennialism," 24.

[39] Hoekema, *The Bible and the Future*, 198–99.

[40] Neil, *The Letter of Paul to the Galatians*, 62.

[41] Ibid.

"Since Christ is the true Israel, the true seed of Abraham, we who are *in Christ* by faith and the working of his Spirit are the true Israel."[42]

UNITY BETWEEN JEWS AND GENTILES

The NT declares that unity has come to believing Jews and Gentiles in Christ. Two primary texts in this regard are Eph 2:11–22 and Rom 11:17–24.[43] Supersessionists often view these passages as evidence that the church is now Israel and that a future restoration of national Israel will not happen.

Ephesians 2:11–22

Barth has observed that of all the books in the NT, nowhere "is the relationship of the church and Israel 'in Christ' described as intensively and strikingly as in Ephesians."[44] At the center of this important letter is Eph 2:11–22, a text Barth calls "the key and high point of the whole epistle."[45]

In Eph 2:11–22, Paul discusses the unity that now exists between Jews and Gentiles as a result of Jesus Christ. Gentiles who were separated from Christ, the "citizenship of Israel," and the "covenants" (Eph 2:12) have now been "brought near by the blood" of Christ (Eph 2:13). Christ, by his death, has now "made both groups one" (Eph 2:14). He has also reconciled both groups "in one body" (Eph 2:16). Now both Gentiles and Jews have equal access to the Father (Eph 2:18) and are "fellow citizens with the saints, and members of God's household" (Eph 2:19).

Two issues must be addressed here. First, does the unity between believing Jews and Gentiles that is referred to in Eph 2:11–22 imply that Gentiles have been incorporated into a new, redefined Israel? And second, does this unity between Jews and Gentiles rule out any future role for national Israel? Those who hold a supersessionist view often answer in the affirmative to both questions.[46]

---

[42]Strimple, "Amillennialism," 88–89. Emphasis in original.

[43]Berkhof writes, "Paul clearly testifies to the spiritual unity of Israel and the Church in Rom. 11:17–21, and in Eph. 2:11–16." L. Berkhof, *Systematic Theology* (Grand Rapids: Eerdmans, 1941; repr. 1991), 572.

[44]M. Barth, "Conversion and Conversation," *Int* 17 (1963): 13.

[45]M. Barth, *Ephesians: Introduction, Translation, and Commentary on Chapters 1–3*, AB 34 (Garden City, NY: Doubleday, 1974), 275.

[46]Those who assert that Eph 2:11–22 teaches that the church is now "Israel" or that a future distinct role for national Israel is not allowed by this passage include the following: K. Riddlebarger, *A Case for Amillennialism: Understanding the End Times* (Grand Rapids: Baker, 2003), 120–21; T. K. Abbott, *A Critical and Exegetical Commentary on the Epistle to the Ephesians and to the Colossians*, ICC (Edinburgh: T&T Clark, 1897; repr. 1979), 59–60; C. Hodge, *An Exposition of Ephesians* (Wilmington, DE: Associated Publishers and Authors, n.d.), 52; Hoekema, *The Bible and the Future*, 200; Zorn, *Christ Triumphant*, 190; Grudem, *Systematic Theology*, 862; LaRondelle, *The Israel of God in Prophecy*, 114.

Concerning the first question, supersessionists have often argued that whereas the former condition of Gentiles was that of exclusion from "the citizenship of Israel" (2:12), the Gentiles are now "fellow citizens" (2:19) of Israel. This means that there is an incorporation of believing Gentiles into Israel. Commenting on Ephesians 2, Abbott writes, "Accordingly in the following verses we have two points of view combined, viz. the reconciliation of the Gentiles to God, and their admission to the [*politeia*] of Israel, namely the true Israel—the Christian Church." [47]

In his interpretation of Eph 2:19, Barth states, "Through his incorporation into Israel a Gentile finds communion with God."[48] Hodge, too, argues that Ephesians 2 teaches the inclusion of Gentiles into a new Israel: "It is not, therefore, to the participation of the privileges of the old, external, visible theocracy, nor simply to the pale of the visible Christian Church, that the apostle here welcomes his Gentile brethren, but to the spiritual Israel, the communion of the saints."[49]

Concerning the second issue, some hold that the logic of Eph 2:11–22 argues against any future role for national Israel in the plan of God. For example, Hoekema declares, "All thought of a separate purpose for believing Jews is here excluded."[50] In reference to Eph 2:11–15, Zorn argues, "Through Christ's fulfilling of the law an end has come to the exclusivity of Israel as a holy nation and a holy people."[51] Grudem says that Ephesians 2 "gives no indication of any distinctive plan for Jewish people ever to be saved apart from inclusion in the one body of Christ, the church."[52]

According to supersessionists it appears unlikely that God would bring Jews and Gentiles together only to make a distinction between the two groups in the future. To do so appears to be going backward. As Hoekema declares, it is like putting the scaffolding back on a finished building:

> To suggest that God has in mind a separate future for Israel, in distinction from the future he has planned for Gentiles, actually goes contrary to God's purpose. It is like putting the scaffolding back up after the building has been finished. It is like turning the clock of history back to Old Testament times. It is imposing Old Testament separateness upon the New Testament, and ignoring the progress of revelation.[53]

---

[47]Abbott, *A Critical and Exegetical Commentary on the Epistle to the Ephesians and to the Colossians*, 59–60.

[48]Barth, *Ephesians 1–3*, 270. Barth says, "The Gentiles are reminded that they are received into the house of God, the community of Israel" (314).

[49]Hodge, *An Exposition of Ephesians*, 52.

[50]Hoekema, *The Bible and the Future*, 200.

[51]Zorn, *Christ Triumphant*, 190.

[52]Grudem, *Systematic Theology*, 862.

[53]Hoekema, *The Bible and the Future*, 201.

Romans 11:17–24

Another text often used as support for supersessionism is Rom 11:17–24.[54] In this passage both believing Jews and Gentiles are said to belong to the same place of blessing that includes the promises and covenants associated with Abraham and the Jewish patriarchs. To illustrate this point, Paul uses the analogy of an olive tree. In this analogy unbelieving Jews represent branches broken off from a natural olive tree while believing Gentiles represent branches from a wild olive tree that are now grafted into the natural olive tree. Some, like Robertson, assert that Gentile inclusion into the place of blessing means that believing Gentiles are now Israelites:

> Believing Gentiles come *into Israel*! Is that not the point Paul made earlier in this chapter [Rom 11]? Gentiles have been "grafted in among" the Israel of God (Rom. 11:17). They have become additional branches, joined to the single stock that is none other than Israel. As a consequence, the believing Gentile community has become a "fellow sharer" (*synkoinonos*) in the rich root of the olive tree that is Israel (Rom. 11:17). In other words, they have become "Israelites."[55]

Allis, too, argues that the unity Paul refers to in Rom 11:17–24 means that believing Gentiles have been incorporated into Israel: "In short, what Paul is saying here is simply by way of illustration and application of his argument in chap. iv., that Abraham is 'the father of all them that believe' (vs. 11), whether Jew or Gentile, circumcision or uncircumcision. They are the true 'Israel of God' (Gal. vi. 16)."[56]

THE CHURCH'S RELATIONSHIP TO THE NEW COVENANT (HEB 8:8–13)

A fourth theological argument made on behalf of supersessionism is related to the new covenant.[57] In Heb 8:8–13, the author of Hebrews quotes Jer 31:31–34, the primary OT text describing the new covenant.[58] This

---

[54] See Robertson, *The Israel of God*, 188; O. T. Allis, *Prophecy and the Church* (Philadelphia: P&R, 1945), 109; Grudem, *Systematic Theology*, 861; LaRondelle, *The Israel of God in Prophecy*, 125–27; Waltke, "Kingdom Promises as Spiritual," 274.

[55] Robertson, *The Israel of God*, 188. Emphases in original.

[56] Allis, *Prophecy and the Church*, 109. See also Grudem, *Systematic Theology*, 861.

[57] The following people believe Heb 8:8–13 conveys the idea that the church now fully inherits the new covenant: Waltke, "Kingdom Promises as Spiritual," 281; Grudem, *Systematic Theology*, 862; Robertson, *The Christ of the Covenants*, 289; LaRondelle, *The Israel of God in Prophecy*, 116–18; Bright, *The Kingdom of God*, 228–29; W. A. VanGemeren, "A Response," in *Dispensationalism, Israel and the Church: The Search for Definition*, ed. C. A. Blaising and D. L. Bock (Grand Rapids: Zondervan, 1992), 337.

[58] The new covenant is mentioned seven times in the New Testament. See Luke 22:20; 1 Cor 11:25; 2 Cor 3:6; Heb 8:8,13; 9:15; and 12:24.

Jeremiah text, as Attridge explains, offered "hope to the Israelites of the exilic period that Yahweh will restore them to their homeland."[59] This quotation of Jeremiah 31 in Hebrews 8 is significant theologically since the new covenant of Jeremiah 31 was originally made with "the house of Israel" and "the house of Judah."[60]

To many supersessionists, this is proof that the new covenant finds its complete fulfillment with the church. As Waltke states, "The writer of Hebrews interprets the New Covenant, originally addressed to the house of Israel and Judah, as fulfilled in the church age (Heb 8:7–13)."[61] This fulfillment in the present age is often thought to rule out a future fulfillment of the covenant with Israel. In reference to Heb 8:8–13, Grudem states, "It seems hard to avoid the conclusion that the author views the church as the true Israel of God in which the Old Testament promises to Israel find their fulfillment."[62]

In addition, supersessionists assert that Heb 8:8–13 is highlighting a typological connection between Israel of the OT and the church in the NT. This is further evidence that all who are related to the new covenant, including Gentile members of the church, are part of Israel. As Robertson observes,

> When Jeremiah specifically indicates that the new covenant will be made "with the house of Judah and with the house of Israel," this perspective must be kept in mind. If the new covenant people of God are the actualized realization of a typological form, and the new covenant is now in effect, those constituting the people of God in the present circumstances must be recognized as the "Israel of God." As a unified people, the participants of the new covenant today are "Israel."[63]

New Testament Silence

Supersessionists sometimes assert that the lack of an explicit reference to a restoration of national Israel in the NT is additional proof that Israel has been superseded by the church. If national Israel is to be restored, supersessionists claim, why are there no discussions about Israel's land or its special role among the nations? This silence on these issues is viewed as evidence against the idea that national Israel will be restored. As Waltke argues, "*Not one* clear NT passage mentions the restoration of

---

[59]H. W. Attridge, *The Epistle to the Hebrews* (Philadelphia: Fortress, 1989), 225.

[60]According to Ladd, this a "very important passage" because it "applies a prophecy given to Israel to the Christian church." Ladd, "Historic Premillennialism," 25.

[61]Waltke, "Kingdom Promises as Spiritual," 281.

[62]Grudem, *Systematic Theology*, 862.

[63]Robertson, *The Christ of the Covenants*, 289.

Israel as a political nation or predicts an earthly reign of Christ before his final appearing. *None* depicts the consummate glory of Christ as an earthly king ruling over the restored nation of Israel. The Spirit's silence is deafening."[64]

Berkhof comes to a similar view. While acknowledging that the OT makes several references to a restoration of Israel, he finds it "remarkable" that the NT does not mention such a restoration: "It is remarkable that the New Testament, which is the fulfillment of the Old, contains no indications whatsoever of the re-establishment of the Old Testament theocracy by Jesus, nor a single undisputed positive prediction of its restoration, while it does contain abundant indications of the spiritual fulfillment of the promises given to Israel."[65]

---

[64]Waltke, "Kingdom Promises as Spiritual," 273. Emphases in original.
[65]Berkhof, *Systematic Theology*, 713.

Chapter 12

Supersessionism and Romans 11:26

The most detailed discussion about Israel in the NT is found in Romans 9–11. While not a supersessionist himself, Diprose has rightly observed that "no serious examination into the legitimacy of *replacement theology* can ignore these chapters."[1] Central to this section is a question asked by Paul in Rom 11:1: "I ask, then, has God rejected His people?" Paul's answer to this question has been a source of debate between supersessionists and nonsupersessionists and even within the supersessionist camp itself. A full discussion of the details and theological implications of Romans 9–11 is beyond the purposes of this work, but this section will survey how supersessionists have interpreted the central text of Rom 11:26a, which reads, "And in this way all Israel will be saved."

Moo observes that Rom 11:26 is the center of Rom 11:25–32, a paragraph that is "the climax to all of Rom. 9–11."[2] He also states that verse 26a is "the storm center in the interpretation of Rom. 9–11 and of NT teaching about the Jews and their future."[3] The debate centers around two key issues: (1) the meaning of "all Israel" and (2) the timing of Israel's salvation.

Supersessionists offer three major interpretations of "all Israel" in Rom 11:26. One view is that "all Israel" refers to all the elect, including believing Jews *and* Gentiles. When Paul says, "All Israel will be saved," he is referring to a current salvation taking place among believing Jews and Gentiles who now make up the true Israel, the church. Those who espouse this view claim that the *kai houtōs*" in 11:26 should not be understood in the temporal sense of "and then." According to Robertson, "Of the approximately 205 times in which the word *houtōs* occurs in the New Testament, not once does it have a temporal significance."[4] Instead, *kai houtōs* should

---

[1] R. E. Diprose, *Israel in the Development of Christian Thought* (Rome: Istituto Biblico Evangelico Italiano, 2000), 56. Emphasis in original.

[2] D. Moo, *The Epistle to the Romans*, NICNT (Grand Rapids: Eerdmans, 1996), 712.

[3] Ibid., 719.

[4] O. P. Robertson, *The Israel of God: Yesterday, Today, and Tomorrow* (Phillipsburg, NJ: P&R, 2000), 181.

be understood as "and in this manner" or "and in this way."[5] Thus, Paul is looking not to the future but to the past. Robertson paraphrases what he believes to be Paul's thought: "'And in this manner' (*kai houtōs*"), by such a fantastic process which shall continue throughout the present age 'up to' (*achris hou*) the point where the full number of the Gentiles is brought in, all Israel is saved."[6]

This view that "all Israel" refers to the church has support in church history. Theodoret, for example, stated, "All Israel means all those who believe, whether they are Jews, who have a natural relationship to Israel, or Gentiles, who are related to Israel by faith."[7] Calvin, too, understood "all Israel" to refer to believing Jews and Gentiles.[8] Moo points out that this view "has received less support in the modern period."[9] Nevertheless, it has been espoused by theologians such as Barth,[10] and more recently it has been defended by Robertson.[11]

A second view held by some supersessionists is that the "all Israel" refers to the sum total of elect Jews throughout history.[12] As Berkhof puts it, "'All Israel' is to be understood as a designation, not of the whole nation, but of the whole number of the elect out of the ancient covenant people."[13] Thus, the sum total of believing Israelites throughout history makes up the "all Israel" to whom Paul was referring. Unlike the first view, this perspective understands "Israel" in verse 26a in a purely ethnic sense; Gentiles are not in view. This second view has received considerable support in modern times. In addition to Berkhof, this perspective has been held by Hoekema, Ridderbos, Berkouwer, and Hendriksen.[14]

---

[5]Ibid.

[6]Ibid., 182.

[7]Theodoret, "Interpretation of the Letter to the Romans," ACCS 6:299.

[8]J. Calvin, *The Epistles of Paul the Apostle to the Romans and to the Thessalonians*, ed. D. W. Torrance and T. F. Torrance, trans. R. Mackenzie (Grand Rapids: Eerdmans, 1961), 255.

[9]Moo, *The Epistle to the Romans*, 720–21.

[10]K. Barth, *The Epistle to the Romans*, trans. E. C. Hoskyns (London: Oxford University Press, 1933), 415–16.

[11]Robertson, *The Israel of God*, 167–92.

[12]S. L. Johnson refers to this view as the "Dutch Interpretation" since it has been held by well-known interpreters from the Netherlands such as Berkouwer and Ridderbos. S. L. Johnson Jr., "Evidence from Romans 9–11," in *A Case for Premillennialism*, ed. D. K. Campbell and J. L. Townsend (Chicago: Moody, 1992), 217.

[13]L. Berkhof, *Systematic Theology* (Grand Rapids: Eerdmans, 1949; repr., 1991), 699.

[14]A. A. Hoekema, *The Bible and the Future* (Grand Rapids: Eerdmans, 1979), 140–41; H. Ridderbos, *Paul: An Outline of His Theology*, trans. J. R. De Witt (Grand Rapids: Eerdmans, 1975), 357–61; G. C. Berkouwer, *The Return of Christ* (Grand Rapids: Eerdmans, 1972), 340–49; W. Hendriksen, *Israel in Prophecy* (Grand Rapids: Baker, 1968), 39–52.

Both of these first two interpretations have two points in common. First, neither views the "Israel" of Rom 11:26 as a generation of Israel in the future. Second, both interpretations stress that the salvation mentioned is a present continuing occurrence and not a future expectation. Robertson, for example, claims that both views "fit into the context of Paul's argument throughout Romans 11."[15] In support of these two views, Robertson claims that Paul's point in Romans 11 is to discuss what God is *presently* doing with Israel; thus, Paul is not writing about some future salvation.

In answer to the question, "I ask, then, has God rejected His people?" Robertson points out that Paul stresses God's current activity among the Jews. In Rom 11:1b, for example, Paul states, "For I too am an Israelite, a descendant of Abraham, from the tribe of Benjamin." According to Robertson, "Paul does not respond to his own question by specifically asserting that God has not cast off his people Israel with respect to some distinctive future reserved for them."[16] Instead, Paul "specifically points to concrete evidence of God's present activity among the Jews. He himself is an Israelite, thus indicating that the grace of God is currently working among Jews."[17]

Further evidence for God's present activity among the Jews, according to Robertson, is also found in Rom 11:5, which states, "In the same way, then, there is also at the present time a remnant chosen by grace." According to Robertson, therefore, "the references in Romans 11 to God's present intention for Israel are pervasive and are highly significant for the total thrust of the chapter."[18]

A third view held by some supersessionists is that Paul is speaking of a future large-scale conversion of the Jews into the Christian church. Those who hold this perspective believe that the "all Israel" refers to the majority of Jews living at the time of the end who will experience salvation when Christ returns to earth. Unlike the first two views, this perspective holds that Paul is speaking of the nation Israel as a whole and that the salvation mentioned was still future from Paul's standpoint.

Merkle points out that this interpretation "is by far the majority view,"[19] and its support in church history is substantial. This view was held by many of the theologians of the patristic era including Origen and Augustine.

---

[15]Robertson, *The Israel of God*, 186.

[16]Ibid., 168.

[17]Ibid.

[18]Ibid., 171. See also B. L. Merkle, "Romans 11 and the Future of Ethnic Israel," *JETS* 43 (2000): 713.

[19]Merkle, "Romans 11 and the Future of Ethnic Israel," 710.

Aquinas held this perspective[20] as did the editors of the 1581 edition of the *Geneva Bible*.[21] More recently, this understanding of Rom 11:26 has been promoted by Moule, Murray, Morris, Bruce, Grudem, and Moo.[22]

Supersessionists who adopt this third position usually deny that national Israel will somehow be *restored* to a place of prominence among the nations. Thus a national *salvation* does not mean a national *restoration*. They do not foresee an earthly restoration of the Davidic kingdom, a rebuilt temple in Jerusalem, or a special role of service for Israel among the nations.

---

[20]See T. Aquinas, *Sancti Thomae de Aquino Super Epistolam B. Pauli ad Romanos lectura*, 11.4, http://www.unav.es/filosofia/alarcon/cro05.html, accessed January 26, 2004.

[21]The comment on Rom 11:26 states, "He [Paul] sheweth that the time shall come that the whole nation of the Jewes, though not every one particularly, shall be joyned to the Church of Christ." *Geneva Bible* (London: 1581).

[22]H. C. G. Moule, *The Epistle of St. Paul to the Romans* (New York: A. C. Armstrong & Son, 1899), 311–12; J. Murray, *The Epistle to the Romans* (Grand Rapids: Eerdmans, 1997), 2:99; L. Morris, *The Epistle to the Romans* (Grand Rapids: Eerdmans, 1988), 421; F. F. Bruce, *The Letter of Paul to the Romans: An Introduction and Commentary*, TNTC 6 (Grand Rapids: Eerdmans, 1985; repr., 1990), 209; W. Grudem, *Systematic Theology: An Introduction to Biblical Doctrine* (Grand Rapids: Zondervan, 1994), 861, n. 17; and Moo, *The Epistle to the Romans*, 723.

Chapter 13

Evaluating the Theological Arguments of Supersessionism

This chapter now moves to an evaluation of the theological arguments for supersessionism. As mentioned earlier, the following are the four primary theological arguments of supersessionism: (1) the NT teaches that national Israel has been permanently rejected as the people of God, (2) the NT's application of OT language to the church shows that the church is now the new Israel, (3) unity between Jews and Gentiles rules out a future role for national Israel, and (4) the church's relationship to the new covenant indicates that the church alone inherits the covenants of national Israel. I will argue that supersessionism is incorrect on all four of the above arguments.

NATIONAL ISRAEL'S PERMANENT REJECTION

Supersessionists often argue that the NT teaches the permanent rejection of national Israel as the people of God. The key text in this regard is Matt 21:43. Supersessionists assert that Matt 21:43 is teaching two main points. First, Jesus is *permanently* removing the kingdom from national Israel. Second, the nation to whom the kingdom will be given is the church with the implication that God's kingdom program does not include any role for Israel as a nation.

While the supersessionist interpretation of Matt 21:43 has considerable support, there is also a significant amount of disagreement with their view of this verse. There have been two different responses to their understanding. Several interpreters have argued that the "you" in Matt 21:43 refers only to the current leaders of Israel and not the nation as a whole. Boring, for instance, states, "Who is represented by the 'you' from whom the kingdom is taken? Who is the 'nation' to whom it is given? In the context the addressees are clearly the chief priests and Pharisees . . . i.e., the Jewish leadership, not the people as a whole."[1] Making a similar point, Kupp

---

[1] M. E. Boring, "The Gospel of Matthew: Introduction, Commentary, and Reflections," *NIB* 8 (Nashville: Abingdon, 1995), 415.

writes, "Jesus' growing antipathy to the Jewish leaders has never spelled outright rejection of the Jewish crowds, the people of Israel. Even in 21.43 the target audience is explicitly the leaders, not the people."[2]

Matthew 21:45 states that the religious leaders "knew He [Jesus] was speaking about them." Saldarini thus argues that the supersessionist view is more in line with supersessionist presuppositions than with the actual meaning of Matt 21:43: "This reading, which fits later Christian supercessionist interpretations of Jewish-Christian relations, is beset by several problems, the most obvious of which is that Matthew makes the chief priests and Pharisees apply the parable to themselves (21:45), not to Israel as a whole."[3]

While this view that Jesus was rejecting Israel's religious leaders and not the Jewish people as a whole has much support, another view better understands the meaning of Matt 21:43. It is not correct to claim that Jesus rejected Israel's religious leaders but not the people of Israel as a whole. Passages such as Matt 23:37–38 and Luke 19:41–44 indicate that Jesus' rejection applies to the whole Jewish nation.

My view of Matt 21:43 is that the kingdom of God would be taken from the current unbelieving nation of Israel and given to a future nation of Israel that would believe. Matthew 23:37–39 indicates several important truths that support this understanding. Verses 37–38 indicate that Jerusalem, the representative city of Israel and the people of Israel, would be judged despite Jesus' attempts to gather it like a hen gathers her chicks. But verse 39 offers hope: "For I tell you, you will never see Me again until you say, 'He who comes in the name of the Lord is the blessed One'!" While the current nation of Israel would be judged, Jesus says the day will come when another generation of Israel will cry out in acceptance of its Messiah. As Fruchtenbaum observes, "The point is that the kingdom while taken from the present Jewish generation, will be given to a future generation of

---

[2]D. D. Kupp, *Matthew's Emmanuel: Divine Presence and God's People in the First Gospel* (Cambridge: Cambridge University Press, 1996), 95. According to D. A. Carson, "Strictly speaking, then, v. 43 does not speak of transferring the locus of the people of God from Jews to Gentiles, though it may hint at this insofar as that locus now extends far beyond the authority of the Jewish rulers . . . instead, it speaks of the ending of the role the Jewish religious leaders played in mediating God's authority." D. A. Carson, "Matthew," *EBC* 8 (Grand Rapids: Zondervan, 1981), 454. Luz writes, "Is Jesus announcing the supersession of Israel by the Gentile Church in the history of mankind's salvation? . . . No, because in this context he is quite clearly speaking to Israel's leaders and to no one else. No, because *ethnos*—that same Greek word for 'people' that means, in the plural, 'nations' or 'Gentiles'—cannot simply be equated with 'church.'" U. Luz, *The Theology of the Gospel of Matthew*, trans. J. B. Robinson (Cambridge: Cambridge University Press, 1995), 119. See also D. L. Turner, "Matthew 21:43 and the Future of Israel," *BSac* 159, no. 633 (2002): 56.

[3]A. J. Saldarini, *Matthew's Christian-Jewish Community* (Chicago: University of Chicago Press, 1994), 59.

Israel."[4] This generation will be the "all Israel" who "will be saved" according to Rom 11:26 and the Israel who will "look on Me whom they have pierced" of Zech 12:10. Thus, I agree with Saldarini when he claims that theologians who interpret "nation" as the church "are reading second-century Christian theology" into Matt 21:43.[5]

Yet even if the "nation" of Matt 21:43 refers to the church, this does not prove supersessionism. The fact that the kingdom can be extended to apply to Gentiles in no way rules out a future restoration of Israel to the kingdom program. Both OT and NT passages explicitly state that God's kingdom program would also include Gentiles, so the inclusion of Gentiles into the kingdom is not proof that Israel is forever removed from God's kingdom program. What supersessionists need to prove is that Matt 21:43 and other texts rule out the possibility that a future nation of Israel will experience the fulfillment of the kingdom. But Matt 21:43 does not do this.

APPLICATION OF "ISRAEL" LANGUAGE TO THE CHURCH

Supersessionists believe the NT applies "Israel" terminology to the church, thus identifying the church as Israel. Several texts are used to support this claim.

Galatians 6:16

The primary text used to show that the church is called Israel is Gal 6:16. Supersessionists interpret the *kai* in Gal 6:16 in the explicative sense of "even" and thus view the "Israel of God" as a reference to the church of believing Jews and Gentiles. They argue that both the copulative ("and") and explicative senses of *kai* are found in the NT, although the explicative sense of *kai* ("even") is used much less often in the NT.[6]

But a strong case has been made that Gal 6:16 is not identifying the church as Israel. Instead, Paul is referring specifically to Jewish Christians.[7] One argument against the supersessionist understanding is that this view interprets the *kai* according to its uncommon usage even though the more common copulative usage makes sense here. In reference to the *kai* in 6:16, Vincent writes, "The explicative *kai* is at best doubtful here, and is

---

[4]A. G. Fruchtenbaum, *Israelology: The Missing Link in Systematic Theology* (Tustin, CA: Ariel, 1989), 405. This is also the view of A. J. McClain, *The Greatness of the Kingdom: An Inductive Study of the Kingdom of God* (Winona Lake, IN: BMH, 1959), 296–97.

[5]Saldarini, *Matthew's Christian-Jewish Community*, 60.

[6]An explicative sense for *kai* may be found in Mark 1:19; Luke 3:18; John 1:16; Rom 1:5; 1 Cor 2:2; 6:6–8; and Eph 2:8.

[7]According to H. D. Betz, the Israel of God refers "to those Jewish-Christians who approve of his καυών ('rule') in v 15." H. D. Betz, *Galatians: A Commentary on Paul's Letter to the Churches in Galatia* (Philadelphia: Fortress, 1979), 323.

rather forced."[8] Fung states, "It is certainly more natural to take the *kai* as simply copulative (= 'and' as in AV, RV, NASB, NEB)."[9]

A second argument against the supersessionist understanding of Gal 6:16 is based on the context of the letter. Paul is defending the concept of salvation by grace through faith against the error of the Judaizers who held that circumcision contributed to salvation. In doing this, Paul singles out Christian Jews in Galatia who correctly believed the gospel of grace and did not follow the error of the Judaizers. Paul, thus, commends these Christian Jews and calls them the "Israel of God." As Johnson puts it, "What more fitting thing could Paul write, it is said, in a work so strongly attacking Jewish professing believers, the Judaizers, than to make it most plain that he was not attacking the true believing Jews. Judaizers are anathematized, but the remnant according to the election of grace are 'the Israel of God.'"[10]

Thus, the context is on the side of the view that Paul was addressing Christian Jews with his "Israel of God" statement. Timothy George has pointed out that the "Israel of God" statement near the end of the epistle makes unlikely that Paul was including Gentile believers in the category of Israel. For George, this is an unlikely place to make a statement of such great theological significance: "It is strange that if Paul intended simply to equate the Gentile believers with the people of Israel that he would make this crucial identification here at the end of the letter and not in the main body where he developed at length his argument for justification by faith."[11]

Another argument against the supersessionist understanding of Gal 6:16 is that no other passages identify the church as "Israel." Alone this does not make the supersessionist view wrong since perhaps this is the one time Paul uses the term *Israel* in regard to Gentiles. Yet the fact that Paul always uses *Israel* for ethnic Jews is significant. As Burton declares, "There is, in fact, no instance of his [Paul] using [Israel] except of the Jewish nation or a part thereof."[12] Is Gal 6:16 the exception? Probably not. Since every other reference to Israel in both the OT and NT carries the ethnic sense,

---

[8]M. R. Vincent, *Vincent's Word Studies of the New Testament* (Peabody, MA: Hendrickson, 1985), 4:180.

[9]R. Y. K. Fung, *The Epistle to the Galatians* (Grand Rapids: Eerdmans, 1988), 310. See also R. L. Saucy, "Israel and the Church: A Case for Discontinuity," in *Continuity and Discontinuity: Perspectives on the Relationship Between the Old and New Testaments*, ed. J. S. Feinberg (Wheaton, IL: Crossway, 1988), 246; S. L. Johnson Jr., "Paul and the 'The Israel of God': An Exegetical and Eschatological Case-Study," in *Essays in Honor of J. Dwight Pentecost*, ed. S. D. Toussaint and C. H. Dyer (Chicago: Moody, 1986), 188; R. E. Diprose, *Israel in the Development of Christian Thought* (Rome: Istituto Biblico Evangelico Italiano, 2000), 47.

[10]Johnson, "Paul and 'The Israel of God,'" 185. See also Saucy, "Israel and the Church," 247.

[11]T. George, *Galatians*, NAC (Nashville: B&H, 1994), 440.

[12]E. D. Burton, *A Critical and Exegetical Commentary on the Epistle to the Galatians*, ICC (Edinburgh: T&T Clark, 1921), 358.

there needs to be particularly strong reasons to go with a nonethnic understanding of the title. But I do not see enough evidence to go with a nonethnic
sense of Israel. Could Gentiles be included in the concept of Israel in Gal
6:16? Yes, it is possible. But it is at the same time improbable. There are
not enough compelling reasons to adopt such a significant redefinition of
the concept of *Israel*. Since Paul was so hard on the Judaizers, he probably
was acknowledging the Jewish believers who had not fallen for the errors
of the Judaizers. To show that his harsh attitude to the Judaizers did not
extend to the true Jewish believers, he reaches out to these Jewish believers
and calls them the "Israel of God."[13]

As George has pointed out, the benediction of a letter is an unlikely place to
make the striking theological assertion that believing Gentiles are now a part
of "Israel." Thus, it is best to understand the *kai* in Gal 6:16 in the more common copulative or connective sense of "and." Diprose is correct that "Galatians
6:16 is insufficient grounds on which to base an innovative theological concept such as understanding the Church to be the *new* and/or *true* Israel."

Romans 9:6

While not referred to as much as Gal 6:16, Rom 9:6 is sometimes used to
show that the title "Israel" has been broadened to include believing
Gentiles. This verse declares, "For not all who are descended from Israel
are Israel." This verse, though, is not a supporting text for supersessionism, as many supersessionists have already admitted.

As Murray has noted, Rom 9:6 is teaching that "there is an 'Israel' within
ethnic Israel."[14] Paul is not saying that believing Gentiles are now part of Israel.
Instead, believing Jews are the true Israel. Sanday and Headlam state, "But St.
Paul does not mean here to distinguish a spiritual Israel (i.e. the Christian
Church) from the fleshly Israel, but to state that the promises made to Israel
might be fulfilled even if some of his descendants were shut out from them.
What he states is that not all the physical descendants of Jacob are necessarily
inheritors of the Divine promises implied in the sacred name Israel."[15] Thus,
Rom 9:6 offers no support for the supersessionist view.

---

[13]Diprose, *Israel in the Development of Christian Thought*, 47. Emphasis in original. See also
J. Jocz, *The Jewish People and Jesus Christ: A Study in the Controversy Between Church and
Synagogue* (London: SPCK, 1962), 422, n. 316.

[14]J. Murray, *The Epistle to the Romans*, NICNT (Grand Rapids: Eerdmans, 1959; repr., 1997), 2:9.

[15]W. Sanday and A. C. Headlam, *The Epistle to the Romans*, ICC (New York: Charles Scribner's
Sons, 1923), 240. See also D. Moo, *The Epistle to the Romans*, NICNT (Grand Rapids: Eerdmans,
1996), 574. About Rom 9:6, Gutbrod writes, "We are not told here that Gentile Christians are the true
Israel. The distinction at R. 9:6 does not go beyond what is presupposed at Jn. 1:47." W. Gutbrod,
"'Ισραήλ κ. τ. λ." in *Theological Dictionary of the New Testament*, ed. G. Kittel (Grand Rapids:
Eerdmans, 1965), 3:387.

Romans 2:28–29

Supersessionists claim that Rom 2:28–29 expands the concept of *Jew* to include believing Gentiles. Nonsupersessionists, though, argue that Paul is not identifying believing Gentiles in his concept of the true Jew. Instead, the true Jew is the ethnic Jew who has trusted in God through faith.

To support this understanding, Fruchtenbaum has argued that ethnic Jews, not Gentiles, are the subject of the broader context of Rom 2:17–3:20: "The Romans 2:25–29 passage does not teach that Gentiles become spiritual Jews," he says.[16] "Paul concluded his discussion of the Gentiles in Romans 2:16. In Rom 2:17–30 he considers the Jewish question."[17]

Fruchtenbaum also argues that Paul, in Rom 2:25–29, is making a distinction between believing and nonbelieving ethnic Jews: "He [Paul] distinguishes between Jews who do not believe and Jews who do believe. This is not a distinction between Jews and Gentiles, nor between Israel and the church, but between the remnant and the nonremnant—between the Jewish believer and the Jewish unbeliever."[18]

Brauch comes to a similar conclusion that there is both an inward and a physical dimension to being a true Jew: "In Romans 2:28–29, he [Paul] argues that there are two kinds of Jews: those who meet only the external requirements (circumcision and physical descent) and those who, in addition, are authentic Jews inwardly, whose circumcision is not only external but also of the heart, worked 'by the Spirit.'"[19] Thus, Paul's point in 2:28–29 is probably similar to that of Rom 9:6, in which it is stated that true Israelites are ethnic Jews who believe in Christ.

Determining whether Paul is expanding the concept of *Jew* to include Gentiles in Rom 2:28–29 is difficult. In the immediate context of Rom 2:26–27, Paul is discussing the "uncircumcised man" (i.e., Gentile) who keeps God's law. Thus, there appears to be a connection between this law-keeping Gentile and the inward Jew Paul mentions in 2:28–29. On the other hand, as Fruchtenbaum has pointed out, the overall discussion of Rom 2:17–3:20 is specifically addressed to those who "bear the name 'Jew'" (2:17). Paul, then, may be using the example of law-keeping Gentiles to show that circumcision alone does not make one right with God. Gentiles, thus, may be introduced for comparison and not redefinition.[20] Ladd may be correct, then,

---

[16] A. G. Fruchtenbaum, "Israel and the Church," in *Issues in Dispensationalism*, ed. W. R. Willis and J. R. Masters (Chicago: Moody, 1994), 128.

[17] Ibid.

[18] Ibid.

[19] W. C. Kaiser Jr., P. H. Davids, F. F. Bruce, and M. T. Brauch, *Hard Sayings of the Bible* (Downers Grove, IL: InterVarsity, 1996), 635. See also C. A. Blaising and D. L. Bock, *Progressive Dispensationalism: An Up-to-Date Handbook of Contemporary Dispensational Thought* (Wheaton, IL: Bridgepoint, 1993), 269; W. MacDonald, *Believer's Bible Commentary* (Nashville: Thomas Nelson, 1995), 1685.

when he states, "He [Paul] may not in these verses [Rom 2:28–29] have Gentiles in view."[21]

I lean toward Fruchtenbaum's understanding that the true Jew is the ethnic Jew who has believed, much like the "Israel of God" of Gal 6:16 refers to ethnic Jews who have trusted in Christ by faith alone. Cranfield, though, has offered what could be considered a third and mediating approach to this passage. He asserts that Rom 2:28–29 may be applying the term *Jew* to believing Gentiles, but he denies that any supersessionist conclusions can be drawn from this finding. To Cranfield, "Paul is in some sense denying the name of Jew to those who are outwardly Jews . . . and at the same time according it to those who are secret, inward Jews but not outward Jews at all."[22]

Thus, I grant that it is possible but not likely that there may be a sense in which believing Gentiles are considered Jews. But even if this were so, Cranfield is correct that these verses cannot be taken to mean that "the Christian church alone is the heir to all the promises" or that Christianity is "the new Israel of God." He notes, "These verses [2:28–29] do not stand by themselves, and if they are to be interpreted in the light of 3.1–4 and also of 9.1–11.36, they can hardly bear this meaning." Thus, for Cranfield, "the true explanation" of these verses is that "Paul is using 'Jew' in a special limited sense to denote the man who in his concrete human existence stands by virtue of his faith in a positive relation to the ongoing purpose of God in history."These verses, however, as Cranfield says, "should not be taken as implying that those who are Jews only outwardly are excluded from the promises."[23]

First Peter 2:9–10

First Peter 2:9–10 applies a cluster of Israelite terms to Peter's readers. Supersessionists interpret this as evidence that the church is now the new Israel. Yet there are several reasons this text does not support supersessionism. First, while I respect the majority opinion of today that Peter was addressing Jews and Gentiles in his letter, I do not take it as a given that Peter was addressing Gentile believers in his epistle. Hiebert points out that "Origen and many others, saw them [Peter's audience] as Jewish Christians."[24]

---

[20]C. B. Hoch Jr., *All Things New: The Significance of Newness for Biblical Theology* (Grand Rapids: Baker, 1995), 288.

[21]G. E. Ladd, "Historic Premillennialism," in *The Meaning of the Millennium: Four Views*, ed. R. G. Clouse (Downers Grove, IL: InterVarsity, 1977), 25.

[22]C. E. B. Cranfield, *A Critical and Exegetical Commentary on the Epistle to the Romans*, ICC 1 (Edinburgh: T&T Clark, 1975), 1:176.

[23]Ibid.

These "others" include Calvin, Bengel, Weiss, Alford, English, and Wuest.[25] In its introductory comments on 1 Peter, the *Ancient Christian Commentary on Scripture* states, "With few exceptions, the Fathers believed that this letter was written by the apostle Peter and sent to Jewish Christians in the Diaspora."[26] It then lists Eusebius of Caesarea, Didymus, Andreas, and Oecumenius as those who held this view of the Jewish audience of 1 Peter.[27]

Peter's letter was written to "sojourners of dispersion" (1:1), which, as Hiebert points out, "has a strong Jewish coloring."[28] Some have argued that the use of the Septuagint in the OT quotations and the thrust of Peter's argument would make Peter's letter largely unintelligible to Peter's readers if they included Gentiles.[29] Plus, Paul points out that Peter was specifically the apostle to the circumcision (see Gal 2:7–8).

Many have pointed out that parts of 1 Peter could be referring to Gentiles.[30] Yet to dismiss the idea that Peter may have been writing specifically to Jewish Christians is not warranted. It is a possible view. Why is it unreasonable to think that the apostle to the Jews wrote a letter to Jews? If Peter did write to Jewish Christians, he is addressing the "Israel of God," the same group Paul was referring to in Gal 6:16—the remnant of Israel made of ethnic Jews who placed their faith in Christ by faith alone.

Yet even if 1 Peter was written with Gentiles in mind, as many believe, it is far from a given that Peter was identifying believing Gentiles as "Israel." As Glenny points out, "Many of the arguments used to suggest the church is a new Israel replacing the nation are based on parallels and correspondences between the two; the obvious error is the belief that such a correspondence or parallel proves identity."[31]

If Gentiles are in view, 1 Pet 2:9–10 may show that the concept of the people of God has been broadened to include Gentiles. And as the chosen people of God, the church has a role and function in the present age that is similar to

---

[24]D. E. Hiebert, *1 Peter* (Chicago: Moody, 1992), 24. Hiebert himself believes that 1 Peter was written to both Jews and Gentiles.

[25]Ibid., 31., n. 79.

[26]G. Bray, ed., "James, 1–2 Peter, 1–3 John, Jude," ACCS 11 (Downers Grove, IL: InterVarsity, 2000), 65.

[27]Ibid.

[28]Hiebert, *1 Peter*, 24.

[29]Ibid. Weiss is one representative of this view.

[30]For a list of these arguments with scriptural support see Hiebert, *1 Peter*, 24.

[31]W. E. Glenny, "The Israelite Imagery of 1 Peter 2," in *Dispensationalism, Israel and the Church: The Search for Definition*, ed. C. A. Blaising and D. L. Bock (Grand Rapids: Zondervan, 1992), 183, n. 126.

[32]Saucy argues, "That many aspects of Israel are applicable to the 'people of God' in the church cannot be denied. The salvation purpose of God is presently being carried out through the church." Saucy, "Israel and the Church," 248.

that of Israel in the OT.[32] So in this sense, there is significant continuity between national Israel and the church. That the church now replaces Israel, however, is not a necessary conclusion. As Hillyer states,

> God's chosen people are no longer confined to the physical descendants of Abraham, the nation of Israel, but by divine decision they are now the body of Christian believers. It is not that ethnic Israel has been irrevocably rejected by God and replaced by Gentiles (Paul makes that clear in Rom. 9–11); rather, for both Jew and Gentile the divine blessings to God's people are available through Jesus the Messiah.[33]

Second, I am not convinced that the application of "Israel" terminology to Gentiles means that Gentiles are now a part of Israel. There are occasions in Scripture in which "Israel" imagery is applied to non-Israelites without these non-Israelites becoming Israel. Isaiah 19:24–25, for instance, predicts that Egypt would someday be called "my people." Yet the context makes clear that Egypt is distinct from Israel since Egypt is mentioned alongside "Israel my inheritance." So even in the OT it was predicted that non-Israelites would someday carry some of the titles of Israel without becoming identified as Israel. As Saucy writes, "Although the term 'people of God' begins with the nation of Israel and has the predominant meaning throughout the Old Testament, there is already in the prophets the anticipation that some outside of Israel will come under its purview."[34] Isaiah 19:24–25 shows, then, that it is possible for non-Jewish groups to have "Israel" imagery applied to them without these groups becoming identified as Israel.[35]

Finally, although Israelite imagery is used for Peter's readers, there is no reference to them being "Israel."[36] Thus, I agree with Michaels when he

---

[33]N. Hillyer, *1 and 2 Peter, Jude*, NIBCNT (Peabody, MA: Hendrickson, 1992), 70. E. A. Blum writes that 1 Pet 2:9–10 "does not mean that the church is Israel or even that the church replaces Israel in the plan of God. Romans 11 should help us to guard against that misinterpretation." E. A. Blum, "1 Peter," *EBC* 12 (Grand Rapids: Zondervan, 1981), 231.

[34]Saucy, *The Case for Progressive Dispensationalism*, 188.

[35]See ibid.

[36]Richardson writes, "In spite of the many attributes, characteristics, privileges and prerogatives of the latter [Israel] which are applied to the former [Church], the Church is not called Israel in the NT." P. Richardson, *Israel in the Apostolic Church* (Cambridge: Cambridge University Press, 1969), 7.

[37]J. R. Michaels, *1 Peter*, WBC 49 (Waco, TX: Word, 1988), 107. Emphases in original. Achtemeier states that it is difficult to prove the relationship between Israel and the church from 1 Peter: "The absence in the letter of any discussion of the relationship between Christian and Jewish communities makes it impossible to determine how the author understood that relationship. . . . That the author is steeped in OT language and the traditions of Israel is evident; how he understands the present status remains unknown." P. J. Achtemeier, *1 Peter: A Commentary on First Peter* (Minneapolis: Fortress, 1996), 167.

says, "Nowhere in 1 Peter are the readers addressed as a *new* Israel or a *new* people of God, as if to displace the Jewish community."[37]

What does 1 Pet 2:9–10 teach about Israel and the church if Gentiles are in view? Glenny has offered an understanding of 1 Pet 2:9–10 that may do justice to the significant continuity between Israel and the church while avoiding the step of identifying the church as Israel. For Glenny, there is "a divinely ordained pattern between Israel and the church (as the people of God)."[38] Peter, then, according to Glenny, uses OT texts that described Israel's relationship with God as a pattern for God's relationship with the church under the new covenant. He does this without identifying the church as Israel:

> Peter is teaching that the church represents a pattern and thus is a fulfillment of the promises made to Israel in these Old Testament passages. He is not saying the church equals Israel; instead he is saying that as Israel in the Old Testament was the people of God by virtue of its relationship with Yahweh, so the church is the present people of God by virtue of its relationship with Jesus, the elect Messiah of God. . . . Peter uses Israel's historical situation as the people of God as a pattern of his recipients' relationship with God; he is not saying that the church is a new Israel replacing the nation.[39]

Glenny, therefore, does hold to some form of a typological connection between the Testaments, but he rejects supersessionist typology. There could be a typological connection between Israel and the church, but the connection is not that of the church superseding Israel.

Galatians 3:7,29

In Gal 3:7, Paul states that those who exercise faith are "Abraham's sons." Galatians 3:29 also declares that those who belong to Christ are "Abraham's seed" and "heirs according to promise." Supersessionists have argued that since Gentiles are sons and descendants of Abraham they must also be spiritual Jews. Nonsupersessionists, however, have contested this understanding. They have done so by challenging the idea that being a "son" or "seed" of Abraham automatically makes one a Jew. Saucy, for example, asserts that Abraham's fatherhood goes beyond being the father of ethnic Israel since he trusted God before he was recognized as a Hebrew:

> If Abraham were merely the father of Israel, we would have to conclude that the Gentiles who are now a part of this seed are therefore a part of Israel. But according to the New Testament, Abraham is more than that; he is portrayed as the father of both the people of Israel and of the Gentiles.

---

[38]Glenny, "The Israelite Imagery of 1 Peter 2," 180.
[39]Ibid., 183.

> On the grounds that Abraham was a believer before he was circumcised—
> that is, before he was recognized as a Hebrew—the Apostle Paul declared
> him to be "the father of all who believe but have not been circumcised . . .
> and . . . also the father of the circumcised" (Ro 4:9–12; cf. v. 16).[40]

For Saucy, the calling of Gentiles does not mean there is a new spiritual Israel: "The fact that the true seed of Abraham includes both Jews and Gentiles does not rule out a continuing distinction for Israel in the New Testament. Nor should the calling of the Gentiles as the seed of Abraham be construed as the formation of a 'new spiritual Israel' that supersedes the Old Testament nation of Israel."[41]

Nonsupersessionists have also argued that the concept of "seed of Abraham" is used in several different ways in the NT. Fruchtenbaum, for example, lists four senses of "seed of Abraham." First, he says it can refer to those who are biological descendants of Abraham. Second, it can refer to the Messiah, who is the unique individual seed of Abraham. Third, Fruchtenbaum says it can refer to the righteous remnant of Israel (cf. Isa 41:8 with Rom 9:6). Fourth, it can be used in a spiritual sense for believing Jews and Gentiles (Gal 3:29).[42] It is context that determines which sense is in mind.

In this last sense—the spiritual sense—believing Gentiles are the seed of Abraham. Feinberg distinguishes between a physical sense and a spiritual sense of being a seed of Abraham. According to him, nonsupersessionists hold that "no sense (spiritual especially) is more important than any other, and that no sense cancels out the meaning and implications of the other senses."[43] Thus, the application of the titles "Abraham's sons" or "seed of Abraham" to believing Gentiles does not mean believing Gentiles are spiritual Jews or part of Israel.[44]

Romans 4:11–12 indicates that Abraham is the father of both the uncircumcised (non-Jews) and the circumcised (Jews) who believe. Thus, being related to Abraham by faith does not automatically make one a Jew. Plus, while much emphasis in Scripture is on the physical seed of Abraham through Isaac and Jacob (Jews), not all descendants of Abraham were Jews. Ishmael was the eldest son of Abraham by Hagar. Ishmael was a blessed descendant of Abraham but was not a Jew.

---

[40]Saucy, *The Case for Progressive Dispensationalism*, 50.

[41]Ibid.

[42]See Fruchtenbaum, *Israelology*, 702.

[43]J. S. Feinberg, "Systems of Discontinuity," in *Continuity and Discontinuity*, 73.

[44]Fruchtenbaum states, "What replacement theologians need to prove their case is a statement in Scripture that all believers are of 'the seed of Jacob.' Such teaching would indicate that the church is spiritual Israel or that Gentile Christians are spiritual Jews." Fruchtenbaum, "Israel and the Church," 126–27.

UNITY BETWEEN JEWS AND GENTILES

Supersessionists believe that unity between Jews and Gentiles means the church is the new Israel and that there is no future role for national Israel. Ephesians 2:11–22 and Rom 11:17–24 are important passages in this regard. If believing Jews and Gentiles are united, in what sense can there be a future distinct role for believing Jews?

Ephesians 2:11–22

In my view, Eph 2:11–22 is not evidence for supersessionism. Some have tried to conclude that since the former condition of Gentiles was that of being "excluded from the citizenship of Israel" this means believing Gentiles must now become Israel or be considered Israelites. Waldron made this point: "I hope the significance of this conclusion is obvious. Just in case it is not, let me spell it out. Gentiles are made near to, or in other words, made participants in 'the commonwealth of Israel.' Now if they are made near to—participants in—the commonwealth of Israel, this means (it seems clear to me) that they are Israelites."[45] According to Waldron, if Gentiles were once excluded from the commonwealth of Israel, then their being "made near" Israel or their being "made participants in 'the commonwealth of Israel'" must mean that believing Gentiles are Israelites.

This logic is not convincing for several reasons. First, while Eph 2:13,17 indicates that the Gentiles are "made near" and are no longer excluded from the "commonwealth of Israel," this does not necessarily mean that believing Gentiles become Israel. Being near to something does not mean assumption of its identity. Paul's discussion of Gentiles going from being "far off" to "near" is reliant on Isa 58:18–19. Thielman observes that Paul is relying on Isaiah's eschatological expectation in which "the nations would come from afar and join Israel in the worship of the one 'who created the heavens, . . . who fashioned the earth and made it' (Isa. 45:18)."[46] The fact that Gentiles have gone from being "far off" to "near," or from "excluded" to "not excluded," does not mean they have assumed the identity of Israel.

Second, if Paul wanted to say that believing Gentiles were now part of Israel, he could have said that, but he did not. Paul will say that God has made both believing Jews and Gentiles "one" (2:14) and "one new man," but he carefully avoids the title "Israel." As Hoch writes, "It seems important to notice carefully what Paul does and does not say. He does not say

---

[45]S. E. Waldron, *MacArthur's Millennial Manifesto: A Friendly Response* (Owensboro, KY: Reformed Baptist Academic Press, 2008), 63.

[46]F. S. Thielman, "Ephesians," in *Commentary on the New Testament Use of the Old Testament*, ed. G. K. Beale and D. A. Carson (Grand Rapids: Baker, 2007), 818.

that the Gentiles are incorporated into the old *politeia* ["commonwealth"] of Israel or into the new *politeia* of Israel or into a new spiritual Israel. He does say that both Jews and Gentiles are created into 'one new man.'"[47]

Perkins, too, disagrees with the idea that Ephesians 2 means believing Gentiles have become part of Israel. As she observes, "Despite the Jewish cast to its depiction of the Gentiles, the 'now' does not speak of Gentiles joining the commonwealth of Israel."[48] She also says, "Although verse 12 might suggest that the Gentiles are to be brought into Israel, Ephesians avoids claiming that the church has replaced Israel."[49]

Third, unlike Israel this "one new man" is a NT organism. It is a soteriological community that is built on the foundation of the NT apostles and prophets and Jesus the cornerstone (see Eph 2:19–20). Israel on the other hand is not a NT entity. It is rooted deeply in the OT with a background going back to Abraham and the promise of the Abrahamic covenant in Genesis 12.

Fourth, in the broader context of Ephesians 2–3, Paul's use of *syn* compounds rules out the idea that Paul is speaking of some "incorporation into Israel" theology. As Hoch explains,

> The key to the sense in which Gentiles are made near to Israel is the preposition suvn. Paul uses six σύν compounds to express the relationship of Gentiles to Jews/Israel in these two chapters: συμπολῖται, "fellow citizens" (2:19); συναρμολογουμένη, "joined together" (2:21); συνοικοδομεῖσθε, "built together" (2:22); συγκληρονόμα, "heirs together" (3:6); σύσσωμα, "members together of one body" (3:6); and συμμέτοχα, "sharers together" (3:6).[50]

Paul's use of these six *syn* compounds indicates that "the Gentiles are brought near to Israel in Christ to share with Israel in its covenants, promise, hope, and God. They do not become Israel; they *share* with Israel."[51] Thielman points out that "the piling up of words compounded with *syn* ('with') shows . . . the equal footing that Gentiles and Jews now have together in the people of God."[52] Ephesians 2–3 emphasizes a *sharing with* Israel and not an *incorporation into* Israel. If Paul were referring to some incorporation

---

[47]C. B. Hoch Jr., "The Significance of the *Syn-Compounds* for Jew-Gentile Relationships in the Body of Christ," *JETS* 25 (1982): 179. Emphases in original.

[48]P. Perkins, *Ephesians*, ANTC (Nashville: Abingdon, 1997), 69.

[49]Ibid., 77.

[50]C. B. Hoch Jr., "The New Man of Ephesians 2," in Blaising and Bock, *Dispensationalism, Israel and the Church*, 113.

[51]Ibid. Emphasis in original.

[52]Thielman, "Ephesians," 819.

of the Gentiles into Israel, he probably would have used "*eis*-compounds, not *syn*-compounds."[53] As Hoch states, Paul is not "presenting some kind of incorporation-into-Israel theology for Gentiles."[54] Instead, Gentiles are now said to *share* with Israel in Israel's covenants and promises: "The key to Paul's theology is not Gentile incorporation into Israel, but a new sharing with Israel in Israel's prior covenants and promise."[55]

Lincoln also points out that the previous unfavorable position of the Gentiles has now "been reversed not by their being incorporated into Israel, even into a renewed Israel of Jewish Christians, but by their being made members of a new community which transcends the categories of Jew and Gentiles, an entity which is a new creation."[56]

In the realm of salvation blessings and status before God, Gentiles are equal with believing Jews. However, salvific unity between Jews and Gentiles does not erase ethnic or functional distinctions between the two groups: "Paul's comments in Ephesians, however, exclude any salvific priority for Israel in the ecclesiological structure of the new man. . . . However, while there is no longer *salvific* advantage, there is still an *ethnic* distinction between Jews and Gentiles. Paul continues to speak of Jews and Gentiles as distinct ethnic groups in his letters (Rom. 1:16; 9:24; 1 Cor. 1:24; 12:13; Gal. 2:14, 15)."[57]

This belief that salvific equality does not rule out functional distinctions is seen in other examples. According to Gal 3:29 men and women share equally in salvation blessings, but the Bible still teaches that men and women have different roles. Thus, in the case of men and women, salvific unity does not nullify functional distinctions. The same is true for elders and nonelders in a church. Both are equal and share the same spiritual blessings, but elders have a distinct role in the plan of God. The same distinction could be made between parents and children. Even within the Trinity, there is an equality of essence yet different roles between the Father, Son, and Spirit. Equality in essence and spiritual blessings does not nullify functional distinctions.

---

[53]Hoch, "The Significance of the *Syn-Compounds* for Jew-Gentile Relationships in the Body of Christ," 179. Hoch also writes, "Paul, however, cannot be arguing for a Gentile incorporation into Israel similar to Jewish proselytizing. Paul never writes of Gentiles as 'in Israel' in any of his letters." Hoch, "The New Man of Ephesians 2," 113.

[54]Ibid., 108. Saucy writes, "The emphasis is not on the nation of Israel as such and the incorporation of the Gentiles into that nation. Rather, the emphasis is on Israel's privileges compared with the place of the Gentiles." Saucy, *The Case for Progressive Dispensationalism*, 159.

[55]Hoch, "The New Man of Ephesians 2," 108.

[56]A. T. Lincoln, "The Church and Israel in Ephesians 2," *CBQ* 49 (1987): 615.

[57]Hoch, "The New Man of Ephesians 2," 118. Emphases in original.

In a real sense, then, believing Jews and Gentiles become the one people of God in regard to salvation. Jews and Gentiles are equal before God. But this unity does not rule out a functional role for national Israel in the future. As Saucy writes, "The union of Jew and Gentile in the church does not rule out the possibility of *functional* distinctions between Israel and the other nations in the future—in the same way that there are functional distinctions among believers in the church today amid spiritual equality."[58]

To sum up, Gentiles are brought near to Israel and Israel's covenants, promises, hope, and God, but they "do not become Israel; they *share* with Israel."[59] Although the Gentiles now share with the Jews, "nothing is said about Gentiles' becoming Jews or part of Israel unless we redefine 'Israel,' which is difficult to justify exegetically."[60] Taylor is correct that "superficial logic" characterizes the supersessionist approach to Ephesians 2 since the supersessionist view does not take into account that unity in salvation does not nullify historical differences:

> Superficial logic has continued to argue that there is no more uniqueness for the Jew and physical Israel. Since it is said Christ has broken down the barrier between Jew and Gentile [Eph. 2:11–18], Israel's election is finished. But this is not the logic of the New Testament. Although there is only one way of salvation for both Jew and Gentile, the New Testament teaches that the Jewish people do still have a unique place in the *historical* working out of God's redemption of the world in Christ.[61]

Romans 11:16b–24

Romans 11:16b–24 stresses unity between believing Gentiles and Jews. This text is similar to Ephesians 2 in that it shows a soteriological unity between believing Jews and Gentiles, but it does not indicate that believing Gentiles are incorporated into Israel.

In this passage, Paul speaks of an olive tree, which appears to represent the place of blessing. The root of this olive tree is likely the Abrahamic covenant. The issue here is the relationship Jews and Gentiles have to the Abrahamic covenant. According to 11:17, "some of the branches were broken off." This refers to unbelieving Jews who are removed from the blessings of the Abraham covenant. Believing Gentiles, though, who are represented by the "wild olive branch," have been grafted into "the rich root of the olive tree." So believing Gentiles are now in the place of blessing as they

---

[58]Saucy, *The Case for Progressive Dispensationalism*, 167. Emphasis in original.

[59]Hoch, "The New Man of Ephesians 2," 113. Emphasis in original.

[60]Saucy, *The Case for Progressive Dispensationalism*, 156.

[61]H. Taylor, "The Continuity of the People of God in Old and New Testaments," *Scottish Bulletin of Evangelical Theology* 3 (1985): 14–15. Emphasis in original.

are benefiting from the Abrahamic covenant. In 11:18, Paul warns Gentile Christians not to be arrogant against the natural branches (Jews) since "God has the power to graft them in again" (11:23), which will clearly be the case according to 11:26, when Paul predicts the salvation of the nation Israel.

It is difficult to see how this passage supports replacement theology. While both the "natural" and "wild" branches have a relationship to the same olive tree, the branches are still distinguished. It is not as though the "wild" branches become "natural" branches. So even within the illustration believing Jews and Gentiles are distinguished. Again, we see the twin concepts of unity and diversity in operation at the same time. Jews and Gentiles are unified in their participation in the Abrahamic covenant but diverse in that Jews and Gentiles do not become the same entity. Das states,

> Certainly gentiles enjoy Israel's privileges as members of God's new people. Gentiles benefit from being grafted onto the olive tree of Israel's gracious heritage. Both believing Israel and the gentiles are together branches on *the same* tree, but instead of Israel losing its identity to the Church, a "third" entity, the gentiles must recognize their dependence upon historic, ethnic Israel's heritage. Although gentiles are benefiting from that heritage, they remain wild branches benefiting *as gentiles*.[62]

The Abrahamic covenant comes through God's promise to Abraham and the "great nation" that would come from him (Gen 12:2). It was also predicted that Gentiles would participate in the blessings of this covenant: "And all the peoples on earth will be blessed through you" (12:3). The roots of the Abrahamic covenant are inherently Jewish, but from its inception, God intended for Gentiles to participate in the covenant. This is what is happening today as believing Gentiles now partake of the Abrahamic covenant (Gal 3:7–8,29). Thus the question is, How does Gentile participation in the Abrahamic covenant, something that was predicted in the OT, mean that national Israel is no longer related to the Abrahamic covenant? This logic does not follow. Paul specifically states that God will graft Israel in again to the rich root of the Abrahamic covenant. This will take place with the second coming (Rom 11:26).

Believing Gentiles are now related to Israel's covenants. Also, believing Jews and Gentiles compose the one people of God in a salvation sense.[63] But this truth does not rule out a future role for national Israel or indicate that the church is now Israel. As House states, "Paul speaks of the grafting

---

[62]A. A. Das, *Solving the Romans Debate* (Minneapolis: Fortress, 2007), 245.
[63]See Moo, *The Epistle to the Romans*, 709.

of the Gentiles into the natural branch (Rom. 11:16–24) but this should not be seen as a diminishing of the promises to Israel but the enhancement of the Gentile position."[64]

To summarize, Eph 2:11–22 and Rom 11:16–24 describe the unity that exists between believing Jews and Gentiles. But unity of Jews and Gentiles in salvation can exist alongside a unique functional role for national Israel. Bock has pointed out that nonsupersessionists view the incorporation language in the NT texts as meaning that there is soteriological unity for Jews and Gentiles in Christ. In addition, "they also acknowledge that these texts have a connection to the promises of the Old Testament, but they argue that this affirmation does not need to eliminate how ethnic Israel has promises to her fulfilled."[65] This approach does justice to the "unity" texts of the NT and the "future for Israel" passages found in both the OT and NT.

New Covenant Fulfilled with the Church

Supersessionists claim that the application of the new covenant to the church in Heb 8:8–13, shows that the church supersedes national Israel. The argument goes like this: If the new covenant was originally made with Israel, and if the new covenant is now said to be fulfilled with the church, then the church must be the new Israel, and the nation Israel is no longer related to the new covenant. This argument, however, is unconvincing for several reasons.

First, while the church is clearly participating in the new covenant, the NT itself links the future salvation of Israel with the new covenant as well. With Rom 11:26, Paul states, "All Israel will be saved." Then he quotes Rom 11:27 as support for the salvation of national Israel: "And this will be My covenant with them when I take away their sins." Paul links the nation Israel's salvation with at least one, if not two, new covenant texts in the OT. According to Kaiser, Rom 11:27 "is nothing less than a reference to the New Covenant of Jer 31:31–34."[66] Murray agrees: "The first part of the quotation is from Isaiah 59:20, 21 and the last part derived from Jeremiah 31:34. There should be no question but Paul regards these Old Testament passages as applicable to the restoration of Israel."[67] Thus, while the church is related to the new covenant, at its salvation Israel will be also. Käsemann

---

[64]H. W. House, "The Church's Appropriation of Israel's Blessings," in *Israel, the Land and the People: An Evangelical Affirmation of God's Promises*, ed. H. W. House (Grand Rapids: Kregel, 1998), 81.

[65]D. L. Bock, "Summary Essay," in *Three Views on the Millennium and Beyond*, ed. D. L. Bock (Grand Rapids: Zondervan, 1999), 291.

[66]Kaiser, "Kingdom Promises as Spiritual and National," 302.

[67]Murray, *The Epistle to the Romans*, 2:98–99. According to Diprose, Rom 11:27 "makes clear that Paul is thinking about Israel's entrance into the new covenant as envisaged by Jeremiah (31:34)." Diprose, *Israel in the Development of Christian Thought*, 151.

rightly states that "Christianity is already living in the new covenant" while "Israel will begin to do so only at the parousia."[68] Application of the new covenant to the church does not cancel a fulfillment of the covenant with national Israel.[69] Pannenberg describes this both-and approach to the new covenant: "The cup that is handed round at the Lord's Supper gives a share in this covenant. This means that the church, which in table fellowship with Jesus is made one as his body, shares already in the new covenant that will be granted to Israel as a whole (Rom. 11:26) when Christ returns as the eschatological Redeemer whose coming Israel awaits."[70]

Pannenberg is correct when he states that there needs to be a balanced approach between viewing the church's current relationship to the new covenant and Israel's promised relationship to the covenant:

> Christian theology today ought to handle the church's relation to the concept of the elect people of God with the openness that we find in Paul's statements on the theme. Undoubtedly the church must understand itself as the people of the new covenant that was concluded in the blood of Jesus Christ and that is renewed at every celebration of the Lord's Supper. But it should not on this account contrast itself as the "new" people of God with the old Jewish people of God as though the latter had been set aside with the old covenant. Jeremiah 31:31–32 and Isaiah in 59:21 promise the new covenant not to another people but to Israel as the eschatological renewal and fulfillment of its covenant relationship with its God.[71]

Second, like other aspects of eschatology, the new covenant also has an "already/not yet" aspect to it in regard to the manner of its fulfillment. Spiritual aspects of the new covenant such as forgiveness of sins and the indwelling Holy Spirit are being realized in the present era while the physical blessings of the covenant await a future fulfillment with national Israel. As Ware writes, "The fulfillment of God's new covenant thus should not now be viewed as an all-or-nothing affair. Rather, it is best seen as partially realized now (spiritual aspects of forgiveness and the indwelling Spirit for

---

[68]E. Käsemann, *Commentary on Romans*, trans. and ed. G. W. Bromiley (Grand Rapids: Eerdmans, 1980), 314.

[69]Those who hold this view include the following: D. Larsen, *Jews, Gentiles and the Church: A New Perspective on History and Prophecy* (Grand Rapids: Discovery House, 1995), 33; B. A. Ware, "The New Covenant and the People(s) of God," in *Dispensationalism, Israel and the Church*, 92–93; D. K. Campbell, "The Church in God's Prophetic Program," in *Essays in Honor of J. Dwight Pentecost*, ed. S. D. Toussaint and C. H. Dyer (Chicago: Moody, 1986), 149; Saucy, *The Case for Progressive Dispensationalism*, 135.

[70]W. Pannenberg, *Systematic Theology* (Grand Rapids: Eerdmans, 1998), 3:473.

[71]Ibid., 3:477.

all covenant participants) and later to be realized in its completeness (when all Israel is saved and restored to its land)."[72]

This application of only the spiritual blessings of the new covenant to the church today is evidence that the church has not replaced Israel. The new covenant promises, as found in the OT, speak of both physical and spiritual blessings. If the church inherits the new covenant in Israel's place, then it could be expected that both the spiritual and physical blessings of the new covenant will be applied to the church. But they are not. Only the spiritual blessings of the new covenant are applied to the church by the NT. As Saucy explains,

> If the New Testament does view the church as a new, reconstituted Israel, as is so often claimed, why are none of the new covenant blessings regarding Israel's restoration and exaltation ever applied by way of "reinterpretation" to the church? It would seem reasonable that if the church is a new "spiritual Israel" and Israel as an ethnic people or nation is outmoded, we might expect to find some of Israel's material blessings reinterpreted and applied by the apostles to the church. The absence of any application of the material blessings—many of which were directly related to the nation Israel—leads to the conclusion that the apostles did not intend to teach that the church was fulfilling the new covenant in the place of Israel.[73]

Another factor is that the new covenant promises addressed to Israel in the OT were never stated in such a way that they excluded the participation of other groups. As Saucy explains, "The fact that the prophetic statements are addressed only to Israel cannot logically be understood to *exclude* others from participating even though they are not a part of Israel. The texts never say that the covenant would relate only to Israel and not to others."[74] Isaiah 52:15 states that the Servant "will sprinkle many nations" with His sacrificial death. Ware claims that Isa 55:3 suggests the new covenant "extends beyond Israel to the nations." [75] He goes on to say that "the new covenant made with Israel includes a host of Gentile participants, not directly addressed as God's covenant partners."[76] So even in the OT it was predicted that the new covenant would eventually extend to other nations.

---

[72]B. A. Ware, "The New Covenant and the People(s) of God," in *Dispensationalism, Israel and the Church*, 95.

[73]Saucy, *The Case for Progressive Dispensationalism*, 135.

[74]Ibid., 114. Emphasis in original.

[75]Ware, "The New Covenant and the People(s) of God," 72. Isaiah 55:3,5 reads, "I will make an everlasting covenant with you, the promises assured to David. . . . so you will summon a nation you do not know, and nations who do not know you will run to you."

[76]Ibid., 73.

Finally, the context of Hebrews makes it unlikely that the writer is indicating a transfer of the people of God from Israel to the church. Hebrews is mostly concerned with establishing the superiority of Jesus Christ and His ultimate sacrifice. More specifically, in Hebrews 8 the writer of Hebrews is stressing that the superior new covenant has replaced the old covenant. He is not, however, addressing the relationship between Israel and the church. As Diprose writes, "What needs to be stressed is that this is not a case of the Church pretending to supersede the Israel of God, but rather of one (presumably Jewish) Christian seeking to convince his fellow Jews that the new covenant has been established through Jesus and that there is no turning back."[77] Thus, "this book appears irrelevant to the question of the origin of *replacement theology*."[78]

ROMANS 11:26

As shown earlier, supersessionists have offered three explanations for the statement "All Israel shall be saved" in Rom 11:26. These three explanations are not satisfactory. The first view that "Israel" refers to the church is the most problematic of the three supersessionist views and is unlikely. The other 10 references to "Israel" in Romans 9–11 clearly refer to ethnic Israel. It is difficult to view "Israel" in verse 26 as referring to anything other than ethnic Israel. As Murray points out, "It is exegetically impossible to give to 'Israel' in this verse any other denotation than that which belongs to the term throughout this chapter. . . . It is of ethnic Israel Paul is speaking and Israel could not possibly include Gentiles."[79] There simply is not enough reason to believe that Paul is switching to a nonethnic understanding of Israel in Rom 11:26.

The second view, that Rom 11:26 is referring to elect Jews throughout history is more possible than the first view, but it is still unlikely. In a section in which Paul is explaining a glorious truth that ends in a wonderful doxology of praise, it seems unlikely that such an obvious truth that all believing Jews throughout history are saved would be the topic of his discussion. As Nanos states, "This [view] too, is redundant and hardly motivates gentiles to humility. They [Paul's readers] already recognize that

---

[77]Diprose, *Israel in the Development of Christian Thought*, 51.

[78]Ibid., 49–50. Emphasis in original.

[79]Murray, *The Epistle to the Romans*, 2:96. Ladd states, "It is quite impossible in light of the context and the course of Paul's thought in this passage to understand 'all Israel' to refer to the Church." G. E. Ladd, *The Gospel of the Kingdom: Popular Expositions on the Kingdom of God* (Grand Rapids: Eerdmans, 1959), 119. See also M. D. Nanos, *The Mystery of Romans: The Jewish Context of Paul's Letter* (Minneapolis: Fortress, 1996), 275–76; C. E. B. Cranfield, *A Critical and Exegetical Commentary on the Epistle to the Romans*, ICC (Edinburgh: T&T Clark, 1975), 2:576.

Jews who believe in Jesus as the Christ are saved, don't they? What does this position tell us about the 'stumbling' of Israel?"[80] To claim that the "all Israel" who will be saved is the trickling in of believing Jews throughout history hardly seems like something connected with a "mystery" (Rom 11:25) or something that is the subject of a great doxology (Rom 11:33–36). Morris asserts that this second view hardly qualifies as a "mystery" (Rom 11:25): "Now it is no 'mystery' that all the elect, Jews as well as Gentiles, will be saved. Nor is the conversion of a few Jews in each generation such as has happened until now the kind of thing that needs to be the subject of a special revelation."[81]

Paul does stress in Romans 11 that there is a present remnant of Israelites who have believed. This is *one* way that shows God's promises to Israel have not failed.[82] But, as Blaising observes, "The second part of the fulfillment of God's word concerning Israel is . . . the glorious blessing upon Israel nationally."[83]

Although the first aspect of God's faithfulness involves the keeping of a remnant, the second involves the eschatological salvation of all Israel. Paul indicates that there is "a twofold bearing of the word of God on the status of Israel—a present time of hardening in which only a remnant from Israel is saved and then an eschatological salvation of Israel as a whole."[84]

The third supersessionist understanding of Rom 11:26 is that Paul is describing a national salvation of Israel into the church but not a restoration of Israel. This view is stronger than the two previous perspectives. With this understanding, "Israel" is being used in an ethnic sense just like the previous 10 references to "Israel" in Romans 9–11. One may wonder what the difference is between this third supersessionist understanding of Rom 11:26, which sees national Israel undergoing a future salvation, and the nonsupersessionist understanding of this verse. The difference, though, is real. For some supersessionists, Romans 11 affirms a future *en masse* salvation of ethnic Jews, but this salvation involves incorporation into the Christian church. With this approach there will be no special role or function for Israel apart from the church. Nonsupersessionists, on the other hand, go beyond believing in a national *salvation* of the Jews. They believe that Israel will also experience a national *restoration*.

---

[80]Nanos, *The Mystery of Romans*, 256.

[81]L. Morris, *The Epistle to the Romans* (Grand Rapids: Eerdmans, 1988), 421.

[82]Blaising writes, "So the first part of God's word about Israel concerns the present time, and that is the fulfillment of the word that only a remnant would be saved (9:4, 6–12, 27–29; 11:5)." C. A. Blaising, "The Future of Israel as a Theological Question," *JETS* 44 (2001): 437–38.

[83]Ibid., 438.

[84]Ibid.

Is this third supersessionist perspective of Rom 11:26 more correct than the nonsupersessionist understanding? The issue is well stated by Bock: "If Romans 11 affirms a response by the Jewish nation viewed as a whole, then does that suggest a future for Israel as a national structure . . . ? Or does Romans 11 merely affirm that many ethnic Jews will come to faith in the future?"[85]

Romans 11:27 links Israel's salvation with the new covenant promises of the OT that predicted Israel's restoration. Thus, Rom 11:27 ties Israel's salvation with the OT promises of a restoration of Israel to its land. As Kaiser writes, "This [Rom 11:27] is nothing less than a reference to the New Covenant of Jer 31:31–34, which is itself an expansion of the very promises God had made with Abraham and David. Thus, we are back to the promise-doctrine again, which also includes the promise of the land."[86]

If Romans 11 teaches a future salvation of Israel based on OT promises, then why would it not be true that there would also be a restoration of the nation in line with the OT promises? In other words, if Israel's salvation is rooted in OT promises, why then would Israel's promised restoration also not occur? As Bock writes, "If there is a future for ethnic Jews, it raises the likelihood—though it need not guarantee it—that national Israel in the midst of the nations has a future as well."[87] Our conclusion, then, is that Rom 11:26 teaches a future salvation of Israel. When taken into consideration with 11:27, it is consistent with a future restoration of Israel.

New Testament Silence

Supersessionists argue that the NT's silence concerning a national restoration of Israel is proof for supersessionism. This assertion, though, is questionable for several reasons. First, since the NT writers were Jews who were familiar with the OT, there was no need for the OT expectations concerning Israel's future to be repeated.[88] Thus, silence by the NT on a matter discussed in the OT should not be taken to mean that the OT teaching has been dropped or transformed. As Johnson has stated,

> There is no need to repeat what is copiously spread over the pages of the Scriptures. There seems to be lurking behind the demand a false principle, namely, that we should not give heed to the OT unless its content is

---

[85]Bock, "Summary Essay," 292.

[86]W. C. Kaiser Jr., "Kingdom Promises as Spiritual and National," in *Continuity and Discontinuity*, 302.

[87]Bock, "Summary Essay," 297.

[88]See R. L. Saucy, *The Case for Progressive Dispensationalism: The Interface Between Dispensational and Nondispensational Theology* (Grand Rapids: Zondervan, 1993), 250.

repeated in the New. The correct principle, however, is that we should not consider invalid and worthy of discard any of the OT unless we are specifically told to do so in the New, as in the case of the law of Moses (the cultus particularly).[89]

Second, as Blaising has pointed out, the conditions of NT times, particularly that of the presence of Israel in its land, made it unlikely that the NT would explicitly address a future return of Israel to the land:

> Some have asked why the New Testament does not stress a return to the land as the Old Testament prophecies do. We must remember, that at the time the New Testament epistles were written, Jews were living in the land. Although there were still many in the dispersion, nevertheless a sufficient return had taken place to constitute a Jewish political presence in the land of covenant promise. The issue in New Testament writings was not a return to the land (since they were already in the land) but the return of the Messiah and a proper relationship to Him which would guarantee everlasting inheritance in the kingdom of glory which He would establish there, in that land.[90]

Third, and most importantly, the claim that the NT is silent about Israel's restoration is simply not true. Acts 1:6 explicitly states that the apostles expected a restoration of the kingdom to Israel. Other passages like Matt 19:28 also refer to a coming restoration of Israel. Although details of a restoration of Israel are not repeated, it is questionable whether the NT is actually silent about Israel's restoration.

In the late nineteenth century, Peters addressed the claims of some who said that if the NT does not repeat what was in the OT then the OT content must be rejected: "They proceed on the principle that whatever is not distinctively repeated, and in detail given, in the New Test. must be rejected." But Peters countered this by saying, "But we have more than this: we have, as will be shown, confirmatory and express evidence in the New sustaining our position. So clear and decisive is this fact that many of our opponents concede the same to us."[81] I think Peters is correct.

---

[89]S. L. Johnson Jr., "Evidence from Romans 9–11," in *A Case for Premillennialism*, ed. D. K. Campbell and J. L. Townsend (Chicago: Moody, 1992), 223. See also W. C. Kaiser Jr., "The Land of Israel and the Future Return (Zechariah 10:6–12)," in *Israel, the Land and the People: An Evangelical Affirmation of God's Promises*, ed. H. W. House (Grand Rapids: Kregel, 1998), 221–22.

[90]Blaising and Bock, *Progressive Dispensationalism*, 267.

[91]G. N. H. Peters, *The Theocratic Kingdom of Our Lord Jesus, the Christ as Covenanted in the Old Testament* (New York: Funk & Wagnalls, 1884; repr., Grand Rapids: Kregel, 1988), 2:50.

SUMMARY

As a theological position, supersessionism has serious weaknesses. In regard to hermeneutics, the view of NT priority over the OT is flawed. It emasculates the OT's ability to speak to the issues it addresses. In addition, the view that Israel was a type that has been superseded by the superior antitype, the church, is in error. Since the NT affirms a future for the nation Israel, Israel can hardly be superseded. Also, the supersessionist view that OT passages regarding Israel have been fully fulfilled in nonliteral ways is not convincing.

As for theological arguments, supersessionists have failed to show that Israel has been forever rejected by God. They also have not been able to offer a compelling case that the NT calls the church "Israel." Supersessionists have also not shown how salvific unity between Jews and Gentiles rules out a future restoration of the nation Israel since equality in salvation does not rule out functional distinctions. Particularly weak is the argument that Heb 8:8–13 teaches that the church is the new Israel. This passage teaches the superiority of the new covenant over the old covenant, but it is not evidence for supersessionism. Supersessionists have incorrectly asserted that church inclusion into the new covenant means national Israel's exclusion.

The issue of NT silence regarding Israel's restoration is also not a strong point for supersessionism. First, it is questionable whether the NT is actually silent on this issue. According to Acts 1:6, the disciples expected a restoration of national Israel after they received 40 days of kingdom instruction from Jesus. Plus, I do not agree with the assumption that the NT has to repeat the details of the OT expectations in order for these expectations still to be in force.

Overall, the doctrine of supersessionism is unconvincing. I see no evidence that demands this view. Since the OT clearly predicted a restoration of national Israel, the burden of proof is on supersessionists to show that this expectation has been cancelled or transformed. The proof texts, typological connections, and promise-fulfillment schemes offered by supersessionists have not proven this. I conclude, therefore, that supersessionism is not consistent with the biblical witness.

Chapter 14

God's Future Plan for Nations

The debate over the relationship between Israel and the church often focuses on God's plans for a single nation—Israel, and rightly so. But in this chapter, I would like to make some general observations about God's plans for nations in general. If we know what God's plans for nations are, we may be able to draw some implications for Israel as a specific nation. I also want first to make some broad observations about God's future purposes for our planet. So I will start with a discussion of God's future plans for the cosmos, and then I will look at implications concerning God's plans for nations and for Israel as a nation.

Just what are God's ultimate purposes for His creation? Are God's plans primarily spiritual? Or are His purposes to transform every aspect of our current universe including its spiritual, physical, social, and political dimensions? Where do nations and Israel fit into this picture?

Blaising has pointed out that there are essentially two models for approaching eschatology—the Spiritual Vision Model and the New Creation Model.[1] According to Blaising, the Spiritual Vision Model emphasizes the spiritual aspects of God's future plans. This model is influenced by Platonism and its dualistic assumption that the spiritual is of higher value than the physical, which is often viewed as a lower level of reality.[2] With the Spiritual Vision Model, heaven is viewed primarily as a spiritual entity. It is the highest level of ontological reality, the realm of spirit as opposed to base matter. With a spiritual vision approach, heaven is viewed as "the destiny of the saved, who will exist in that nonearthly, spiritual place as spiritual beings engaged eternally in spiritual activity."[3] The Spiritual Vision Model, Blaising argues, is a combination of biblical themes and cultural ideas that were common to the

---

[1]C. A. Blaising, "Premillennialism," in *Three Views on the Millennium and Beyond*, ed. D. L. Bock (Grand Rapids: Zondervan, 1999), 161.

[2]Snyder calls this approach "the kingdom as inner spiritual experience model." "As a distinct model it may be traced to the influence of Platonist and Neoplatonist ideas on Christian thinking and especially to Origen." H. A. Snyder, *Models of the Kingdom* (Eugene, OR: Wipf and Stock, 1991), 42.

[3]Blaising, "Premillennialism," 161.

classical philosophical tradition. The biblical themes the Spiritual Vision Model draws upon include the following:

1. The promise that believers will see God
2. The promise that believers will receive full knowledge
3. The description of heaven as the dwelling place of God
4. The description of heaven as the destiny of the believing dead prior to the resurrection

In addition to the biblical themes, the Spiritual Vision Model also draws upon cultural (Greek) ideas that were common to the classical philosophical tradition:

1. A basic contrast between spirit and matter
2. An identification of spirit with mind or intellect
3. A belief that eternal perfection entails the absence of change

According to Blaising, central to all three of these ideas is "the classical tradition's notion of an ontological hierarchy in which spirit is located at the top of a descending order of being. Elemental matter occupies the lowest place."[4] Thus, heaven is the realm of spirit as opposed to matter. It is a nonearthly spiritual place for spiritual beings who are engaged only in spiritual activity. This heaven is viewed as being free from all change. Eternal life, therefore, is viewed primarily as "cognitive, meditative, or contemplative."[5] The Spiritual Vision Model has led many Christians to view eternal life "as the *beatific vision* of God—an unbroken, unchanging contemplation of the infinite reality of God."[6]

In his book *Models of the Kingdom*, Snyder points out that a purely spiritual view of the kingdom, which he calls "the kingdom as inner spiritual experience model," "may be traced to the influence of Platonist and Neoplatonist ideas on Christian thinking."[7] According to Snyder, this model "draws to some degree on Greek philosophical roots."[8] He also states that "one can sense the Platonism lying behind this model."[9] He then goes on to

---

[4]Ibid.
[5]Ibid.
[6]Ibid., 162.
[7]Snyder, *Models of the Kingdom*, 42.
[8]Ibid., 52.
[9]Ibid.

say, "Historically this model has often been tainted with a sort of Platonic disdain for things material, perhaps seeing the body or matter as evil or at least imperfect and imperfectible. It is thus dualistic, viewing the 'higher' spiritual world as essentially separate from the material world."[10]

The Spiritual Vision Model was inherently linked to allegorical and spiritual methods of interpretation that were opposed to literal interpretation based on historical-grammatical contexts. Blaising also notes that the Spiritual Vision Model "was intimately connected with practices of 'spiritual interpretation' that were openly acknowledged to be contrary to the literal meaning of the words being interpreted."[11] He adds, "The long-term practice of reading Scripture in this way so conditioned the Christian mind that by the late Middle Ages, the spiritual vision model had become an accepted fact of the Christian worldview."[12]

In contrast to the Spiritual Vision Model is the New Creation Model. This model emphasizes the physical, social, political, and geographical aspects of eternal life more so than does the Spiritual Vision Model. It emphasizes a coming new earth, the renewal of life on this new earth, bodily resurrection, and social and political interactions among the redeemed. As Blaising states, "The new creation model expects that the ontological order and scope of eternal life is essentially continuous with that of present earthly life except for the absence of sin and death."[13]

Eternal life with a New Creation Model is an embodied life on earth. This model "does not reject physicality or materiality, but affirms them as essential both to a holistic anthropology and to the biblical idea of a redeemed creation."[14] This approach follows the language of passages like Isaiah 25, 65–66; Revelation 21; and Romans 8—passages that speak of a regenerated earth in which life is largely continuous with our current life but dramatically better because of the reduction and removal of the effects of sin and the curse. This regenerated earth involves matters like nations, kings, economics, culture, and other matters linked to a physical planet.

The New Creation Model appears to have been the primary approach of the church of the late first and early second centuries AD. It was found in apocalyptic and rabbinic Judaism and in second-century Christian writers such as Irenaeus of Lyons. But, as Blaising asserts, the Spiritual Vision

---

[10]Ibid., 54.
[11]Blaising, "Premillennialism," 165.
[12]Ibid.
[13]Ibid., 162.
[14]Ibid.

Model would take over and become "the dominant view of eternal life from roughly the third century to the early modern period."[15]

To summarize, the New Creation Model emphasizes the transformation of all aspects of our world including its physical, social, political, and economic dimensions. As Moore states, "The picture then is not of an eschatological flight from creation but the restoration and redemption of creation with all that entails: table fellowship, community, culture, economics, agriculture and animal husbandry, art, architecture, worship—in short, *life* and that abundantly."[16]

Thus, God is not just interested in the spiritual aspects of man; He is intent on renewing every aspect of our environment on earth. There will be a "regeneration" of the earth (see Matt 19:28 NASB) and a "restoration of all things" (see Acts 3:19–21). A New Creation Model asserts that the eternal state will be much like the world before the fall and will be like what the world would have been if the fall had never happened.

I hold that the New Creation Model is more true to Scripture than the Spiritual Vision Model. God's end-game plan for this world is to restore it to its intended purpose as expressed in Genesis 1–2. Thus, the kingdom of God and its final phase as described in Revelation 21–22 is largely a return to Edenic conditions before the fall of Genesis 3. This restoration includes every aspect of life including its physical, social, political, economic, and spiritual dimensions. The second coming of Jesus will usher in a transformation of society in every area. The kingdom of God is not primarily a spiritual entity, although it certainly includes a spiritual dimension with spiritual qualities (see Rom 14:17). The culmination of the kingdom includes a restoration of the physical, social, political, and economic dimensions as well. Thus, it is legitimate to reject any dualism that emphasizes the spiritual over the physical. That is why I respectfully disagree with Waltke when he states, "The kingdom's character is 'heavenly' and 'spiritual,' not 'earthly' and "political.'"[17] This is a false dichotomy and smacks of Platonism more than the Bible.

IMPLICATIONS OF A NEW CREATION MODEL FOR NATIONS AND ISRAEL

So what are the implications for adopting a New Creation Model? One implication is that we should not assume that physical things are inherently unspiritual. The physical universe God created was deemed "very

---

[15]Ibid., 164.

[16]R. D. Moore, "Personal and Cosmic Eschatology," in *A Theology for the Church*, ed. D. L. Akin (Nashville: B&H, 2007), 859.

[17]B. Waltke, "Kingdom Promises as Spiritual," in *Continuity and Discontinuity: Perspectives on the Relationship Between the Old and New Testaments*, ed. J. S. Feinberg (Wheaton, IL: Crossway, 1988), 270.

good" (Gen 1:31), not something that needed to be escaped or transcended. We should not assume that things like land, temples, and nations are unspiritual. Nor should we think that such things must necessarily be types or pictures of greater spiritual realities in some Platonic fashion. Instead, we view things like geography, land, nations, and other physical matters as essential aspects of our existence. In eternity, we will inhabit a literal new earth in literal physical bodies.

Such an approach has implications for Israel. When we come across passages where God promises physical blessings and a land for Israel, we should not assume that these things are somehow inferior or that they were solely intended as shadows of spiritual blessings to come. Physical blessings are not necessarily antithetical to spiritual blessings. Nor is it true that physical blessings promised in the OT cannot be harmonized with spiritual blessings in the NT. This is not an either-or situation but is often a both-and. Both physical blessings and spiritual blessings can work together in harmony.

Now specifically, what does a New Creation Model mean for nations? The implications here are significant. Nations appear to have a place in God's future plans. Although nations are a postfall development and they often act contrary to God's purposes in this present age, there is no indication that the concept of nations is inherently unspiritual or wrong. As Christopher Wright states, "Although we first meet the nations in the context of the fallenness and arrogance of humanity even after the flood, the Bible does not imply that ethnic or national diversity is in itself sinful or the product of the fall—even if the deleterious effects of strife among nations certainly are."[18]

Nations are a major theme of Scripture. As Wright states, "The nations of humanity preoccupy the biblical narrative from beginning to end." In fact, there is a real sense in which "the conflict of nations mirrors the brokenness of humanity as a whole."[19] Nations, thus, are a major theme of God's redemptive plan. Wright points out that "God's mission is what fills the gap between the scattering of the nations in Genesis 11 and the healing of the nations in Revelation 22." Thus, it is "God's mission in relation to nations" perhaps more than any other theme "that provides the key that unlocks the biblical grand narrative."[20]

---

[18]C. Wright, *The Mission of God: Unlocking the Bible's Grand Narrative* (Downers Grove, IL: InterVarsity, 2006), 455–56.

[19]Ibid., 454.

[20]Ibid., 455.

Scripture states that God created nations. Paul attributes the diversity of nations to the Creator in Acts 17:26: "From one man He has made every nation of men to live all over the earth and has determined their appointed times and the boundaries of where they live". Thus, God made every nation and determines their longevity and boundaries. Nations are also an important part of God's plans and purposes. In the OT God chose a nation, Israel, to be His chosen people (see Deut 7:6–8). Israel's role was to bring blessings to the other nations. This was promised in Gen 12:2–3. God promised that a great nation would come from Abraham (12:2), but He also declared, "And all the peoples on earth will be blessed through you" (12:3). Thus, the purpose of Abraham's blessing and that of the great nation Israel was to bring blessings to the whole world. As Wright states, "Beyond doubt, then, there was a universal purpose in God's election of Abraham, and therefore also a universal dimension to the very existence of Israel. Israel as a people was called into existence because of God's mission to bless the nations and restore his creation."[21] Christensen is correct when he states, "It is clear that 'Israel as a light to the nations' is no peripheral theme within the canonical process. The nations are the matrix of Israel's life, the *raison d'être* of her very existence."[22]

In addition, the OT indicates that God often used nations to fulfill His purposes and even His judgments. God would even use wicked nations for His purposes (see Isa 10:5). Prophetic passages also spoke of coming blessings for the nations. Isaiah 19 promised that someday God would send Egypt a "savior" and a "leader" who will "rescue them" (19:20). Isaiah 19:23–25 then states, "On that day there will be a highway from Egypt to Assyria. Assyria will go to Egypt, Egypt to Assyria, and Egypt will worship with Assyria. On that day Israel will form a triple [alliance] with Egypt and Assyria—a blessing within the land. The LORD of Hosts will bless them, saying, 'Blessed be Egypt My people, Assyria my handiwork, and Israel My inheritance'".

There are several things to note from this passage. First, God has a plan for nations, even specific nations. This passage alone mentions blessings for Egypt, Assyria, and Israel. Second, while most of the attention in the OT is on God's plans for the nation Israel, Israel is not the only nation who will be blessed by God. God mentions Egypt and Assyria as nations that will

---

[21]Ibid., 251.

[22]D. L. Christensen, "Nations," in *Anchor Bible Dictionary*, ed. D. N. Freedman et al. (New York: Doubleday, 1992), 4:1037.

experience His favor. Third, terminology that was used to describe Israel in the OT is also applied to other people groups. Israel is referred to as God's "people" in the OT, but here we see the concept of the people of God also being applied to Egypt in the future. Fourth, we see that even though "Israel" language will be applied to other nations it is not done so at the expense of national Israel's identity. After mentioning "Egypt My people" and "Assyria my handiwork," God mentions "Israel My inheritance." The nations who are blessed are not incorporated into Israel, but they are blessed alongside Israel. Spiritual unity does not cancel national distinctions.

Other passages tell us more about God's plans for nations in the future. Zechariah 14 indicates that when Jesus becomes "king over all the earth" (Zech 14:9), there will be nations. Jerusalem, the capital city of Israel, will be there (14:11). Zechariah 14:17 states that "the families of the earth" will be there. One nation singled out is Egypt (14:18–19). Zephaniah 3:8–10 clearly speaks of a coming judgment and restoration of nations:

> Therefore, wait for Me—this is the LORD's declaration—until the day I rise up for plunder. For My decision is to gather nations, to assemble kingdoms, in order to pour out My indignation on them, all My burning anger; for the whole earth will be consumed by the fire of My jealousy. For I will then restore pure speech to the peoples so that all of them may call on the name of Yahweh and serve Him with a single purpose. From beyond the rivers of Cush My supplicants, My dispersed people, will bring an offering to Me.

This passage indicates a progression in God's plan for the nations. He will "gather nations" and "assemble kingdoms" to pour out His "indignation" upon them. But He will then purify them, and they will serve the Lord "with a single purpose." This even includes Gentiles "beyond the rivers of Cush." Thus, God's plans for the nations include more than judgment. God will also save and restore them.

Perhaps some will say, "Yes, but these are OT passages, and we don't take the OT literally." Or some may say that the promise of God's blessings to nations was entirely fulfilled with the gospel's being taken to the nations (see Matt 28:19; Acts 2:5–13). Yet while I acknowledge and rejoice in the fact that the gospel is being taken to the world, it is difficult to see that the spread of the gospel throughout the world is the final fulfillment of the promises regarding nations. Are the nations of our world joining together "with a single purpose" with purified lips to worship the Lord (see Zeph 3:8–10)? It appears that there is more to God's plans for nations than select members of each nation being saved. The nations of the world as a whole also appear headed for some form of restoration. Romans 11:12 indicates a staged progression in blessings to the Gentiles. The "riches" Gentiles are experiencing now during the state of Israel's "stumbling" will escalate with the "full number" of national Israel's salvation (see Rom 11:26). It may be that the salvation of Israel as a nation has implications for other nations in a positive sense.

Plus, it should be noted that this age before the bodily return of Christ includes persecution at the hands of "kings and governors" (Luke 21:12). These are enemies of the gospel. Also, the nations are currently at war with the Lord. As Psalm 2:1–3 indicates, ""The nations rebel. . . . The kings of the earth take their stand, and the rulers conspire together against the LORD and His Anointed One: 'Let us tear off their chains and free ourselves from their restraints.'" While representatives of every nation come to know the Lord, the nations as a whole do not. They hate the Lord and want to hurt God's people. Revelation 19:15 indicates that at the second coming of Jesus, God's Anointed One (Ps 2:2) will "strike the nations" and rule them with a rod of iron (see Ps 2:8–9). This is a future event.

All authority on heaven and earth has been given to Jesus (Matt 28:18), but the full exercise of that authority awaits the time of His second coming. Matthew 25:31–32 says, "When the Son of Man comes in His glory, and all the angels with Him, then He will sit on the throne of His glory. All the nations will be gathered before Him, and He will separate them one from another". At the time of Jesus' glorious return with His angels, Jesus will sit upon His throne to judge the nations.

In Rev 2:26, Jesus makes a significant promise to Christians at Thyatira: "The one who is victorious and keeps My works to the end: I will give him authority over the nations." Two points should be noted here. First, in this present age of persecution and turmoil, Christians are called to stand fast and overcome. They currently are not ruling with Christ, but when He comes again, they will. When Jesus comes again, one of the things He will have believers do is assist Him in His rule over the nations. Christians do not have authority over the nations now, but they will when Jesus comes again. Second, after Jesus' second coming nations still exist. If there are no nations after Jesus comes, how can He give us authority over the nations?

With the heavenly throne scene of Revelation 4–5, it was revealed to John that Jesus the Lamb had purchased with His blood men "from every tribe and language and people and nation" (Rev 5:9). According to Rev 5:10

these individuals, who represent all ethnic groups, are identified as "a kingdom and priests to our God." But then it is said that "they will reign on the earth" (Rev 5:10). The reign of the saints with the Lamb will take place in the future ("will reign") in accordance with the thousand-year reign of Christ (Rev 20:4–6) that takes place after the second coming of Jesus (see Rev 19:11–21). So the reign of Jesus over the nations with His saints is future from our standpoint.

Nations and ethnic identity are still important in the NT. Revelation 7:9 makes note of the saved from every ethnic group: "After this I looked, and there was a vast multitude from every nation, tribe, people, and language, which no one could number, standing before the throne and before the Lamb. They were robed in white with palm branches in their hands".

The representatives before the throne are *not* people who *formerly* were from every, nation, tribe, people, and language. Their ethnic identity continues even as they compose a unified people of God. Alcorn makes a good observation when he states, "Racial identities will continue (Revelation 5:9; 7:9), and this involves a genetic carryover from the old body to the new."[23] Alcorn also notes that "tribes, peoples, and nations will all make their own particular contribution to the enrichment of life in the New Jerusalem."[24] As a premillennialist, I see a role for nations in the plan of God when Jesus' millennial kingdom begins. But even in the eternal state, it appears there are nations as the following passages from Rev 21:23–24,26; 22:1–2 indicate:

> The city does not need the sun or the moon to shine on it, because God's glory illuminates it, and its lamp is the Lamb. The *nations* will walk in its light, and the kings of the earth will bring their glory into it. . . . They will bring the glory and the honor of the *nations* into it. . . . Then he showed me the river of living water, sparkling like crystal, flowing from the throne of God and of the Lamb down the middle of the broad street [of the city]. On both sides of the river was the tree of life bearing 12 kinds of fruit, producing its fruit every month. The leaves of the tree are for healing the *nations*. (Rev 21:23–24,26; 22:1–2)[25]

---

[23]R. C. Alcorn, *Heaven* (n.p.: Eternal Perspective Ministries, 2004), 290.
[24]Ibid., 380.
[25]The emphases in these three passages are mine.

Sometimes premillennialists will affirm strongly that there are nations in the millennial kingdom, but they oppose the idea of nations in eternity.[26] But these passages in Revelation explicitly state that there will be multiple nations in the eternal state. According to Rev 21:24, there are not only nations; there are also "kings." These appear to be human rulers who have jurisdiction over geographical boundaries. Aune states, "The pilgrimage of the kings of the earth to the new Jerusalem presupposes the existence of the nations of the world and their rulers as well as the location of the eschatological Jerusalem on the earth."[27] The fact that the kings bring "their glory" into the new Jerusalem indicates that the new Jerusalem is not all there is to the new earth. Kings come from their nations to bring contributions to the new Jerusalem. According to Aune, "The bringing of glory and honor to the eschatological city of God is surely a sign of the conversion of the nations and the kings of the earth, reflecting the Jewish hope for the eschatological conversion of the heathen."[28]

Revelation 21:24 also appears to teach that there are economic-social-political dimensions to the nations in the eternal state. Alcorn says, "Surely these kings and culture who bring their 'splendor' and 'glory' into the new world won't start from scratch. They'll bring into the new world a national and personal history, and ethnic identity, and a wealth of customs, art forms, and knowledge."[29]

I grant that there are difficulties with trying to understand what the eternal state will be like, and there is a kernel of truth in Niebuhr's assertion that we should be leery of those who are overly concerned with the furniture of heaven and the temperature of hell, but it appears that there is good reason to think that nations will exist on the new earth. The amillennialist, Hoekema, appeared to teach that there will be multiple nations on the new earth: "From chapter 22 [of Revelation] we learn that on the new earth the

---

[26]Newell claims that premillennialists should not be closed to the idea of nations on the new earth. He states, "We know positively that at least *one* nation and *one* seed, ISRAEL, will belong upon the new earth." He then goes on to say, "Yet, if Israel be the elect nation, the existence of other nations is presupposed." W. R. Newell, *Revelation: A Complete Commentary* (Grand Rapids: Baker, 1935; repr., 1987), 344. D. McDougall also points out that Isa 66:22, an explicit new heavens and new earth passage, mentions the perpetuity of the nation Israel in the new heavens and new earth. He says, "This then testifies to the fact that there will be at least one distinct nation." D. G. McDougall, "Revelation 21:9 to 22:5: Millennium or Eternal State?" (Th.M. thesis, Talbot Theological Seminary, 1969), 168. McDougall also says, "The leaves used for the healing of the nations [in Rev 22:2] are not a major problem, since due to the fact that there will be nations who become a part of the eternal state immediately at the end of the millennium, there must be a means by which they may be spiritually healed for the full and final blessings being ushered in" (177).

[27]D. E. Aune, *Revelation 17–22*, in WBC 52c (Nashville: Thomas Nelson, 1998), 1171.

[28]Ibid, 1173.

29 Alcorn, *Heaven*, 382.

nations will live together in peace." In regard to Rev 21:24,26, Hoekema asked, "Is it too much to say that, according to these verses, the unique contributions of each nation to the life of the present earth will enrich the life of the new earth?" These contributions include "the best products of culture and art which this earth has produced."[30]

Support for the idea of multiple nations in the eternal state may also be found in Rev 21:3: "Look! God's dwelling is with humanity, and He will live with them. They will be His people, and God Himself will be with them and be their God." But "His people" is the translation of *laoi autou*, which is literally "His peoples" (plural). John did not use the singular *laos* ("people") but the plural *laoi* ("peoples"). This mentioning of "peoples" may have reference to the nations and kings of Rev 21:24,26. In his comments on Rev 21:3 Vincent declares, "Notice the plural, *peoples* . . . because many nations shall partake of the fulfillment of the promise." Vincent then links this verse with the mention of plural nations in Rev 21:24.[31] Aune argues that "Rev 21:3 should read [*laoi*] 'peoples,' rather than simply [*laos*] 'people.'"[32] Since Rev 21:24,26 refers to multiple nations and kings, it makes sense that John may be referring to plural "peoples" in Rev 21:3. Keener points out that understanding "peoples" in the plural "may fulfill the promise that many nations will become God's people and He will live among them (Zech 2:11; cf. Isa. 19:25)."[33] Zechariah 2:11 declares, "Many nations will join themselves to the Lord on that day and become My people. I will dwell among you, and you will know that the Lord of Hosts has sent Me to you".

While dogmatism on this issue must be avoided, the possibility and importance of nations on the new earth must be considered. As McDougall has observed, "The reference to nations existing during the eternal state is not inconsistent with any teaching in the Bible."[34] This leads to an important theological implication. *If one recognizes that there are nations in*

---

[30]A. A. Hoekema, *The Bible and the Future* (Grand Rapids: Eerdmans, 1979), 286.

[31]M. R. Vincent, *Vincent's Word Studies in the New Testament* (Peabody, MA: Hendrickson, n.d.), 2:563.

[32]Aune, *Revelation 17–22*, 1123. I acknowledge that there are disputed textual issues over whether the text should read *laos* or *laoi*, although more recent scholarship appears to prefer *laoi*.

[33]C. S. Keener, *Revelation*, The NIV Application Commentary (Grand Rapids: Zondervan, 2000), 487.

[34]McDougall, "Revelation 21:9 to 22:5: Millennium or Eternal State?" 177.

eternity with specific roles and identities, why would there not be a special role and identity for the nation Israel?

In response to Hoekema's declaration concerning the presence of nations and culture on the new earth, Horner points out that "the mention of distinctive national contributions . . . would surely have to include the cultural benefactions of Israel!"[35] Horner's point cannot be ignored. If there are nations on the new earth, why would Israel not be one of these nations contributing to the new order? Plus, the presence of plural nations in the eternal state indicates that it is not God's purpose to make everyone Israel as amillennialists and covenant theologians often claim. There is no indication that the nations in Revelation 21–22 are all identified as "Israel." Israel's role is to bring blessings to the nations, but not to make everybody Israel.

The concept of nations in eternity does not contradict passages that speak of unity among God's people (see Rev 5:9–10). Nations can coexist in harmony with the equality of salvation and spiritual blessings of which all believers partake. In regard to salvation, there is one people of God, but this concept does not rule out all ethnic, geographical, or gender distinctions. Hays is correct when he states, "God's intention is for his people to be multi-ethnic and multi-cultural, but yet united in their fellowship and their worship of him."[36] This truth can apply to the future eternal kingdom. Some may appeal to Eph 2:11–22 and its discussion of unity between Jews and Gentiles. But Eph 2:11–22 does not rule out what other Bible passages say about the importance of nations even in the future. Ephesians 2:11–22 discusses the salvific unity that takes place between believing Gentiles and Jews since Christ removed the barrier of the Mosaic law, but it does not remove all distinctions. God often brings glory to Himself through the concepts of *unity* and *diversity*. The Trinity evidences unity (one God) and diversity (three persons). The church is the body of Christ, which evidences unity (one body) with diversity (many parts of the one body). With men and women we find equality in essence (see Gal 3:28) with distinctions in function (see 1 Tim 2:9–12).

To summarize, God's plans for the future are consistent with a New Creation Model approach in which both physical and spiritual blessings will occur. God appears to have a future plan for nations. One of these nations will be Israel. The final eternal state, thus, will see the final and complete fulfillment of Gen 12:2–3 in which God's plan for Abraham and Israel is to bring blessings to all the families of the earth.

---

[35] B. E. Horner, *Future Israel: Why Christian Anti-Judaism Must Be Challenged*, NACSBT (Nashville: B&H Academic, 2007), 217.

[36] J. D. Hays, *From Every People and Nation: A Biblical Theology of Race* (Downers Grove, IL: InterVarsity, 2003), 199.

Chapter 15

A Case for the Restoration
of National Israel, Part 1

The case against supersessionism does not depend solely on the refutation of the arguments of supersessionism. There are ample scriptural reasons to believe in a future salvation and restoration of the nation Israel. In fact, this is my main reason for rejecting replacement theology. I reject replacement theology mainly because multiple explicit passages predict a future salvation and restoration of the nation Israel in both the Old and New Testaments. The positive case for a restoration of Israel can be categorized in seven positive declarations:

1. The Bible explicitly teaches the restoration of the nation Israel.
2. The Bible explicitly promises the perpetuity of the nation Israel.
3. The NT reaffirms a future restoration for the nation Israel.
4. The NT reaffirms that the OT promises and covenants to Israel are still the possession of Israel.
5. New Testament prophecy affirms a future for Israel.
6. The NT maintains a distinction between Israel and the church.
7. The doctrine of election is proof that God has a future for Israel.

THE BIBLE EXPLICITLY TEACHES THE RESTORATION OF ISRAEL

The Bible on many occasions teaches that Israel will be restored to its land. Below I will mention a few of these. Deuteronomy 30:1–6 is a strategic passage regarding God's plans for Israel:

> When all these things happen to you—the blessings and curses I have set before you—and you come to your senses [while you are] in all the nations where the LORD your God has driven you, and you and your children return to the LORD your God and obey Him with all your heart and all your soul by doing everything I am giving you today, then He will restore your fortunes, have compassion on you, and gather you again from all the peoples where the LORD your God has scattered you. Even if your exiles are at

the ends of the earth, He will gather you and bring you back from there. The LORD your God will bring you into the land your fathers possessed, and you will take possession of it. He will cause you to prosper and multiply you more than [He did] your fathers. The LORD your God will circumcise your heart and the hearts of your descendants, and you will love Him with all your heart and all your soul, so that you will live.

This passage details a big-picture prophecy concerning Israel's future. God had dramatically delivered Israel from Egypt. He also gave Israel the law. In Deuteronomy 28–29 God described the blessings that would come upon Israel if the nation obeyed Him, and He discussed the curses that would come because of disobedience. God then discusses what the distant future will hold for Israel. After proclaiming blessings and curses, God would banish Israel to all the nations. But a time would come when Israel would "return" to God and God would "restore" Israel. This includes a spiritual salvation ("your God will circumcise your heart") and a restoration "into the land your fathers possessed." In sum, God promised Israel that after a period of banishment the nation would be saved and restored to its promised land.

Some have claimed that the land promises to Israel were fulfilled entirely in Joshua's day according to Josh 21:43–45. In this passage we are told that "everything was fulfilled" in regard to Israel possessing their land. But Josh 21:43–45 must be understood in light of the big-picture prediction of Deut 30:1–6. In Josh 21:43–45, we have a snapshot of God's faithfulness at the time of Israel's initial occupation of the land of Canaan. But Josh 21:43–45 cannot be the entire fulfillment of the land promise to Israel because Israel had not even been cursed and banished to the nations yet, which must come before Israel's salvation and restoration. God's plan for Israel's restoration to the Promised Land is reaffirmed later in Jer 16:14–15:

> "However, take note! The days are coming"—the LORD's declaration—
> "when it will no longer be said: As the LORD lives who brought the Israelites from the land of Egypt, but rather: As the LORD lives who brought the Israelites from the land of the north and from all the other lands where He had banished them. For I will return them to their land that I gave to their ancestors."

Centuries after the events of Joshua 21 and during a time of great disobedience by Israel, God promises that He will "return" Israel "to their land." This land is linked with the land He gave "to their ancestors." Thus, the future restoration of Israel to her land is linked with the promise of the Abrahamic covenant given to the patriarchs of Israel.

Many other passages reaffirm the expectation of Deut 30:1–6. Ezekiel 36:22–30 predicts that after a period of dispersion Israel will experience salvation and a restoration to her land:

> "Therefore, say to the house of Israel: This is what the Lord GOD says: It is not for your sake that I will act, house of Israel, but for My holy name, which you profaned among the nations where you went. I will honor the holiness of My great name, which has been profaned among the nations— the name you have profaned among them. The nations will know that I am Yahweh"—the declaration of the Lord GOD—"when I demonstrate My holiness through you in their sight.
>
> "For I will take you from the nations and gather you from all the countries, and will bring you into your own land. I will also sprinkle clean water on you, and you will be clean. I will cleanse you from all your impurities and all your idols. I will give you a new heart and put a new spirit within you; I will remove your heart of stone and give you a heart of flesh. I will place My Spirit within you and cause you to follow My statutes and carefully observe My ordinances. Then you will live in the land that I gave your fathers; you will be My people, and I will be your God. I will save you from all your uncleanness. I will summon the grain and make it plentiful, and will not bring famine on you. I will also make the fruit of the trees and the produce of the field plentiful, so that you will no longer experience reproach among the nations on account of famine."

Ezekiel 37:21–29 also predicts the restoration of Israel:

> "Tell them: This is what the Lord GOD says: I am going to take the Israelites out of the nations where they have gone. I will gather them from all around and bring them into their own land. I will make them one nation in the land, on the mountains of Israel, and one king will rule over all of them. They will no longer be two nations and will no longer be divided into two kingdoms. They will not defile themselves any more with their idols, their detestable things, and all their transgressions. I will save them from all their apostasies by which they sinned, and I will cleanse them. Then they will be My people, and I will be their God. My servant David will be king over them, and there will be one shepherd for all of them. They will follow My ordinances, and keep My statutes and obey them.
>
> "They will live in the land that I gave to My servant Jacob, where your fathers lived. They will live in it forever with their children and grandchildren, and My servant David will be their prince forever. I will make a covenant of peace with them; it will be an everlasting covenant with them. I will establish and multiply them, and will set My sanctuary among them forever. My dwelling place will be with them; I will be their God, and they will be My people. When My sanctuary is among them forever, the nations will know that I, the LORD, sanctify Israel."

Jeremiah 30:1–3 tells of a restoration of Israel to her land:

> [This is] the word that came to Jeremiah from the LORD. This is what the
> LORD, the God of Israel, says: "Write down on a scroll all the words that I
> have spoken to you, for the days are certainly coming"—[this is] the
> LORD's declaration—"when I will restore the fortunes of My people Israel
> and Judah"—the LORD's declaration. "I will restore them to the land I
> gave to their ancestors and they will possess it."

Many other passages teach the restoration of Israel. Isaiah 66:22 teaches
that in connection with "the new heavens and the new earth" the "offspring" and "name" of Israel will "endure." Joel 3:20 indicates that as a
result of the Day of the Lord (3:18) "Judah will be inhabited forever, and
Jerusalem from generation to generation." With Zeph 3:20, God promises
to "restore" the "fortunes" of Israel. When examining these and other restoration texts in the Bible, certain truths emerge:

1. The restoration of Israel involves both spiritual salvation and physical blessings, including possession of the land of promise.
2. The promise of restoration is based not on Israel's greatness but on
   God's choice and God's character.
3. The promise for restoration takes place after the period of Israel's
   disobedience.

As the passages above and many others indicate, the restoration of Israel
is a major theme of the OT. It is an explicit doctrine. As such, we should
be skeptical of any perspective that says Israel will not be restored as a
nation, especially when no NT text explicitly revokes or transfers the OT
expectation.

The future of national Israel is not just an OT matter. The statement in Rom
11:26—"And in this way Israel shall be saved"—is consistent with the view that
Israel will experience a national salvation and restoration at some point in the
future. As Blaising and Bock assert, "In Romans 11:26, the term 'thus' [Gk.
houtōs, "in this way"] is best interpreted with a view to 'just as' indicating that
the salvation of 'all Israel' (most definitely a national reference in light of the
contextual use of the term Israel) will take place as predicted by the prophets."[1]

The other 10 references to "Israel" in Romans 9–11 refer to ethnic Israel,
so the Israel who "will be saved" in 11:26 must also refer to ethnic Israel.
Johnson writes, "It is exegetically and theologically highly unlikely that the

---

[1]C. A. Blaising and D. L. Bock, *Progressive Dispensationalism: An Up-to-Date Handbook of
Contemporary Dispensational Thought* (Wheaton, IL: Bridgepoint, 1993), 318, n. 18.

term 'Israel,' having been used 10 times for the nation in the theodicy of Romans 9–11, should now suddenly without any special explanation refer to 'spiritual Israel,' composed of elect Jews and Gentiles."[2]

Romans 11:27–28 ties Israel's salvation and restoration to the promises of the new covenant in the OT. Burns writes, "Paul seems to be teaching that Messiah's eschatological Parousia will be the time of God's sovereign ratification of the new-covenant promise with Israel."[3] Kaiser sees a restoration of Israel to its land based on Rom 11:27: "Thus we are brought back to the land promise and to the destiny that God has shaped from the beginning for his people Israel. Indeed, in the very context from which the New Covenant comes (Jer 31:31–34), there is a renewed emphasis on the land promise once again (Jer 31:35–40)!"[4] Thus, Romans 11 is evidence for a special future for Israel. According to Blaising, "Are there theological reasons for believing that Israel has a future? Yes, because God is faithful to his word. Yes, because, 'For I, the Lord, do not change; therefore you, O sons of Jacob, are not consumed' (Mal. 3:10). Yes, because, 'The gifts and calling of God are irrevocable' (Rom 11:29)."[5] As Cranfield writes, "It seems . . . probable that Paul was thinking of a restoration of the nation Israel as a whole to God *at the end*, an eschatological event in the strict sense."[6]

The view that Rom 11:26 is teaching a future salvation of national Israel has considerable support among commentators and Christian theologians. In fact, I believe this view is the historic view of the Christian church. Nothing in this text would refute the OT expectation of a restoration of Israel. Romans 11:27 does link the OT promises of the new covenant with Israel's salvation mentioned in 11:26. This may be evidence that all of the new covenant, including its promised physical blessings, may still be the coming possession of national Israel. In conclusion, one major reason to believe in a restoration of the nation Israel is because the Bible teaches it.

THE BIBLE EXPLICITLY PROMISES THE PERPETUITY OF THE NATION ISRAEL

Another proof for the coming restoration of Israel is that the Bible teaches the perpetuity of the nation Israel. Israel will always be a nation before God. Jeremiah 31:35–37 states,

---

[2] S. L. Johnson Jr., "Evidence from Romans 9–11," in *A Case for Premillennialism*, ed. D. K. Campbell and J. L. Townsend (Grand Rapids: Kregel, 1997), 202.

[3] J. L. Burns, "The Future of Ethnic Israel in Romans 11," in *Dispensationalism, Israel and the Church: The Search for Definition*, ed. C. A. Blaising and D. L. Bock (Grand Rapids: Zondervan, 1992), 214.

[4] W. C. Kaiser Jr., "An Assessment of 'Replacement' Theology," *Mishkan* 21 (1994): 16.

[5] C. A. Blaising, "The Future of Israel as a Theological Question," *JETS* 44 (2001): 439–40.

[6] C. E. B. Cranfield, *A Critical and Exegetical Commentary on the Epistle to the Romans*, ICC 2 (Edinburgh: T&T Clark, 1979), 2:577. Emphasis in original.

This is what the LORD says:

The One who gives the sun for light by day, the fixed order of moon and stars for light by night, who stirs up the sea and makes its waves roar—the LORD of Hosts is His name: If this fixed order departs from My presence—[this is] the LORD's declaration— then also Israel's descendants will cease to be a nation before Me forever. This is what the LORD says: If the heavens above can be measured and the foundations of the earth below explored, I will reject all of Israel's descendants because of all they have done—[this is] the LORD's declaration.

In this poem made up of two sayings (vv. 35–36 and 37), the Lord declares what Nicholson has called "the impossibility of Israel being forsaken forever by God."[7] Notice that Israel's everlasting existence as a "nation" is linked to the continued existence of the sun, moon, and stars. One who looks into the sky and sees these cosmic bodies can have assurance that Israel's existence as a nation before God is assured. Claims that this passage has been reinterpreted so that the church is the true Israel that fulfills this passage are not satisfactory. The *nation* Israel is promised a perpetual place in the plan of God, and the nation will always endure as a special object of God's love.

THE NEW TESTAMENT REAFFIRMS A FUTURE FOR NATIONAL ISRAEL

Even if the NT never discussed a future salvation and restoration of Israel, there is still justification for believing in it since God has already spoken on this matter and has not revoked what He promised earlier. Thus, we reject any perspective that says God has to repeat what He said earlier in order for the previous revelation still to be in effect. Yet the fact that God does reaffirm a salvation and restoration of Israel in the NT gives even more reason to believe in a future for Israel. Texts that support and reaffirm the restoration of Israel include Matt 19:28/Luke 22:30; Matt 23:37–39/Luke 13:35; Luke 21:24; Acts 1:6; and Romans 11.

Matthew 19:28 and Luke 22:30

Jesus' words in Matt 19:28 and Luke 22:29–30 are explicit evidence that Jesus expected a restoration of national Israel.[8] Matthew 19:28 states, "Jesus said to them, 'I assure you: In the Messianic Age, when the Son of Man sits on His glorious throne, you who have followed Me will also sit on 12

---

[7]E. W. Nicholson, *The Book of the Prophet Jeremiah: Chapters 26—52* (Cambridge, UK: Cambridge University Press, 1975), 72.

thrones, judging the 12 tribes of Israel.'"

In Luke's account of the Lord's Supper, Jesus declared, "I bestow on you a kingdom, just as My Father bestowed one on Me, so that you may eat and drink at My table in My kingdom. And you will sit on thrones judging the 12 tribes of Israel."

Jesus is speaking about what will take place in the future. In the day when the earth experiences regeneration and the kingdom is established, the apostles will sit on 12 thrones judging the 12 tribes of Israel. Saucy is correct when he states that these two passages offer "support for a future restoration of Israel."[9] In his discussion of the term "kingdom," Schmidt points out that Jesus shared the hope of His Jewish contemporaries of a national restoration of Israel because of Jesus' words in Matt 19:28 and Luke 22:29–30:

> Even where national and political hopes were not to the fore, but salvation was expected for the whole world in the last time, His [Jesus'] contemporaries still thought it important that there should be a place of privilege for Israel. Israel was to arise with new glory, and the scattered tribes, and indeed the Gentiles, were to stream towards the new Jerusalem. Jesus shares this hope. He gives to His disciples, the twelve, as representatives of the twelve tribes of the people of God, the holy people, judicial and administrative office in the reign of God (Mt. 19:28 = Lk. 22:29 *f.*).[10]

Lowery states that "Matthew . . . encourages a continuing mission to Israel as a means to the realization of the hope that one day Israel will be restored." Thus, Jesus' statement in 19:28 "is a confident assertion that this restoration will indeed take place."[11] Blaising, too, believes that Matt 19:28 confirms OT prophecy and its assertion that the Messiah would rule Israel and the nations in a political kingdom: "In summary, we see that Jesus affirmed the tradition of Old Testament prophecy and apocalypticism and proclaimed a coming worldwide political kingdom in which He as Messiah

---

[8]Those who believe these texts teach a future restoration of national Israel include E. P. Sanders, *Jesus and Judaism* (Philadelphia: Fortress, 1985), 103; R. L. Saucy, *The Case for Progressive Dispensationalism: The Interface Between Dispensational and Nondispensational Theology* (Grand Rapids: Zondervan, 1993), 267; K. L. Schmidt, "Βασιλεία" in *TDNT*, ed. G. Kittel (Grand Rapids: Eerdmans, 1964), 1:586; D. K. Lowery, "Evidence from Matthew," in *A Case for Premillennialism*, ed. D. K. Campbell and J. L. Townsend (Chicago: Moody, 1992), 180; Blaising and Bock, *Progressive Dispensationalism*, 238; R. H. Gundry, *Matthew: A Commentary on His Literary and Theological Arts* (Grand Rapids: Eerdmans, 1982), 393; P. K. Nelson, *Leadership and Discipleship: A Study of Luke 22:24–30*, SBL Dissertation Series 138 (Atlanta: Scholars Press, 1994), 221–22; A. G. Fruchtenbaum, *Israelology: The Missing Link in Systematic Theology* (Tustin, CA: Ariel, 1989), 203.

[9]Saucy, *The Case for Progressive Dispensationalism*, 267.

[10]Schmidt, "Βασιλεία," 586.

[11]Lowery, "Evidence from Matthew," 180.

of the house of David would rule Israel and all the nations. We see Him making preparations for the administration of that coming kingdom by promising His disciples ruling positions along with Him."[12]

Is it possible, though, that Jesus is referring to the church in Matt 19:28 or Luke 22:30? Are the 12 tribes representative of a new people of God, the church, that transcends ethnic distinctions? Supersessionists have claimed this. For example, commenting on Matt 19:28, Hill states, "The twelve tribes are the new Israel, probably the Church."[13] Mounce declares, "The symbolism of the twelve tribes is carried over into the New Testament to represent the Christian church."[14] In his comments on Matt 19:28, France writes, "This remarkable transfer of imagery graphically illustrates the theme of a 'true Israel' of the followers of Jesus who take the place of the unbelieving nation."[15] Lange holds that the reference to the 12 tribes of Israel "must be taken in a symbolical sense, as applying to the whole body of believers (*see* Rev. xxi. 12)."[16]

I find these claims unconvincing. As Saucy argues, "The idea that Jesus is referring to some new spiritual Israel in this promise must be rejected. Matthew always makes a clear distinction between Gentiles and Jews. Similarly, Luke always uses the word 'Israel' to refer to the Jewish people."[17] Referring specifically to Matt 19:28, Lowery writes, "This authority is to be exercised in relation to Israel, which means the Jews and not the church. Interpreters may refer to the church as a 'new Israel' or 'true Israel' but Matthew and other NT writers did not do so."[18] Gundry likewise says, "Neither in Jesus' intention nor in Matthew's does 'Israel' mean the church."[19] Thus, I agree with Harrington when he declares, "There is no reason to interpret the twelve tribes as a symbol for the Church. Matthew meant Israel."[20]

Almost certainly the apostles understood Jesus' words in Matt 19:28 to refer to a restored national Israel. Even after 40 days of kingdom instruction, the apostles were still thinking of a restoration of Israel (see Acts 1:3,6). I conclude, therefore, with Sanders that Matt 19:28 "confirms the view that Jesus looked for the restoration of Israel."[21]

---

[12]Blaising and Bock, *Progressive Dispensationalism*, 238.

[13]D. Hill, *The Gospel of Matthew*, NCBC (Grand Rapids: Eerdmans, 1972), 284.

[14]R. H. Mounce, *Matthew*, NIBCNT (Peabody, MA: Hendrickson, 1991), 185.

[15]R. T. France, *Matthew: An Introduction and Commentary*, TNTC (Grand Rapids: Eerdmans, 1985; repr., 1987), 288.

[16]J. P. Lange, *A Commentary on the Holy Scriptures: Matthew*, trans. and ed. P. Schaff (Grand Rapids: Zondervan, n.d.), 349. Emphasis in original.

[17]Saucy, *The Case for Progressive Dispensationalism*, 268.

[18]Lowery, "Evidence from Matthew," 178. See also A. J. Saldarini, *Matthew's Christian-Jewish Community* (Chicago: University of Chicago Press, 1994), 28.

[19]Gundry, *Matthew*, 393.

[20]D. J. Harrington, *The Gospel of Matthew*, Sacra Pagina (Collegeville, MN: Liturgical Press, 2007), 279.

The same conclusion can be made for Luke 22:29–30. Nelson observes that the reference to the "twelve tribes" in 22:30 is a reference not to the church but to the Jewish people. There is no use of "Israel" in the Synoptics or Acts "which does not refer to the Jewish people/nation, the Israel of the OT. . . . Thus it does not appear that Luke attaches a new Christian meaning to the various terms and phrases that have traditionally been used to describe Israel of old (contrast Gal 6:16)."[22] In light of Luke's literal sense of "Israel," Luke 22:30 is probably speaking of national Israel: "It is best to take the 'twelve tribes of Israel' in Luke 22:30b as referring to the Israel of the OT, the people of God. Luke does not envision a new Israel which becomes marked off from Israel of old, but an Israel which has returned to its roots and whose Messiah has come welcoming all who would repent and believe."[23]

The attempts to explain Israel as the church in these passages are not convincing. Boring has argued that the view that the church is the new Israel in Matt 19:28 is a "misinterpretation."[24] He states, "The concept of the church as the 'new Israel' is foreign to Matthew, who always uses 'Israel' in the empirical sense. Because even eschatologically restored Israel must be judged and sorted out like the church, the church is not simply identified with Israel."[25] The same is true for Luke's Gospel. When it comes to the church, Wainwright points out that Luke "never explicitly calls it 'Israel,' and there is not good reason to suppose that when he speaks of the restoration of Israel he is alluding to the Church. He is referring to the Jewish nation."[26] According to Jervell, "The concept 'Israel' is never used by Luke as a term for a church made up of Jews and Gentiles."[27] Thus, Matt 19:28 and Luke 22:30 explicitly show that the NT reaffirms a restoration of national Israel. The NT is not silent about Israel's restoration.

Matthew 23:37–39 and Luke 13:34–35

Matthew 23:37–39 and Luke 13:34–35 also are evidence that Jesus

---

[21]Sanders, *Jesus and Judaism*, 103.

[22]Nelson, *Leadership and Discipleship*, 221–22.

[23]Ibid., 223.

[24]M. E. Boring, "The Gospel of Matthew: Introduction, Commentary, and Reflections," *NIB* 8 (Nashville: Abingdon, 1995), 392. In his thoughts on Matt 19:28, H. A. W. Meyer says, "It is a mistake, therefore, to take the people of Israel as intended to represent the people of God in the *Christian* sense." H. A. W. Meyer, *Critical and Exegetical Hand-Book to the Gospel of Matthew*, trans. P. Christie (New York: Funk & Wagnalls, 1890), 347.

[25]Boring, "The Gospel of Matthew," 392.

[26]A. W. Wainwright, "Luke and the Restoration of the Kingdom to Israel," *ExpTim* 89 (1977): 76.

[27]J. Jervell, *Luke and the People of God: A New Look at Luke–Acts* (Augsburg: Fortress, 1972; repr., Eugene, OR: Wipf & Stock, 2002), 72, n. 22.

expected a future restoration of Israel.[28] Matthew 23:37–39 records Jesus' words to the inhabitants of Jerusalem:

"Jerusalem, Jerusalem! She who kills the prophets and stones those who are sent to her. How often I wanted to gather your children together, as a hen gathers her chicks under her wings, yet you were not willing! See, your house is left to you desolate. For I tell you, you will never see Me again until you say, 'He who comes in the name of the Lord is the blessed One'!" (Matt 23:37– 39)

The text in Luke 13:34–35 is similar:

Jerusalem, Jerusalem! She who kills the prophets and stones those who are sent to her. How often I wanted to gather your childrend together, as a hen gathers her chicks under her wings, but you were not willing! See, your house is abandoned to you. And I tell you, you will not see Me until the time comes when you say, 'He who comes in the name of the Lord is the blessed One'! (Luke 13:34–35)

In these two parallel texts, Jesus announced that desolation would come to Jerusalem and its temple because the Jewish inhabitants of Jerusalem rejected Him. Jesus also announced that He would be hidden from the people of Jerusalem until the day they say, "He who comes in the name of the Lord is the blessed One!"

The prediction that the Jews will one day cry out that Jesus is "blessed" is clear, but the manner in which they will do so is disputed. Is this the exclamation of disobedient Jews facing eschatological judgment, or is it the cry of a repentant Israel at the time of its restoration? The latter view is preferred. Blomberg notes that Jesus' words in Matt 23:39 indicate "genuine belief" on the part of Israel.[29] This declaration of blessedness upon Jesus will come from a repentant nation at the time of its restoration. Gundry, for example, argues that Matt 23:37–39 refers to "Israel's restoration in the

---

[28]Those who assert that these texts are consistent with the idea of a restoration of national Israel include the following: Gundry, *Matthew*, 394; C. S. Keener, *Matthew*, IVPNTCS (Downers Grove, IL: InterVarsity, 1997), 341; Lowery, "Evidence from Matthew," 179–80; R. C. Tannehill, *Luke*, ANTC (Nashville: Abingdon, 1996), 226–27; C. A. Evans, "Prophecy and Polemic: 'Jews in Luke's Scriptural Apologetic,'" in *Luke and Scripture: The Function of Sacred Tradition in Luke-Acts*, ed. C. A. Evans and J. A. Sanders (Minneapolis: Fortress, 1993), 179; J. Koening, *Jews and Christians in Dialogue: New Testament Foundations* (Philadelphia: Westminster, 1979), 11–12; D. L. Bock, *Luke 9:51–24:53*, BECNT 2 (Grand Rapids: Baker, 1996), 1251; Saucy, *The Case for Progressive Dispensationalism*, 265; L. R. Helyer, "Luke and the Restoration of Israel," *JETS* 36 (1993): 324–25; Fruchtenbaum, *Israelology*, 783–84.

[29]C. L. Blomberg, "Matthew," in *Commentary on the New Testament Use of the Old Testament*, ed. G. K. Beale and D. A. Carson (Grand Rapids: Baker, 2007), 85.

kingdom of the Son of man."[30] He also says, "The limitation of the woes to the scribes and Pharisees (vv 13–36) forestalls a contradiction between the woes and the implied conversion of Israel."[31]

Matthew 23:37–39 teaches both judgment and hope. There is judgment for the present generation of Israel, but there is also the hope of restoration in the future. As Keener states,

> This passage reminds us that God does not forget his promises to his people. . . . Matthew places it among the woes of coming judgment, but in so doing transforms this into a promise of future hope. . . . Israel's restoration was a major theme of the biblical prophets and reappeared at least occasionally in early Christianity (Rom 11:26), though the emphasis of early Christian apologetic came to focus on the Gentile mission.[32]

Luke 13:34–35 also holds out hope for a restoration of national Israel. In reference to Luke 13:35, Tannehill declares, "This lament over Jerusalem includes a continuing hope that a restored Jerusalem will find this salvation."[33] Evans believes a positive reception of Jesus by the Jews, as described in Luke 13:35, is linked to the *parousia*: "The saying, therefore, likely alludes to the parousia, at the time the kingdom is finally restored to Israel (Acts 1:6, 11); then stubborn Jerusalem will finally bless the Messiah. But not until then will the inhabitants be gathered together under the wings of Messiah's care and protection. The expectation is that someday, but not now, the Jewish nation will respond and be reconciled to the Messiah."[34]

Koenig also links a joyful welcome of Jesus by the Jews with the *parousia* and the restoration of Israel: "But this means that the prophecy recorded in Lk. 13:35 must look forward to some *other* future event. This other is probably Jesus' Parousia descent to Jerusalem as Son of Man Messiah in the Kingdom of God (Lk. 21:27; Acts 1:11). On that day Jerusalemites will repent of their blindness and welcome Jesus with blessings. Thereafter the final restoration of Israel can proceed."[35]

Bock points out that hope for a future restoration of Israel in Luke 13:35 can be supported by other statements in Luke and Acts:

---

[30]Gundry, *Matthew*, 394.

[31]Ibid., 474.

[32]Keener, *Matthew*, 341.

[33]Tannehill, *Luke*, 226–27.

[34]Evans, "Prophecy and Polemic," 179.

[35]Koening, *Jews and Christians in Dialogue*, 11–12. Emphasis in original.

It is debated whether Luke by this remark holds out hope for Israel's future. Luke 21:24 and the speech of Acts 3 show that Jesus and the church continued to extend hope to Israel. They believed that God would restore the nation in the end. In fact, the NT suggests that such a response will precede Christ's return, thus Luke's later reference to the current period as "the time of the Gentiles."[36]

Important to this understanding of the exclamation "He who comes in the name of the Lord is the blessed One!" is the belief that this is a joyful cry of a repentant Israel undergoing restoration and not the woeful cry of a condemned Israel undergoing judgment. This exclamation, referred to in Matt 23:39 and Luke 13:35, is taken from Ps 118:26. Psalm 118 is a psalm of thanksgiving for God's saving goodness. As Evans states, "The rabbis understood Ps 118:26 in reference to the day of redemption."[37]

The joyful context of Psalm 118 makes likely that the quotation of this psalm in Matt 23:39 and Luke 13:35 refers to a joyful deliverance of a restored Israel. Noting that the Jews regarded Psalm 118 as a messianic psalm of praise, Saucy declares, "It is far more likely that this statement following the pronouncement of judgment is to be taken as a promise of a joyful greeting of their Messiah by the people of Jerusalem."[38] According to Helyer, "It is hard not to see here a reference to the future conversion of Israel (cf. Rom 11:25–26). The suggestion that the cry is a reluctant admission of sovereignty has little to commend it, especially in view of the context of the quotation from Ps 118:26."[39]

Bock, too, argues against the idea that the exclamation of the Jews is a forced recognition of Jesus: "Still another faulty explanation is that Jews will be forced to recognize him at the second coming. . . . The quotation from Ps. 118 is positive and anticipates a positive recognition, not a forced one."[40] Thus, Matt 23:39 and Luke 13:35 are evidences for the restoration of national Israel.

Supersessionists have criticized this interpretation of these passages. France, for example, argues that there are "two factors" against the view that Jesus is speaking of a national salvation of Israel. First, he claims that the statement

---

[36]Bock, *Luke*, 2:1251.

[37]Evans, "Prophecy and Polemic," 179, n. 33.

[38]Saucy, *The Case for Progressive Dispensationalism*, 265.

[39]Helyer, "Luke and the Restoration of Israel," 324–25. Although not a nonsupersessionist, D. A. Hagner states, "It is possible to link the future acceptance of Christ implied in the words of Ps 118:26 to the eschatological salvation of Israel referred to by Paul in Rom 11:26, 31." D. A. Hagner, *Matthew 14–28*, WBC 33b (Dallas: Word, 1995), 681.

[40]Bock, *Luke*, 2:1251. M. Elliott claims the message of Matt 23:39 and Luke 13:35 "implies the warm reception of the Son of Man by Israel at some future date." M. Elliott, "Israel," in *Dictionary of Jesus and the Gospels*, ed. J. B. Green, S. McKnight, and I. H. Marshall (Downers Grove, IL: InterVarsity, 1992), 363.

"until you say" in Matt 23:39 is "expressed in Greek as an indefinite possibility rather than as a firm prediction." Thus, "this is the condition on which they will see him again; but there is no promise that the condition will be fulfilled."[41] Second, France believes the judgment context of Matthew 23 and 24 argues against the idea that Jesus was speaking of a future hope for the nation Israel:

> A prediction of future repentance would be quite out of keeping not only with the flow of thought throughout ch. 23 (of which this is the climax) and ch. 24 which deals with judgment to come, but also with the perspective of the Gospel as a whole, which has repeatedly spoken of Israel's last chance, and of a new international people of God (8:11–12; 12:38–45; 21:40–43; 22:7; 23:32–36; *etc.*).[42]

Supersessionists stress that the judgment context of Matt 23:39 is evidence that Jesus was not referring to a future salvation or restoration of Israel. But while the context heavily speaks of judgment, this does not logically mean that that there cannot be hope for Israel after a period of judgment. As Goppelt writes, Matthew "may in fact have had in mind a saving encounter of Israel with the returning One at the *parousia* in 23:39."[43] Lange, too, states that Matt 23:39 "is an intimation of a future conversion."[44]

But a glimmer of hope can be offered in the midst of somber predictions of judgment. Thus, Matt 23:37–39 and the parallel teaching in Luke 13:35 foretell a day when the inhabitants of Jerusalem will joyfully recognize their king. As Senior states, "In Matthew's perspective, the rejection of Jesus by the leaders is indeed a grave sin, one that brings divine judgment. Yet the story of God's relationship to Israel is not concluded, and the day will come when

---

[41]France, *Matthew*, 332.

[42]Ibid., 333. Commenting on Matt 23:37–39, J. C. Fenton states that Israel's judgment is irreversible: "So judgment will come upon them [people of Jerusalem]; Jesus himself will not be seen again by the crowds until he comes in glory, and then it will be too late for them to repent." J. C. Fenton, *Saint Matthew*, WPC (Philadelphia: Westminster, 1963), 377. Commenting on Matt 23:39, D. A. Hagner states, "It is possible to link the future acceptance of Christ implied in the words of Ps 118:26 to the eschatological salvation of Israel referred to by Paul in Romans 11:26, 31, but this probably goes well beyond what Matthew and his readers understood by this concluding statement." D. A. Hagner, *Matthew 14–28*, 681. See also D. R. A. Hare, *Matthew*, IBC (Louisville, KY: John Knox, 1993), 272.

[43]L. Goppelt, *Theology of the New Testament: The Variety and Unity of the Apostolic Witness to Christ*, trans. J. Alsup (Grand Rapids: Eerdmans, 1982), 2:231, n. 29. Emphasis in original.

[44]Lange, *Matthew*, 415. S. Toussaint notes the significance of the word, "until" in 23:39 when he writes, "It is extremely important for one to note that Christ's rejection of Israel is not an eternal one. The word 'until' . . . of verse thirty-nine together with the following statement affirms the fact that Christ will come again to a repentant nation." S. D. Toussaint, *Behold the King: A Study of Matthew* (Eugene, OR: Multnomah Press, 1980), 265–66.

[45]D. Senior, *Matthew*, ANTC (Nashville: Abingdon, 1998), 264.

Jerusalem will again receive its Messiah with shouts of praise."[45] Ladd, too, rightly points out that Matt 23:37–39 is evidence that "Israel is yet to be saved."[46] It is also evidence that Israel's rejection is not final: "This rejection [of Israel] is not final and ultimate; the day will come when Israel will say, 'Blessed is he who comes in the name of the Lord' (vv. 37–39). The Kingdom of God is not taken from the Jews that they might be forever abandoned; 'all Israel' is yet to be saved and brought within the redemptive purpose of God."[47]

Acts 1:6–7

Another passage that supports the idea of a restoration of national Israel is Acts 1:6–7: "So when they had come together, they asked Him, 'Lord, at this time are You restoring the kingdom to Israel?' He said to them, 'It is not for you to know times or periods that the Father has set by His own authority.'"

This text, which describes Jesus' final interchange with his apostles before His ascension, affirms the idea of a restoration of the nation Israel.[48] It does so in two ways. First, it shows that at this late date in the earthly ministry of Jesus the apostles fully expected a restoration of the nation Israel. Second, Jesus' response includes no rebuke or correction for this belief, thus affirming the correct nature of their understanding. Concerning the first point, Acts 1:6 shows that the disciples clearly expected a future restoration of the Davidic kingdom to national Israel. As McLean states,

> The terms "Israel" and "Israelite" occur 32 times in Luke-Acts. In each occurrence the terms refer to the people of Israel as a national entity. Therefore it seems correct to understand that the disciples' question in Acts 1:6 referred to a restoration of a kingdom to the nation of Israel. They were asking Jesus about the timing of the future restoration of the Davidic kingdom of Israel as described and defined in the Old Testament.[49]

---

[46]G. E. Ladd, *The Gospel of the Kingdom: Popular Expositions on the Kingdom of God* (Grand Rapids: Eerdmans, 1959), 120.

[47]G. E. Ladd, "Matthew," *The Biblical Expositor*, ed. C. F. Henry (Philadelphia: Holman, 1960), 847.

[48]The following people view this text as affirming a future restoration of national Israel: P. W. Walaskay, *"And So We Came to Rome": The Political Perspective of St Luke* (Cambridge: Cambridge University Press, 1983), 17; J. A. McLean, "Did Jesus Correct the Disciples' View of the Kingdom?" *BSac* 151, no. 602 (1994): 222; Saucy, *The Case for Progressive Dispensationalism*, 268; L. Helyer, "Luke and the Restoration of Israel," 327; J. M. Penny, *The Missionary Emphasis of Lukan Pneumatology* (Sheffield: Sheffield Academic Press, 1997), 69; Blaising and Bock, *Progressive Dispensationalism*, 237; D. L. Tiede, "The Exaltation of Jesus and the Restoration of Israel in Acts 1," *HTR* 79 (1986): 278; D. Larsen, *Jews, Gentiles and the Church: A New Perspective on History and Prophecy* (Grand Rapids: Discovery House, 1995), 35; Fruchtenbaum, *Israelology*, 104–5.

[49]McLean, "Did Jesus Correct the Disciples' View of the Kingdom?" 222. See also Saucy, *The Case for Progressive Dispensationalism*, 268.

This belief of the disciples was not misguided. Two reasons are given to support this view. First, Acts 1:3 states that Jesus met with the disciples for a period of 40 days after His resurrection "speaking about the kingdom of God." It seems unlikely that the disciples could be misguided in their perceptions of the kingdom after having received 40 days of instruction about it from the risen Lord. As Penney states, "The disciples' question here (1.6) is hardly to be construed as a nationalistic misunderstanding. It echoes Gabriel's language from the opening chapter of the Gospel."[50]

Second, the lack of correction from Jesus in Acts 1:7 is validation that the disciples were correct in their beliefs about Israel's restoration. If the disciples had been wrong, Jesus probably would have corrected their misconception as He did on other occasions. But Jesus' lack of correction can be viewed as affirmation of their idea. As McLean asserts,

> The ministry of Jesus focused, in part, on correcting false doctrine and rebuking errant teachers. However, it is noteworthy that Jesus did not correct the disciples' question about the restoration of the kingdom to Israel. Therefore in view of the consistent ministry of Jesus to correct the disciples when they were in error, it seems correct to conclude that in their question in Acts 1:6 they properly anticipated a future restoration of the kingdom for Israel.[51]

Jesus refused to address the timing of the kingdom, but He offered no correction to their idea that a restoration of national Israel would take place. Chance writes, "In short, Jesus' response challenges the hope for an immediate restoration of Israel. It does not challenge the hope of such a restoration itself."[52]

While supersessionists have often acknowledged that the disciples at this point had nationalistic expectations on their minds,[53] they disagree with the idea that Acts 1:6 is evidence for the idea of a future national restoration of Israel. Supersessionists have offered two alternative explanations for the meaning of Acts 1:6. First, some have claimed that the disciples were simply misguided in their understanding of the kingdom or that they had not grasped

---

[50]Penney, *The Missionary Emphasis of Lukan Pneumatology*, 69. "The issue at stake here was not whether the land would be restored to Israel but only the issue of timing." W. C. Kaiser Jr., "The Land of Israel and the Future Return (Zechariah 10:6–12)," in *Israel, the Land and the People: An Evangelical Affirmation of God's Promises*, ed. H. W. House (Grand Rapids: Kregel, 1998), 223.

[51]McLean, "Did Jesus Correct the Disciples' View of the Kingdom?" 219.

[52]J. B. Chance, *Jerusalem, the Temple, and the New Age in Luke–Acts* (Macon, GA: Mercer University Press, 1988), 133.

[53]Robertson states,: "What can be said about the nature of this kingdom as understood by the disciples? The fact that they spoke of its being 'restored to Israel' indicates that they were thinking of it as a national entity with its center located in Jerusalem and its domain encompassing the land of their fathers. They were expressing the Jewish hope that God would establish his rule, so that Israel would

the true meaning of Jesus' kingdom message.[54] Zorn states that Acts 1:6 indicates "the last flicker on the apostles' part . . . concerning their hope that national Israel would once again be a political theocracy."[55]

Second, others like Robertson hold that Israel would indeed be restored, but it would be restored in a way different from the nationalistic expectations of the apostles. As he states, "The kingdom of God would be restored to Israel in the rule of the Messiah, which would be realized by the working of the Holy Spirit through the disciples of Christ as they extended their witness to the ends of the earth."[56] Thus, as the kingdom message was carried to the world through the Holy Spirit, Israel's kingdom was being restored. To support this view, Robertson ties the question of the disciples in Acts 1:6 with Jesus' statement in 1:8 that the disciples would receive the power of the Holy Spirit and they would be Jesus' witnesses throughout the earth: "This statement [in 1:8] should not be regarded as peripheral to the question asked by the disciples. Instead, it is germane to the whole issue of the restoration of the kingdom to Israel."[57]

In spite of these explanations, however, Acts 1:6 seems to be significant evidence for the nonsupersessionist view. The fact that these disciples had immediately experienced 40 days of kingdom instruction from the risen Jesus (see Acts 1:3) makes it unlikely they could be so wrong about the nature of the kingdom and national Israel's relationship to it. Also, Jesus' answer, although not an explicit affirmation of their hope, appears to assume the correctness of their expectation. McKnight is correct when he states, "Since Jesus was such a good teacher, we have every right to think that the impulsive hopes of his audience were on target."[58] I thus conclude with Walaskay that Jesus said nothing that "dampened the hope of his disciples for a national kingdom."[59]

---

be freed from its enemies and reconstituted as the great nation it once was." O. P. Robertson, *The Israel of God: Yesterday, Today, and Tomorrow* (Phillipsburg, NJ: P&R, 2000), 130. N. T. Wright says the disciples "still cherished ambitions for the nation of Israel."

[54]According to N. T. Wright, Acts 1:6 shows that the disciples "had not grasped the radical nature of Jesus' agenda." N. T. Wright, *Jesus and the Victory of God* (Minneapolis: Fortress, 1996), 463.

[55]R. O. Zorn, *Christ Triumphant: Biblical Perspectives on His Church and Kingdom* (Carlisle, PA: Banner of Truth, 1997), 50. Zorn also states, "How persistent the mistaken thinking of the disciples was in terms of the old economy's continuance" (194, n. 1).

[56]Robertson, *The Israel of God*, 134. Wright states that "Jesus reaffirms the expectation, but alters the interpretation." N. T. Wright, *The New Testament and the People of God* (Minneapolis: Fortress, 1992), 374.

[57]Robertson, *The Israel of God*, 133.

[58]S. McKnight, *A New Vision for Israel: The Teachings of Jesus in National Context* (Grand Rapids: Eerdmans, 1999), 130–31.

[59]Walaskay, "*And So We Came to Rome*," 17. Blaising writes, "The national hope of Israel in their question appears as a given. The question has to do only with the time of fulfillment." Blaising and Bock, *Progressive Dispensationalism*, 237. See also Tiede, "The Exaltation of Jesus and the Restoration of Israel in Acts 1," 278. See also Larsen, *Jews, Gentiles and the Church*, 35.

Chapter 16

A Case for the Restoration
of National Israel, Part 2

In this chapter, I am continuing discussion of the case for a restoration of the nation Israel. Other reasons are discussed in this chapter.

THE NEW TESTAMENT REAFFIRMS THE OLD TESTAMENT PROMISES, AND COVENANTS ARE STILL THE POSSESSION OF ISRAEL

If the nation Israel has been permanently superseded by the church, one would not expect a statement in the NT declaring that the covenants and promises of the OT are still the possession of the nation Israel. But this is what is found in Rom 9:3b–4 when Paul refers to "my countrymen by physical descent. They are Israelites, and to them belong the adoption, the glory, the covenants, the giving of the law, the temple service, and the promises".

According to Paul, the "covenants" and "promises" and even "temple service" are still seen as being the possession of Israel even with the church existing and even during a time in which Israel's disobedience is evident. Paul is referring to ethnic Israel here. When Paul states, "To them belong" the "covenants" and the "promises," he is stating this as a present reality. Saucy correctly observes that "the present tense of the verb shows that Paul affirms these privileges, including the covenants and promises, as the present possession of Israel. . . . They still belong to Israel in unbelief."[1] If the church were now the true Israel and if it were true that the nation Israel was no longer related to the OT covenants and promises, why then does Paul state that the covenants and promises still belong to Israel?

We find a similar affirmation in Acts 3:11–26. In Peter's second sermon to the "Men of Israel," he reminds the representatives of Israel that "you are the sons of the prophets and of the covenant that God made with your forefathers, saying to Abraham, And in your seed all the families of the earth will be blessed" (3:25). Even in a state of unbelief, there is a sense in which Israel is still related to the Abrahamic covenant.[2]

---

[1]R. L. Saucy, *The Case for Progressive Dispensationalism: The Interface Between Dispensational and Nondispensational Theology* (Grand Rapids: Zondervan, 1993), 248.

NEW TESTAMENT PROPHECY AFFIRMS A FUTURE FOR ISRAEL

Evidence for a future salvation and restoration of Israel is found in NT prophetic passages. Put simply, the fact that NT prophecy mentions Israel, Jerusalem, and the temple as having continuing relevance is supplemental proof that national Israel still has a role to play in God's plan.

For example, in Matt 24:15–20, Jesus discusses the coming "abomination that causes desolation" that will occur in the "holy place" (v. 15), which is a reference to a horrible and blasphemous event in the Jewish temple in Jerusalem. Those who are in Judea are told to flee to the mountains (v. 16). What Jesus discusses is consistent with what Dan 9:24–27 predicts concerning the nation Israel. But if the nation Israel has no future significance in the plan of God, then why is there prophetic significance to Judea, Jerusalem, and the temple? If the church is the new Israel that transcends geographical and ethnic boundaries, why would Jesus be so concerned about the land of Israel and its temple? The better conclusion is that the land of Israel and the temple have a future significance because Israel itself has future significance in the plan of God.

A parallel passage to Matt 24:15 is found in 2 Thessalonians 2. In regard to Jesus' coming and our being gathered to Him (2 Thess 2:1), which are future events, Paul predicted that a day was coming when the man of lawlessness would take his seat in the temple of God and declare himself to be God (see 2 Thess 2:3–4). This is probably the same event Jesus discussed when He referred to the "abomination that causes desolation" in Matt 24:15. The temple is a Jewish object. The fact that this is a temple "of God" rules out the idea that this is a pagan or illegitimate temple.[3] Hiebert points out, "The whole picture seems naturally to suggest an eschatological Jewish temple. This was the view of Irenaeus (*Against Heresies*, V. 30.4) and other early church fathers."[4] The implications of this passage are important. If Israel has been transcended by the church and there is no role for a future land and temple for Israel, why then does Paul mention a temple? It appears that Paul assumes the predictions concerning the abomination of desolation as discussed in Dan 9:24–27 will still come to pass. Revelation 11:1–2 also mentions the specific dimensions of a temple in the last days.

---

[2]They are related not because they are saved at this point but because God has committed Himself to Israel.

[3]Beale objects to the idea of a future literal physical temple in Jerusalem, claiming that the temple refers to the church. See G. K. Beale, *The Temple and the Church's Mission: A Biblical Theology of the Dwelling Place of God* (Downers Grove, IL: InterVarsity, 2004), 269–92. However, I see no reason to abandon the plain sense of the passage which appears to be referring to a literal temple, and thus parallels what Daniel predicted in Dan 9:24–27.

[4]D. E. Hiebert, *1 & 2 Thessalonians* (Chicago: Moody, 1992), 334.

Luke 21 also discusses important eschatological events. Verse 24 is evidence for a restoration of Israel. Jesus states, "They will fall by the edge of the sword and be led captive into all the nations, and Jerusalem will be trampled by the Gentiles until the times of the Gentiles are fulfilled". Jesus predicts that Jerusalem will be under Gentile control for a period known as "the times of the Gentiles." But is there any indication of a restoration of Israel in this verse? The answer is yes. The word "until" signifies a limit to the judgment on Israel discussed in 21:24. While admitting that Luke 21:24 does not explicitly state what is to happen after the time of Gentile domination of Israel ends, this text is compatible with the OT expectation of a restoration of Israel after a period of judgment. As Saucy explains,

> But it might be asked, if Jesus was merely teaching that Jerusalem is to be trodden down by Gentiles until the Lord returns to conclude salvation history in the setting up of the eternal kingdom, why did he not say, "Jerusalem will be trampled . . . until I come" or something to that effect rather than "until the times of the Gentiles are fulfilled"? The times of the Gentiles will terminate with the coming of Christ. But the use of this particular language suggests the reversal of the situation for the down-trodden city as a result of the end of the gentile domination at the appearance of the Messiah. Such a scenario would be in perfect harmony with the Jewish prophecy. The motif of the treading down of Jerusalem was "a set theme in prophecy." But the subsequent restoration of the nation was also a theme of that expectation. Thus, although the force of Jesus' teaching in this passage is on the coming judgment, its temporary nature makes it perfectly compatible with the rest of the Old Testament hope of the restoration of Israel.[5]

Tannehill, too, admits that Luke 21:24 does not explicitly state what will happen to Jerusalem after the time of Gentile domination is over. He does believe, though, that Luke 21:24 is consistent with the OT, other Jewish writings, and the book of Acts in speaking of a restoration of Jerusalem:

> We are not told explicitly what will happen then, but if we return to the other texts that speak of this trampling, we find the expectation that Jerusalem will be restored. Zechariah 12:1–9 is an oracle of salvation for Jerusalem, and *Pss. Sol.* 17:21–25 is a prayer that the Messiah may come to rescue Jerusalem (cf. also Isa 65:17–25; Dan 8:14; 1 Macc 4:36–60; 2 *Baruch* 68:1–5; and cf. Chance 1988, 133–38). Furthermore, Acts 3:21 indicates that the "times of restoration of all that God spoke" through the prophets (my literal translation) can still come to the people of Jerusalem.[6]

---

[5]See Saucy, *The Case for Progressive Dispensationalism*, 266.
[6]R. C. Tannehill, *Luke*, ANTC (Nashville: Abingdon, 1996), 306.

In tying Luke 21:24 with other statements in Luke, Franklin asserts that the destruction of Jerusalem spoken of in 21:24 "is not the last word" for the nation Israel. In fact, its restoration is still to come:

> In Jesus, the promises to David have received their guarantee (1.32–33) so that the restoration of the kingdom to Israel is still part of the Christian hope (Acts 1:6). At the moment, Jerusalem's house is forsaken (13.35), but this is only until 'the times of the Gentiles are fulfilled' (21.24) when, at the day of her restoration, she will cry, 'Blessed be he who comes in the name of the Lord' (13.35). The destruction of Jerusalem in no way contradicts Luke's theme, for he is confident of her restoration and future supremacy.[7]

Bock places significant stress on the phrase "times of the Gentiles" and the limit on this time period as mentioned in Luke 21:24. The phrase "times of the Gentiles," according to him, "denotes . . . Gentile domination (Dan. 2:44; 8:13–14; 12:5–13) and the subsequent hope for Israel (Ezek. 39:24–29; Zech. 12:4–9)."[8] In regard to the limit for the "times of the Gentiles," Bock asserts that "the city's fall is of limited duration, or why else mention a time limit."[9] The wording in Luke 21:24 is also significant according to Bock. He states, "Why describe this period this way unless there is an intended contrast between Israel and the Gentiles?"[10] Bock thus describes the "times of the Gentiles" as "the current period in God's plan when Gentiles are prominent but that will culminate in judgment on those nations."[11] This means there will be a future for Israel: "It would thus seem that this view of Israelite judgment now but vindication later suggests what Paul also argues in Rom. 11:25–26: Israel has a future in God's plan. Israel will be grafted back in when the fullness of Gentiles leads it to respond (see also Rom. 11:11–12, 15, 30–32)."[12]

Commenting on the significance of Luke 21:24 along with Matt 23:38–39, Kaiser asserts that the OT expectation regarding Israel is still alive:

> While the emphasis falls on the expected judgment (being "desolate" and being "trampled on"), what is taken as a divine matter-of-fact is that the OT promises to Israel are still in the picture—Jerusalem will belong to

---

[7]E. Franklin, *Christ the Lord: A Study in the Purpose and Theology of Luke–Acts* (London: SPCK, 1975), 130.

[8]D. L. Bock, *Luke 9:51–24:53*, BECNT (Grand Rapids: Baker, 1996), 2:1680.

[9]Ibid.

[10]Ibid., 1681.

[11]Ibid.

[12]Ibid.

Israel once the "times of the Gentiles" have ended and once Israel greets "he who comes" (an obvious use of OT terminology for the Messiah) with blessing rather than curses.[13]

Luke 21:24 is not an explicit statement about a future restoration of Israel. But as Plummer has stated, it does teach that "the punishment of Israel has a limit."[14] I thus agree with Tannehill that although not explicit evidence for the restoration of Israel, Luke 21:24 is consistent with the OT expectation of a restoration for the Jewish inhabitants of Jerusalem.[15] I also agree with Chance when he states, "Close examination of L. 21:24b, c provides a strong hint that Luke did foresee the restoration of Jerusalem."[16] Ladd is correct when he connects Luke 21:24 with the salvation of all Israel mentioned in Rom 11:26: "The divine judgment is to rest upon Jerusalem and upon the Jewish nation until the 'times of the Gentiles,' i.e., the divine visitation of the Gentiles is accomplished. When God's purpose for the Gentiles is fulfilled, so this verse implies, Jerusalem will no longer be trodden down. There will be a restoration of Israel; 'all Israel will be saved.'"[17]

In addition, Rev 7:4–8 specifically foretells the sealing of the 12 tribes of Israel during the time of tribulation upon the world:

> And I heard the number of those who were sealed: 144,000 sealed from every tribe of the sons of Israel: 12,000 sealed from the tribe of Judah, 12,000 from the tribe of Reuben, 12,000 from the tribe of Gad, 12,000 from the tribe of Asher, 12,000 from the tribe of Naphtali, 12,000 from the tribe of Manasseh, 12,000 from the tribe of Simeon, 12,000 from the tribe of Levi, 12,000 from the tribe of Issachar, 12,000 from the tribe of Zebulun, 12,000 from the tribe of Joseph, 12,000 sealed from the tribe of Benjamin.

---

[13]W. C. Kaiser Jr., "Kingdom Promises as Spiritual and National," in *Continuity and Discontinuity: Perspectives on the Relationship Between the Old and New Testaments*, ed. J. S. Feinberg (Wheaton, IL: Crossway, 1988), 301.

[14]A. Plummer, *A Critical and Exegetical Commentary on the Gospel According to St. Luke*, ICC (Edinburgh: T&T Clark, 1960), 483.

[15]Tannehill, *Luke*, 306. Commenting on the phrase, "until the times of the Gentiles are fulfilled," R. A. Culpepper says, "God's promise of a limit to the period of Israel's oppression by the Gentiles can also be found in the Scriptures (Tob 14:5; Dan 12:7; Rom 11:25)." R. A. Culpepper, "The Gospel of Luke: Introduction, Commentary, and Reflections," *NIB* 9 (Nashville: Abingdon, 1995), 405.

[16]J. B. Chance, *Jerusalem, the Temple, and the New Age in Luke–Acts* (Macon, GA: Mercer University Press, 1988), 134.

[17]G. E. Ladd, *The Gospel of the Kingdom: Popular Expositions on the Kingdom of God* (Grand Rapids: Eerdmans, 1959), 120.

The specific mentioning of each of the 12 tribes of Israel emphasizes the continuing role of the tribes of Israel in the plan of God. This is not a reference to Gentiles or the "church militant" as some assert.[18] Immediately after this section, Rev 7:9 states, "After this I looked, and there was a vast multitude from every nation, tribe, people, and language, which no one could number, standing before the throne and before the Lamb". John distinguishes Jews (Rev 7:4–8) and Gentiles (Rev 7:9). The group in 7:4–8 is made of ethnic Jews while the group in 7:9 is a multitude from "every nation." Also, the group in 7:4–8 is finite; it is a group of 144,000, while the group in 7:9 is "a great multitude which no one could count." These are not the same groups of people.

Revelation 21:10–14 also emphasizes the continuing relevance of the tribes of Israel in God's plan:

> He then carried me away in the Spirit to a great and high mountain and showed me the holy city, Jerusalem, coming down out of heaven from God, arrayed with God's glory. Her radiance was like a very precious stone, like a jasper stone, bright as crystal. The city had a massive high wall, with 12 gates. Twelve angels were at the gates; the names of the 12 tribes of Israel's sons were inscribed on the gates. There were three gates on the east, three gates on the north, three gates on the south, and three gates on the west. The city wall had 12 foundations, and the 12 names of the Lamb's 12 apostles were on the foundations.

This passage is significant because of its reference to the "12 tribes of the sons of Israel" (v. 12) in the eternal state. As Thomas states, the names of Israel serve "explicit notice of the distinct role of national Israel in this eternal city in fulfillment of their distinctive role in history throughout the centuries of their existence (cf. 7:1–8)."[19]

The 12 tribes of Israel are distinguished from the "Lamb's 12 apostles" of verse 14. Thus, this passage shows that the Israel-church distinction is still maintained to some degree even in the eternal state. This passage also rules out any idea that the 12 tribes of Israel were only a temporary type that has been superseded by the 12 apostles. The 12 tribes of Israel, who are the foundation of national Israel, are viewed as distinct from the 12 apostles (see Eph 2:20). As Thomas puts it, "It is significant that John brings together the 12 tribes of Israel and the 12 apostles here, and makes

---

[18]See G. K. Beale and S. M. McDonough, "Revelation," in *Commentary on the New Testament Use of the Old Testament*, ed. G. K. Beale and D. A. Carson (Grand Rapids: Baker, 2007), 1107.

[19]R. L. Thomas, *Revelation 8–22: An Exegetical Commentary* (Chicago: Moody, 1995), 463.

a distinction between them. Jesus did the same earlier (Matt 19:28; Luke 22:30). This distinction shows the wrongness of identifying the 12 tribes in 7:4–8 with the church."[20]

New Testament prophecy stresses prophetic themes such as Jerusalem and the temple that are related to Israel. This only makes sense if there is prophetic significance for the nation Israel. That is why Peters was accurate when he declared, "The union of the doctrine of the restoration [of Israel] with the events of the Second Advent make it easy for any believer to join the declarations of the Old with those of the New Test."[21]

NEW TESTAMENT KEEPS ISRAEL AND THE CHURCH DISTINCT

The NT distinguishes Israel and the church in such a way that rules out the idea that the church is now identified as Israel or that the church entirely inherits Israel's promises and covenants to the exclusion of Israel. Fruchtenbaum, for example, points out that the title *Israel* is used a total of 73 times in the NT, but it is always used of ethnic Jews: "Of these seventy-three citations, the vast majority refer to national, ethnic Israel. A few refer specifically to Jewish believers who still are ethnic Jews."[22] Saucy confirms this point when he says, "The NT evidence reveals that outside of a few disputed references . . . the name Israel is related to the 'national' covenant people of the OT."[23]

The NT still consistently refers to the nation Israel as "Israel" even after the establishment of the church. Israel is addressed as a nation in contrast to Gentiles *after* the church was established at Pentecost (Acts 3:12; 4:8, 10; 5:21, 31, 35; 21:28). As Ryrie points out, "In Paul's prayer for natural Israel (Rom. 10:1) there is a clear reference to Israel as a national people distinct from and outside the church."[24] Paul's linking of national Israel to the covenants and promises of the OT, even while in a state of unbelief, is further proof that the church has not entirely absorbed Israel's blessings:

> Paul, obviously referring to natural Israel as his "kinsmen according to the flesh," ascribes to them the covenants and the promises (Rom. 9:3–4). That these words were written after the beginning of the church is proof

---

[20]Ibid., 465.

[21]G. N. H. Peters, *The Theocratic Kingdom of Our Lord Jesus, the Christ as Covenanted in the Old Testament* (New York: Funk & Wagnalls, 1884; repr., Grand Rapids: Kregel, 1988), 2:51.

[22]A. G. Fruchtenbaum, "Israel and the Church," in *Issues in Dispensationalism*, ed. W. R. Willis and J. R. Master (Chicago: Moody, 1994), 120.

[23]R. L. Saucy, "Israel and the Church: A Case for Discontinuity," in *Continuity and Discontinuity*, 244–45.

[24]C. C. Ryrie, *Dispensationalism* (Chicago: Moody, 1995), 127. Emphasis in original.

that the church does not rob Israel of her blessings. The term *Israel* continues to be used for the natural (not spiritual) descendants of Abraham after the church was instituted, and it is not equated with the church.[25]

The book of Acts maintains a distinction between Israel and the church. In the book of Acts, both Israel and the church exist simultaneously, but the term *Israel* is used 20 times and *ekklesia* ("church") 19 times. But the two groups are always kept distinct.[26] Thus the continued use of the term *Israel* for the physical descendants of Jacob is evidence that the church is not Israel. As Saucy explains, "The church is not . . . identified with 'Israel.' They share a similar identity as the people of God enjoying equally, the blessings of the promised eschatological salvation. But this commonality does not eliminate all distinctions between them."[27]

The Doctrine of Election Ensures Israel's Place in God's Plan

From the beginning of Israel's existence, God's choice of this nation was based on His unconditional electing purposes. It was not because of anything Israel had done that made her the chosen people of God (see Deut 7:6–8). The NT reaffirms Israel's election as the reason God can never remove or replace Israel. With Rom 11:1–2a, Paul states, "I ask, then, has God rejected His people? Absolutely not! For I too am an Israelite, a descendant of Abraham, from the tribe of Benjamin. God has not rejected His people whom He foreknew". In what Murray has called "the most emphatic negative available,"[28] Paul denies the possibility of Israel's being permanently rejected by God.

The impossibility of God's casting Israel away is linked to God's foreknowledge in 11:2. As Cranfield writes, "The fact that God foreknew them (i.e., deliberately joined them to Himself in faithful love) excludes the possibility of His casting them off."[29] Pannenberg points out the importance of God's election of Israel from another standpoint. If Israel's election could be set aside, in what way could Christians be sure of their own election? But since God has not rejected Israel, Christians can be sure of their own election: "How could Christians be certain of their own comparatively

---

[25]Ibid. Emphasis in original.

[26]Fruchtenbaum, "Israel and the Church," 118. Emphases in original.

[27]Saucy, *The Case for Progressive Dispensationalism*, 210. For Saucy, "it is the lack of national characteristics that distinguishes the church from Israel" (210).

[28]J. Murray, *The Epistle to the Romans*, NICNT (Grand Rapids: Eerdmans, 1959; repr., 1997), 2:66.

[29]Cranfield, *Epistle to the Romans*, 2:545. See also H. W. Hoehner, "Israel in Romans 11," in *Israel, the Land and the People: An Evangelical Affirmation of God's Promises*, ed. H. W. House (Grand Rapids: Kregel, 1998), 150.

new membership in the circle of God's elect if God for his part did not remain faithful to his election in spite of Israel's unbelief? This is the apostle's point when he advocates the inviolability of the election of the Jewish people (11:29; cf. 9:6). He has in mind also Christian assurance of election."[30]

Moltmann, too, points out that Israel's election means that God's promises cannot be transferred entirely to the church:

> There can be no question of God's having finally rejected the people of his choice—he would then have to reject his own election (11.29)—and of his then having sought out instead another people, the church. Israel's promises remain Israel's promises. They have not been transferred to the church. Nor does the church push Israel out of its place in the divine history. In the perspective of the gospel, Israel has by no means become "like all the nations."[31]

This issue of Israel's election is significant. In Scripture, God's election is based on His sovereign choice and is not revoked by the disobedient actions of those with whom He has elected. This appears to be a problem for those who take a punitive supersessionist approach or assert that Israel is no longer the people of God because of their disobedience. If Israel's restoration is linked to God's election, which Romans 11 indicates, then Israel's restoration is surely based on the character of God. Thus, Israel's restoration is sure because God is faithful and He keeps His promises.

---

[30]W. Pannenberg, *Systematic Theology*, trans. G. Bromiley (Grand Rapids: Eerdmans, 1993), 3:471.

[31]J. Moltmann, *The Way of Jesus Christ: Christology in Messianic Dimensions*, trans. M. Kohl (San Francisco: HarperSanFrancisco, 1990), 35.

Conclusion

Based on the arguments presented in this book, I conclude that supersessionism is not a biblical doctrine. As I have argued, the case against supersessionism can be made on two fronts. First, a strong positive case can be made for the salvation and restoration of national Israel. Second, a strong negative case can be offered against the doctrine of supersessionism.

Concerning the first point, the case for a salvation and restoration of Israel starts with a New Creation Model of eschatology in which there is room for matters such as nations and land. A New Creation Model rejects the assumption that material or physical matters are lesser entities that must give way to purely spiritual things. Plus, this model understands that spiritual blessings in Christ do not transcend or cancel physical blessings or promises made to the nation Israel. Thus, the spiritual and the physical blessings work together in harmony. This is a both-and situation and not an either-or one. Also, a study of the purpose of Israel shows that Israel's purpose was to bring blessings to the families of the earth (Gen 12:2–3). It never has been God's intention to make everyone Israel. Also significant are the multiple explicit texts that teach and reaffirm a future salvation and restoration of the nation Israel (see Deuteronomy 30; Isaiah 2; Ezekiel 36–37; Zephaniah 3; Zechariah 14; Matt 19:28; 23:39; Acts 1:6; Romans 11).

Concerning the second point, supersessionists have not made a compelling case that the church is the new Israel or that the church fulfills national Israel's place to such an extent that the nation Israel will not be restored. Often supersessionists draw inferences that are not demanded from the biblical text, or they conclude too much from passages that are not directly addressing Israel's role in God's plan. For instance, the attempt to show that the church is now called Israel because of passages like Gal 6:16 and Rom 9:6 is not convincing. Both passages have ethnic Jews in mind and are not calling Gentiles "Israel." Plus, even if it could be shown that these passages include Gentiles in the concept of Israel, these texts do not indicate that national Israel no longer has a role to play in God's plans.

What about Israelite terminology applied to the church? Several Israelite images are used of the church. Members of the church are now the people of God, the temple of God, and the true circumcision. But

Isa 19:24–25 predicted that non-Jews would inherit imagery and titles used to describe Israel without becoming Israel. Thus, sharing descriptive titles with Israel does not mean the church is Israel. Similarity does not mean identity. Groups can share many descriptive titles and characteristics without being the same.

The attempt to demonstrate that Eph 2:11–22 supports supersessionism is also not convincing. This passage affirms the unity in salvation that Gentiles and Jews experience, but this passage does not rule out a future role for Israel to the nations. Salvific equality in Christ does not rule out functional distinctions. The addition of believing Gentiles into the people of God does not have to mean the subtraction of Israel from its place in the plan of God.

Claims that Acts 15 and Hebrews 8 teach that the NT has reinterpreted the OT expectation of a restoration of Israel are not persuasive. James quotes Amos 9 in Acts 15 as one example of an OT prophet who predicted that Gentiles would be saved without having to become Jews. The issue at hand here is Gentile inclusion in salvation, not whether Israel's restoration is being fulfilled entirely with the church. The purpose of this passage is primarily soteriological and not eschatological. Hebrews 8 shows that Jesus is the mediator of the superior new covenant. But it is difficult to see how the inauguration of the new covenant means that national Israel has been separated from this covenant. The new covenant was promised to Israel, but it was never given in such a way that ruled out Gentile participation. Romans 11:26–27 links national Israel's future salvation with the new covenant.

Of course, any discussion of Israel must wrestle with the implications of Romans 9–11. The historic view of the church is that this is speaking of a national salvation of Israel. The attempts to claim otherwise simply are not convincing. I do find it interesting that many supersessionists admit this. Yet they are often quick to say, "Yes, there is a national salvation of Israel, but no restoration of Israel is mentioned in Romans 9–11." But my question is this: if one is willing to admit that Israel as a nation will be saved in line with the new covenant passages Paul quotes, why wouldn't one believe in a restoration as well? In other words, if Israel's salvation is linked with OT promises, why wouldn't the OT expectation about a restoration of Israel still be in effect too? What evidence is there that the salvation of Israel is to be expected but not a restoration?

The primary error of supersessionism is this: *In their desire to emphasize the unity in salvation that Jews and Gentiles have experienced, supersessionists have mistakenly concluded that such unity excludes a special role for Israel in the future.* But salvific unity does not erase all ethnic and functional distinctions. Gentiles are now partakers of Israel's covenants, *and* national Israel will be saved and restored with a role of service to the nations.

Diprose has correctly pointed out that on their own certain texts "may be . . . compatible with *replacement theology*." But he also states, "They do not require it."[1] This is a key distinction. There is an important difference between saying that some texts may be consistent with supersessionism and asserting that certain texts demand supersessionism. From our perspective, no texts, whether individually or collectively, demand the conclusion that national Israel has been permanently replaced or superseded by the church as the people of God. Diprose is also right when he states that in order for replacement theology to qualify as a biblical doctrine, "passages which *allow* such an interpretation are not enough." Instead, there needs to be "positively, passages which clearly teach it and negatively, no passages which actually exclude it."[2] Blaising has pointed out that much of the NT's discussion concerning "the extension of present kingdom blessings to Gentile believers" is "consistent with Old Testament promises about Gentiles." But he also mentions, "The New Testament never presents these events as a *replacement* of the specific hopes of Israel. Instead, they are argued as *compatible* or *complementary* to the hopes of Israel."[3]

The NT reaffirms the OT expectations concerning a restoration of Israel. When this is coupled with the fact that no texts clearly identify the church as Israel or teach the permanent rejection of Israel, the case for supersessionism is unconvincing, and the case for Israel's restoration is strong. Thus, we agree with Kaiser when he says, "To argue that God replaced Israel with the church is to depart from an enormous body of biblical evidence."[4]

Cranfield is an example of a scholar who let the biblical evidence change his views toward Israel. Cranfield admitted that he used to hold to the view that the church replaced Israel in the plan of God. He said, "And

---

[1] R. E. Diprose, *Israel in the Development of Christian Thought* (Rome: Istituto Biblico Evangelico Italiano, 2000), 69–70. Emphasis in original.

[2] Ibid. Emphasis in original.

[3] C. A. Blaising and D. L. Bock, *Progressive Dispensationalism: An Up-to-Date Handbook of Contemporary Dispensational Thought* (Wheaton, IL: Bridgepoint, 1993), 267. Emphases in original. Bock states, "Fulfillment can take place in the church without removing the hope of fulfillment for Jews or Israel." D. L. Bock, "Summary Essay," in *Three Views on the Millennium and Beyond*, ed. D. L. Bock (Grand Rapids: Zondervan, 1999), 292. See also G. B. Caird, *New Testament Theology* (Oxford: Clarendon, 1994), 51; J. Moltmann, *The Way of Jesus Christ: Christology in Messianic Dimensions*, trans. M. Kohl (San Francisco: HarperSanFrancisco, 1990), 35.

[4] W. C. Kaiser Jr., "An Epangelical Response," in *Dispensationalism, Israel and the Church: The Search for Definition*, ed. C. A. Blaising and D. L. Bock (Grand Rapids: Zondervan, 1992), 364.

I confess with shame to having also myself used in print on more than one occasion this language of the replacement of Israel by the Church."[5] His study of Romans 9–11, including its implications for God's electing purposes, though, convinced him otherwise:

> It is only where the Church persists in refusing to learn this message, where it secretly—perhaps unconsciously!—believes that its own existence is based on human achievement, and so fails to understand God's mercy to itself, that it is unable to believe in God's mercy for still unbelieving Israel, and so entertains the ugly and unscriptural notion that God has cast off His people Israel and simply replaced it by the Christian Church. These three chapters [Rom 9–11] emphatically forbid us to speak of the Church as having once and for all taken the place of the Jewish people.[6]

I hope that many Christians, too, would embrace the explicit biblical evidence concerning Israel and give God the glory that His electing purposes for Israel still stand. After all, God's faithfulness to Israel is a testimony that His promises for us will never fail: "For from Him and through Him and to Him are all things. To Him be the glory forever. Amen" (Rom 11:36).

---

[5]C. E. B. Cranfield, *A Critical and Exegetical Commentary on the Epistle to the Romans*, ICC (Edinburgh: T&T Clark, 1979), 2:448, n. 2.

[6]Ibid., 448.

Appendix

The Origin of the Church

Those who identify the church as Israel sometimes claim that the church did not begin in the NT era but instead has roots in the OT. As Grudem states, "The church is the community of all true believers for all time." For him, the church encompasses "both believers in the New Testament age and believers in the Old Testament age as well."[1] This argument is often supported by linking the NT concept of *ekklesia*, which is often translated "church," with the OT term *qahal*, which sometimes referred to the gathering of Israel. Allegedly, because the Septuagint uses *ekklesia* to translate *qahal*, this must mean the church existed in some form in the OT. I will argue that this argument is incorrect and that the Bible teaches that the church is a NT entity. I will do so by looking at the term *ekklesia* and how it is understood in the Bible.

Lothar Coenen explains that the term *ekklesia* is derived from *ek-kaleō*, which was used for a summons to an army to assemble.[2] In classical Greek, the term *ekklesia* is found in the writings of Herodotus, Thucydides, Xenophon, Plato, and Euripides (fifth century BC onward). In these writings, the word refers to an assembly of the citizens of a Greek city[3] In the secular sense, *ekklesia* most often refers simply to a gathering or assembly of persons. This general sense of *ekklesia* as an assembly is found in Acts 19:32,39,41 in reference to a riotous mob. In only three cases in classical Greek is *ekklesia* used of a religious fellowship.[4] According to Saucy, "the secular use, therefore, provides little for an appreciation of the rich meaning of the New Testament term outside of the formal analogy of an assembly of people meeting for a particular purpose."[5]

---

[1] W. Grudem, *Systematic Theology: An Introduction to Biblical Doctrine* (Grand Rapids: Zondervan, 1994), 853.

[2] L. Coenen, "ἐκκλησία," *NIDNTT* 1:291, ed. C. Brown (Grand Rapids: Zondervan, 1975), 1:291.

[3] M. J. Erickson, *Christian Theology* (Grand Rapids: Baker, 1998), 1041.

[4] Coenen, "ἐκκλησία," 1:291–92.

[5] R. L. Saucy, *The Church in God's Program* (Chicago: Moody, 1972), 13.

In the OT, the term *qahal* refers to a summons to an assembly and the act of assembling. As Erickson points out, "It is not so much a specification of the members of the assembly as a designation of the occurrence of assembling."[6] A religious significance is sometimes attached to the word (e.g. Deut 9:10; 10:4; 23:1–3). Also, the term can refer to a general assembly of the people (1 Kings 12:3), women (Jer 44:15), children (Ezra 10:1; Neh 8:2), or nations other than Israel (in Ezekiel used of Egypt, 17:17; Tyre 27:27; Assyria 32:22). The Septuagint, the Greek translation of the OT, uses *ekklesia* 77 times to translate *qahal*.

A survey of the uses of *qahal* indicates that no technical meaning was attached to this term in the OT or to the Septuagint Greek translation of *ekklesia*. But in the attempt to show continuity between the church and Israel, some supersessionists claim that *qahal* was a technical term for Israel as the people of God in the OT. In addition, *qahal* is viewed as the background for the NT concept of *ekklesia*. It is claimed, then, that the apostles viewed the church as the new Israel and the continuation of OT Israel. But as Saucy points out, "There is no evidence, however, that such is the case. *Qahal* and its Greek translation simply mean an assembly."[7] The NT gives a religious technical meaning to *ekklesia*, but the attempt to link the technical NT sense of *ekklesia* with OT *qahal* is not warranted. In fact, it is close to the logical fallacy of semantic anachronism in which the late use of a word is read back into earlier literature.[8]

Ekklesia occurs 114 times in the NT. Five of these references have no reference to the NT church, leaving 109 references with such a relationship.[9] While *ekklesia* is a common term in the NT, it is unevenly distributed. There are only two references to *ekklesia* in the Gospels: Matt 16:18 and Matt 18:17. The majority of references to *ekklesia* appear in Paul's letters. Paul uses the term 46 times, including nine usages in Ephesians and four in Colossians. In Revelation John uses *ekklesia* 20 times.

The sparse references to "church" in the Gospels contrasted with the many references to "church" in Acts, the Epistles, and Revelation support the idea that the church began after the earthly ministry of Christ. Coenen makes this contrast between Luke's Gospel and Acts: "The fact that Luke, on the other hand, uses the word 23 times in Acts suggests the conclusion

---

[6]Erickson, *Christian Theology*, 1042.

[7]Saucy, *The Church in God's Program*, 13–14.

[8]See D. A. Carson, *Exegetical Fallacies*, 2nd ed. (Grand Rapids: Baker, 1996), 33. See also B. Norman, "The Origin of the Church" (M.Div. thesis, The Master's Seminary April 28, 2009).

[9]Saucy, *The Church in God's Program*, 16.

that he, at least, consciously avoided using it for a group that belonged to the period of Jesus' earthly activity."[10]

The NT develops *ekklesia* from the nontechnical meaning of "assembly" or "gathering" to the technical meaning of the Christian people of God.[11] The word often refers to a group of believers in a specific city such as "the church of God in Corinth" (1 Cor 1:2; 2 Cor 1:1) or "the churches in Galatia" (Gal 1:2). The book of Revelation was written to seven specific churches (Revelation 1–3). *Ekklesia* is used of Christians who lived and met in various areas in the book of Acts (Acts 5:11; 8:1; 13:1). The term is used for meetings in individual homes (Rom 16:5; Col 4:15) or to believers in a larger geographical area such as Judea, Galilee, and Samaria (Acts 9:31) and the province of Asia (1 Cor 16:19). Most references to *ekklesia* are to a local assembly of those committed to Christ (1 Thess 1:1; 1 Cor 4:17). The term also is used to refer to a universal body of believers (Matt 16:18; 1 Cor 10:32; Eph 1:22; 5:23–32; Col 1:18, 24).

In sum, before the NT *ekklesia* often had a general nonreligious understanding. With the NT, the term took on a more technical religious meaning for those who were followers of Christ, although a few references still maintained a nonreligious meaning. It is incorrect, therefore, to conclude that the relationship of *ekklesia* to *qahal* means that the church existed in the OT.

Also, there are good biblical reasons to view the church as beginning in the NT era and not in the OT. In Matt 16:18, Jesus declared, "And I also say to you that you are Peter, and on this rock I will build My church, and the forces of Hades will not overpower it". This verse, which is the first of two references to *ekklesia* in the Gospels, is strong evidence for a NT origin for the church for two reasons. First, Jesus' words are an explicit statement that the church from that standpoint in history was future. The verb *oikodomēsō*, "I will build," is future tense. Thus, when Jesus made this statement, the church did not exist; it was still future. Second, the church was to be built on "this rock." There is debate concerning what "this rock" refers to. Some say the rock is Peter himself, and others say it is Peter's profession that Jesus is the Messiah, the Son of the living God (Matt 16:18). But regardless of which option is correct, the one thing we know is that the church would be built on something related to the NT era and not to the OT.

---

[10]Coenen, "ἐκκλησία," 1:298.
[11]Saucy, *The Church in God's Program*, 15.

Closely related to Matt 16:18 is Eph 2:19–20, which states that "God's household" (2:19), the church, is "built on the foundation of the apostles and prophets, with Christ Jesus Himself as the cornerstone" (2:20). This passage reveals that the foundation of the church is built on NT persons—the apostles, prophets,[12] and Christ Jesus. If the foundation of the church is built on NT persons, then the church itself must be a NT entity.

Another evidence for the NT origin of the church is linked with the outpouring of the Holy Spirit. The church is inherently tied to the NT baptizing ministry of the Holy Spirit. First Corinthians 12:13 states, "For we were all baptized by one Spirit into one body—whether Jews or Greeks, whether slaves or free—and we were all made to drink of one Spirit." Those who are members of the body of Christ have all experienced Spirit baptism. But Spirit baptism is a NT experience that started with the events of Acts 2 when the Spirit was first given to Christians. While the Holy Spirit is omnipresent and was at work in the OT era, His role took on a unique function with the events of the day of Pentecost. Shortly before His ascension, Jesus declared that the disciples would be baptized with the Holy Spirit in a matter of days (Acts 1:5). Then in Acts 2 the Holy Spirit was poured out upon the believers in Jerusalem (2:3–4). Since the church is linked with Spirit baptism and Spirit baptism occurred with the events of Acts 2, we can conclude that the church began with the events of Acts 2 and is a NT entity.

Another evidence for the NT origin of the church is found in Eph 2:14–15. In discussing the relationship of believing Jews and Gentiles in the church, Paul says, "For He is our peace, who made both groups one and tore down the dividing wall of hostility. In His flesh, He made of no effect the law consisting of commands and expressed in regulations, so that He might create in Himself one new man from the two, resulting in peace." Paul describes the church as "one new man." The church is "new," not old, from his perspective. Also, this "one new man" is tied to the doing away of "the law consisting of commands," which occurred "through the cross" (2:16). The church as "one new man" from the death of Christ and the end of the law of commands. The reasonable conclusion to draw is that the church began in the NT in connection with Christ's ministry.

The theological factors in favor of a NT origin of the church are impressive and are more decisive than the claim that semantic considerations equate the technical meaning of *ekklesia* ("church") in the NT with *qahal* of the OT.

---

[12]That NT prophets are in view and not OT prophets is supported by the fact that the other references to "prophets" in Ephesians clearly refer to NT prophets (see Eph 3:5; 4:11).

Selected Bibliography

Berding, Kenneth, and Jonathan Lunde, eds. *Three Views on the New Testament Use of the Old Testament*. Grand Rapids: Zondervan, 2007.

Blaising, Craig A. "The Future of Israel as a Theological Question." *Journal of the Evangelical Theological Society* 44:3 (2001): 435–50.

———, and Darrell L. Bock, eds. *Dispensationalism, Israel and the Church: The Search for Definition*. Grand Rapids: Zondervan, 1992.

———, and Darrell L. Bock, *Progressive Dispensationalism: An Up-to-Date Handbook of Contemporary Dispensational Thought*. Wheaton, IL: Bridge-Point, 1993.

Bock, D. L., ed. *Three Views on the Millennium and Beyond*. Grand Rapids: Zondervan, 1999.

Boettner, Loraine. *The Millennium*. Philadelphia: Presbyterian & Reformed, 1957.

Campbell, Donald K., and Jeffrey L. Townsend, eds. *A Case for Premillennialism: A New Consensus*. Chicago: Moody, 1992.

Carroll, James. *Constantine's Sword: The Church and the Jews*. Boston: Houghton Mifflin, 2001.

Charlesworth, James H., ed. *Jews and Christians: Exploring the Past, Present, and Future*. New York: Crossroad, 1990.

Clouse, R. G., ed. *The Meaning of the Millennium: Four Views*. Downers Grove, IL: InterVarsity, 1977.

Cohen, Jeremy, ed. *Essential Papers on Judaism and Christianity in Conflict: From Late Antiquity to the Reformation*. New York: New York University Press, 1991.

———. "The Mystery of Israel's Salvation: Romans 11:25–26 in Patristic and Medieval Exegesis." *Harvard Theological Review* 98/3 (2005): 247–81.

Cranfield, C. E. B. *A Critical and Exegetical Commentary on the Epistle to the Romans*. 2 volumes. ICC. Edinburgh: T&T Clark, 1979.

De Lange, N. R. M. *Origen and the Jews: Studies in Jewish-Christian Relations in Third-Century Palestine*. Cambridge: Cambridge University Press, 1976.

Diprose, Ronald E. *Israel in the Development of Christian Thought*. Rome: Istituto Biblico Evangelico Italiano, 2000.

Dunn, James D. G., ed. *Jews and Christians: The Parting of the Ways A.D. 70 to 135*. Grand Rapids: Eerdmans, 1999.

Evans, Craig A., and Donald A. Hagner, eds. *Anti-Semitism and Early Christianity: Issues of Polemic and Faith*. Minneapolis: Fortress, 1993.

Feinberg, John S., ed. *Continuity and Discontinuity: Perspectives on the Relationship Between the Old and New Testaments*. Wheaton, IL: Crossway, 1988.

Fruchtenbaum, A. G. *Israelology: The Missing Link in Systematic Theology*. Tustin, CA: Ariel, 1989.

Glenny, W. Edward. "Typology: A Summary of the Present Evangelical Discussion." *Journal of the Evangelical Theological Society* 40:4 (1997): 627–38.

Goppelt, L. *Typos: The Typological Interpretation of the Old Testament in the New*. Translated by D. H. Madvig. Grand Rapids: Eerdmans, 1982.

Helyer, L. R. "Luke and the Restoration of Israel." *Journal of the Evangelical Theological Society* 36 (1993): 317–30.

Holwerda, David E. *Jesus & Israel: One Covenant or Two*? Grand Rapids: Eerdmans, 1995.

Hood, John Y. B. *Aquinas and the Jews*. Philadelphia: University of Pennsylvania Press, 1995.

Horner, Barry E. *Future Israel: Why Christian Anti-Judaism Must Be Challenged*. Nashville: B&H, 2008.

House, H. Wayne, ed. *Israel, the Land and the People: An Evangelical Affirmation of God's Promises*. Grand Rapids: Kregel, 1998.

Johnson, John J. "A New Testament Understanding of the Jewish Rejection of Jesus: Four Theologians on the Salvation of Israel." *Journal of the Evangelical Theological Society* 43 (June 2000): 229–46.

Johnson, S. L., Jr. "Paul and the 'The Israel of God': An Exegetical and Eschatological Case-Study." In *Essays in Honor of J. Dwight Pentecost*. Edited by S. D. Toussaint and C. H. Dyer. Chicago: Moody, 1986.

Kaiser, Walter C., Jr. "An Assessment of 'Replacement Theology': The Relationship Between the Israel of the Abrahamic–Davidic Covenant and the Christian Church." *Mishkan* 21 (1994): 9–20.

Karlberg, Mark W. "Legitimate Discontinuities Between the Testaments." *Journal of the Evangelical Theological Society* 28:1 (1985): 9–20.

———. "The Significance of Israel in Biblical Typology." *Journal of the Evangelical Theological Society* 31:3 (1988): 257–69.

Köstenberger, A. J. "The Identity of the ΙΣΡΑΗΛ ΤΟΥ ΘΕΟΥ (Israel of God) in Galatians 6:16." *Faith and Mission* 19 (2001): 3–24.

LaRondelle, Hans K. *The Israel of God in Prophecy: Principles of Prophetic Interpretation*. Berrien Springs, MI: Andrews University Press, 1983.

Larsen, David. *Jews, Gentiles and the Church: A New Perspective on History and Prophecy*. Grand Rapids: Discovery House, 1995.

McClain, Alva J. *The Greatness of the Kingdom: An Inductive Study of the Kingdom of God*. Winona Lake, IN: BMH Books, 1959.

McKnight, Scot. *A New Vision for Israel: The Teachings of Jesus in National Context*. Grand Rapids: Eerdmans, 1999.

Merkle, B. L. "Romans 11 and the Future of Ethnic Israel." *Journal of the Evangelical Theological Society* 43 (2000): 709–21.

Pentecost, J. Dwight. *Things to Come: A Study in Biblical Eschatology*. Grand Rapids: Zondervan, 1958.

Peters, George N. H. *The Theocratic Kingdom of Our Lord Jesus, the Christ as Covenanted in the Old Testament.* 3 volumes. New York: Funk & Wagnalls, 1884; reprint, Grand Rapids: Kregel, 1988.

Poythress, Vern S. *Understanding Dispensationalists,* 2d. ed. Phillipsburg, NJ: P&R, 1994.

Richardson, Peter. *Israel in the Apostolic Church.* Cambridge: Cambridge University Press, 1969.

Ridderbos, Herman. "The Future of Israel." In *Prophecy in the Making: Messages Prepared for Jerusalem Conference on Biblical Prophecy.* Edited by Carl F. H. Henry. Carol Stream, IL: Creation, 1971.

———. *Paul: An Outline of His Theology.* Translated by John Richard De Witt. Grand Rapids: Eerdmans, 1975.

Riddlebarger, Kim. *A Case for Amillennialism: Understanding the End Times.* Grand Rapids: Baker, 2003.

Robertson, O. P. *The Christ of the Covenants.* Phillipsburg, NJ: P&R, 1980.

———. *The Israel of God: Yesterday, Today, and Tomorrow.* Phillipsburg, NJ: P&R, 2000.

Rydelnik, Michael. *The Messianic Hope: Is the Hebrew Bible Really Messianic?* NACSBT. Nashville: B&H, 2010.

Ryrie, Charles C. *Dispensationalism.* Chicago: Moody, 1995.

Sanders, E. P. *Jesus and Judaism.* Philadelphia: Fortress, 1985.

Saucy, Robert L. *The Case for Progressive Dispensationalism: The Interface Between Dispensational & Non-Dispensational Theology.* Grand Rapids: Zondervan, 1993.

Siker, Jeffrey S. *Disinheriting the Jews: Abraham in Early Christian Controversy.* Louisville, KY: Westminster/John Knox, 1991.

Simon, Marcel. *Versus Israel: A Study of the Relations Between Christians and Jews in the Roman Empire (135–425).* Translated by H. McKeating. Oxford: Oxford University Press, 1986.

Sizer, Stephen. *Zion's Christian Soldiers: The Bible, Israel and the Church.* Nottingham, England: Inter-Varsity, 2008.

Snyder, Howard A. *Models of the Kingdom.* Eugene, OR: Wipf and Stock, 1991.

Soulen, Kendall. *The God of Israel and Christian Theology.* Minneapolis: Fortress, 1996.

Taylor, H. "The Continuity of the People of God in Old and New Testaments." *Scottish Bulletin of Evangelical Theology* 3 (1985): 13–26.

Tiede, D. L. "The Exaltation of Jesus and the Restoration of Israel in Acts 1." *Harvard Theological Review* 79 (1986): 278–86.

Turner, David L. "The Continuity of Scripture and Eschatology: Key Hermeneutical Issues." *Grace Theological Journal* 6:2 (1985): 275–88.

———. "Matthew 21:43 and the Future of Israel." *Bibliotheca Sacra* 159 (2002): 46–61.

VanGemeren, Willem. "Israel as the Hermeneutical Crux in the Interpretation of Prophecy." *Westminster Theological Journal* 45:1 (1983): 132–44.

Walton, John H. *Covenant: God's Purpose, God's Plan*. Grand Rapids: Zondervan, 1994.

Walvoord, John F. *The Millennial Kingdom*. Grand Rapids: Zondervan, 1959.

Williamson, Clark M. *A Guest in the House of Israel: Post-Holocaust Church Theology*. Louisville, KY: Westminster/John Knox, 1993.

Willis, W. R., and J. R. Master. *Issues in Dispensationalism*. Chicago: Moody, 1994.

Wright, N. T. *Jesus and the Victory of God*. Minneapolis: Fortress, 1996.

———. *The New Testament and the People of God*. Minneapolis: Fortress, 1992.

Wylen, Stephen M. *The Jews in the Time of Jesus*. Mahwah: Paulist Press, 1996.

Subject Index

Author Index

Scripture Index